Structures and Time

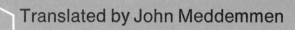

Translated by John Meddemmen

Cesare Segre

Structures and Time

Narration, Poetry, Models

The University of Chicago Press
Chicago and London

CESARE SEGRE is professor of Romance philology
at the University of Pavia and president of the
International Association for Semiotic Studies.
He is the editor of *Strumenti critici* and the series
Critica e filologia, and the author of half a dozen
books, among them *Semiotics and Literary Criticism*,
1973; he has also prepared critical editions of the
Chanson de Roland and some of the works of
Fournival, Ariosto, and Giamboni.

The University of Chicago Press, Chicago 60637
The University of Chicago Press, Ltd., London

Library of Congress Cataloging in Publication Data

Segre, Cesare.
  Structures and time.

  Translation of Le strutture e il tempo.
  Includes bibliographical references and index.
  1. Literature—History and criticism—Addresses,
essays, lectures. I. Title.
PN515.S3713   809   79-68
ISBN 0-226-74476-0

Contents

Preface

Chapters 2–9 of this volume bring together essays written between 1969, the year in which *I segni e la critica* appeared (translated into English as *Semiotics and Literary Criticism* [The Hague, 1973]), and 1973. Chapter 2 was published in Italian as "Strutture romanzesche, strutture novellistiche e funzioni," in *Collected Essays on Italian Language and Literature Presented to Kathleen Speight* (Manchester, 1971). Chapters 3–5 and 7–8 have also been published in Italian: chapter 3 appeared in *Strumenti critici* 6 (1972): 133–62; chapter 4 in *Studi sul Boccaccio* 6 (1971): 81–108; chapter 5 in *Letteratura e critica: studi in onore di N. Sapegno* (Rome, 1975), vol. 2; chapter 7 as the introduction to the Meridiani *Don Chisciotte* (Milan, 1974), in a somewhat shortened version; and chapter 8 in *Strumenti critici* 7 (1973): 186–215, reprinted in the Brazilian translation of *I segni e la critica: os signos e a crítica* (São Paulo, 1974). Chapter 6 has appeared in English, in a somewhat different form, in the *Journal for Descriptive Poetics and Theory of Literature* 2 (1977): 313–38; and chapter 9 was prepared for the volume *Semiología del teatro: textos reunidos y presentados por J. M. Díez Borque y Luciano García Lorenzo* (Barcelona, 1974) and appeared in French translation in *Documents de travail et pré-publications*, no. 29, Centro Internazionale di Semiotica e di Linguistica di Urbino, December 1973.

Each essay sets out, in the act of examining a text, to investigate a theoretical problem: a way of working which seems to be, and is, the deliberate assumption of a methodological position. The reader will be in a position to note, moreover, that while some chapters move rather far in the direction of formalization, others have a more straightforward, essay-like character. Formalization is the means to an end, not an end in itself.

Such close chronological limits have meant that apart from the differences of the specific problems they deal with, all the chapters follow a common thematic thread, though it was only in the act of putting the book together as such that I became aware of its persistence: the theme is time. Time appears again and again in chapters 2–9 in many different aspects; basically, however, these can be reduced to two: time within the text, that of the succession of its narrative and poetic moments; and external time, that of reading or recreating the text itself.

Structuralist interpretation actuates in general a deconstruction or breaking down of the text, which it subsequently reconstructs according to categories, formulae, tables. The text ends up in some measure "detemporalized." But that the critic should use such an approach is in no sense impermissible: indeed it is very similar to the approach used by the ordinary reader. During reading itself, in fact, one dwells on a single linear segment, that on which the reading rests for a moment during its progressive unfolding. What has already been read is rearranged achronically in memory.

But it is advisable to insist on the importance of the temporal aspect. Along the time axis lie not only narrative and poetic moments but also verbal and conceptual rhythm, recursivity, and disambiguation techniques: reading is an adventure which has been programmed in its phases and duration. Thus all my chapters insist, for various aspects, on the impossibility of separating syntagm from paradigm, succession from achrony. Let us think of the work of literature as a machine: better knowledge of its structures satisfies us to the degree that it brings us into fuller contact with its functioning in time. If its functioning (in time) is left out of account, the machine is no more than an assemblage of pieces.

The internal temporal aspect and relations in general between diachrony and achrony constitute one of the central themes of narratological research. In putting a chapter on narratology at the beginning of the book, I wished to treat in more detail an argument which had already been developed in sectors in various chapters (2–5). Thus chapter 1, besides dealing with almost all of the problematic aspects of narratology from Tomashevsky and Propp to Greimas and Bremond, provides a more solid foundation for the particular analyses of the chapters that follow. The thesis for which narrative models are themselves historical models falls within the ideological coordinates put forward in my earlier book.

Chapter 1 is thus not really a theoretical foreword to a group of critical essays so much as a systematic and independent treatment of one part—the most compact part—of the themes dealt with in chapters that proceed to illustrate other and more varied problems: from the problem of stylistic "vectors" to that of registers, from "point of view" to poetic parallelism, to semic bifurcation between written theatrical action and action as represented onstage.

In part, these problems are directly suggested by the semiotic approach of the work; in part, they grow out of an undertaking to preserve the polyhedric nature of the literary work, at the formal level as well, from the overwhelming violence of formalization. It is just such recourse to meaningful values which can, in the approach here adopted, assign to schemata, statistics, and formulae a well-defined role in critical inquiry. Furthermore, it is through meaningful values that the work of literature becomes once more a tributary of history: from history it comes, and into history it flows yet again through the continuity of our readings.

One

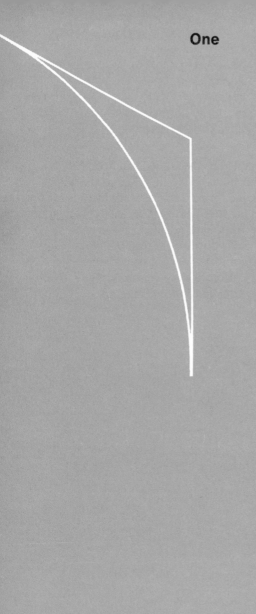

Analysis of the Tale,
Narrative Logic, and Time

Narrative Analysis and Semiotics

The printed characters which run in parallel lines across the pages of a book, if placed end to end, would stretch for hundreds of yards, sometimes for miles. If the text is narrative in character, reading it would seem to consist quite simply in recognizing and understanding along this line the words and sentences of which these characters are the sign. Naturally, however entertaining the reading, the operations to be performed are not so elementary as they seem, and research over the last decades has discovered the principal motifs.

In a text, what signifies (signifiers) and what is signified (meanings)—the dichotomy is Saussure's—are superimposed upon each other, indeed stratified. Each word is made up of letters (signifiers) which symbolize groups of phonemes (meanings), and these together constitute the signifier of the (conceptual) signification. Furthermore, groups of words which are enclosed between two strong punctuation marks or between the beginning and the first such mark stand as signifiers of a synthetic (sentential) meaning; in their turn groups of sentences are the signifiers of a (narrative) meaning, and it is precisely when we go beyond the frontiers of the sentence that we reach the (almost) unknown country of narrativity (the subject of narrative analysis).

As a general rule, narration can be looked at from at least two points of view: (1) as a discourse, essentially the narrative itself, to be considered as signifier, and (2) as content, that is, the meaning of the narrative. Such a dichotomy seems to be reflected in the opposition of *syuzhet* and *fabula* proposed by the Russian Formalists, or plot and story in English; *discours* and *histoire* as Todorov uses them,[1] *récit* and *histoire* in Genette,[2] or *récit racontant* and *récit raconté* in Bremond.[3] The uncertainty of the terminology, aggravated by the now habitual *analyse du récit* in place of "analysis of the fabula," derives from the fact that a mere dichotomy is inadequate to represent the field of research effectively. Plot and fabula are in reality (sec. 1.1) two ways of representing narrative content, while what is lacking is a term which will indicate its signifying aspect. Thus I shall adopt, at least at the outset, a three-part division: *discourse* (the narrative text as signifier), *plot* (textual content in the order of its presentation), and *fabula* (content or, better, its cardinal elements, as rearranged in logical and chronological order).

It is my aim in the pages which follow to provide a critical panorama of the principal attempts at narrative analysis that have been made up to the present. They spring from a belief that such researches are useful, but also from an experience of certain innate contradictions, certain insuperable limits, which are part and parcel of this approach and which we should not seek to hide from ourselves. Enthusiasm in proposing new analytical techniques or in applying, and often contaminating, those already in existence (our age is one of epigonism and eclecticism) have caused meditation on the theoretical foundations to be neglected. Worse still, some have preferred to oppose to it a dogmatic *fin de non recevoir*.

There is a widespread misunderstanding which I would like to clear away at the outset. Discourse and fabula (and even plot) seem to lend themselves all too readily to the by now inevitable image of levels: surface level, the discourse; deep level, the fabula (or else, in descending order of depth, first the plot and then the fabula). These images derive from Chomsky, as does the other no less frequent symmetry which sees the discourse as *generated* by the plot and the plot by the fabula. As long as it is levels one refers to, little harm is done. Levels, however, multiply rapidly, and it becomes clear that it would be better to consider them as ideal sections rather than as involving measures of depth.[4] But it is misleading to talk in generative terms if this involves, in some measure, a genetic conception.

It is incorrect to think of discourse as a development (by amplification or addition of details) of a "deep level" of, say, plot, because the plot does not exist prior to the discourse except perhaps as an unformed project, subject to continual adjustments. The plot achieves its settled form the moment the work as a linguistic construction is brought to completion. Expression and content are the two faces of a single object, like signifier and signified in Saussure: it is useful to distinguish them, impossible to separate them. To confirm this, try imagining "transformation rules" which would explain the passage from a deep narrative structure to a narrative discourse. It is a project which, though perhaps conceivable in a phenomenological study of relations between plot and fabula (where it would, however, be a question simply of expository schemata or traditions), would become absurd if the intention were to arrive at the surface—the discourse, complete with all its lexical and stylistic elements.

Levels and generation thus remain two quite acceptable metaphors, but only if explicitly recognized as such. It is better still if in "generation" one senses a trace of creativity, of freedom of invention, all the more striking in that the book, defined once and for all as a whole and in its single sentences, is already fixed *ne varietur* in its discursive expression, a perfect mechanism, forever immobile. The sender does not speak to us; *he has spoken to us*. The only freedom involved is ours as receivers of his message, to understand and interpret it in progressively greater depth. It is we who move backward and forward in the space between the surface and the other (supposed) levels, we who think up the most complex itineraries between the various structures in and of the text.

The fact remains that this type of investigation falls well within the confines of literary semiotics. A text (in our case, a narrative text) is a whole made up of signs whose progressively larger groupings—arrived at in terms of techniques which, though not fully specified, are neither casual nor infinite—serve in their turn as signs. The rules for the coherence of these sign complexes (a better designation than "macrosign," in that it allows for the at least theoretical possibility of taking apart and substituting its components) are in part linguistic—traditional linguistics up to and including Chomsky, holding good for sentences and *Textlinguistik* (at least as programmed) over even wider extensions—but they are also related in part to rules of nonlinguistic meaning which attempts are made to define.

If discourse, plot, and fabula are ranged in the area mapped out for this investigation, it may be affirmed that for the zone which lies between discourse and plot, rules of meaning of a linguistic type always obtain: rules which govern our ability to perceive sentential and transsentential meanings (e.g., those of a sequence or episode). But between plot and fabula rules of meaning are much more difficult to define, since we are dealing with relations not between signifiers and signified but between differently articulated signifiers. This is so even though they are coextensive at least in terms of the terrain of their pertinence. What can be stated at once is that the "competence" we show in conceiving or understanding a tale proves the existence of an inventory and a certain number of possible combinations of communicable narrative meanings. Narrative analysis sets itself the task—and it is a difficult one—of sketching out this inventory and describing these possibilities.

As will soon become evident, the main difference between fabula and plot lies in the fact that the former respects the chronological order of events (however fantastic it may be), while the latter keeps to the order in which the writer has described them.

Time, as an irreversible order of succession, is thus the basic element of discrimination between various modes of linking events: a sort of ideal "measuring rod." On the other hand, reading too takes place in time (always in an irreversible order of succession, leaving aside as of no theoretical importance the eventuality of a reader's rereading certain passages before going on). An interlacement of some complexity exists among reading (or discourse) time, plot time, and fabula time.[5]

Finally, it is in the temporal dimension that one is made aware of recursive phenomena, and it is primarily on this plane that they function. They are fundamental not only for their expressive and stylistic effects (I am thinking of the well-motivated persistence in the study of parallelisms)[6] but also for their communicative and in particular their narrative effects (it is recurrence which reaffirms the identity of places, characters, events; which aligns facts along a curve of tonal modulations and atmosphere; which drafts the semiotic framework of a tale). For this reason the problem of time will be dominant in this book and will give unity, I hope, to its introductory chapter and to many of those which follow.

If the reader is sufficiently clear-sighted to marvel over the fact that studies on narration increase and multiply at a moment when the novel (be it alive, dying, or dead) is less and less the narration of events, and hardly ever of adventures, he is at liberty to consider these researches as the inventory of a bankruptcy, or else as yet another demonstration of the irrepressible human urge to fabulate and to tell tales.

Plot, Fabula, and Narrative Model

1.1. At the beginning (and convention requires that we have one) we might put Veselovsky. Erlich writes that "to formalist morphological analysis no small contribution was made by the distinction introduced by Veselovsky in his incomplete *Poetics* of plots, between 'motif,' the unity of narrative measure, and 'plot,' or group of different motifs."[7] Shklovsky quotes him, in fact: "By motif I mean the simplest narrative unit that in the form of an image corresponds to the diversified exigencies of the primitive intellect or to its day-to-day observations. . . . By plot I mean an accumulation of different situations (or motifs)."[8]

If, however, we examine what Veselovsky meant by "motif," it is clear that he alludes to two quite different orders of things: "(1) the so-called *légendes des origines*: the representation of the sun as an eye; the idea that the sun and moon are brother and sister or else husband and wife; myths of the rising and setting of the sun, of sun spots, of eclipses of sun and moon, and so forth; (2) real-life situations: the carrying off of the bride (a peasant marriage custom), the farewell banquet (in folk tales), and other such customs."[9]

Veselovsky's starting point was taken up and developed particularly by Shklovsky and Tomashevsky. Shklovsky, in *Literatura i kinematograf* (Berlin 1923)[10] and then in *O theorii prozy*, sets up an opposition between plot and fabula: "The concept of plot is all too often confused with that of the illustration of events, with what I should conventionally define as fabula. In reality, the fabula is merely the material used to give form to the plot. The plot of *Evgeny Onegin*, for example, is not the love affair of Onegin and Tatyana but an elaboration of this fabula obtained by inserting digressions which break it up."[11] This should be compared with the definition of fabula given by Tomashevsky: "The theme of a work with fabula represents a more or less unified system of events, deriving one from the other, connected one to the other. It is precisely the ensemble of such events in their reciprocal internal relationships that we call fabula"; and also his definition of plot: "The distribution in terms of an aesthetic construction of the events in a work is called its plot."[12]

If the two definitions are combined, it appears that fabula is the system of events in their temporal and causal order which the writer uses as his material; but he expounds it in an artificial-artistic order, and it is this which constitutes the plot. Veselovsky, however, after ordering motifs in classes as simple elements, opposed simple and compound (motif and plot). Yet their definition was not univocal. In Veselovsky's terminology, what we should say is that the fabula is a system of logical and chronological connections of type 2 motifs, while plot is their literary manipulation.

The opposition of fabula and plot is a clear step forward with respect to Veselovsky. Shklovsky and Tomashevsky have with remarkable insight disengaged two compresent syntagmatic lines, one of which, the fabula, acts as a neutral double, ingeniously employed to throw into relief, by contrast, the techniques of composition which writers adopt.

As for techniques of composition (and plot construction), how much attention was given to them by Shklovsky and Eikhenbaum, and with what imaginative insights, is well known. However, they dealt in less detail with the question of the minimal elements which make up the fabula, Veselovsky's motifs. Tomashevsky is enlightening here, for he points out the need to arrive at elements that are not susceptible of further analysis: "As we go on thus breaking down the work into thematic fractions, we finally reach segments which *cannot be broken down further*, for they constitute minimal portions of thematic material: 'Evening came'; 'Raskolnikov killed the old woman'; 'The hero died'; 'A letter was received'; etc. In practice every sentence contains a motif of its own." And he continues, "These motifs, by their combination, form the work's thematic structure. From this point of view, the fabula is made up of the ensemble of its motifs in their causal-temporal logical relationships, while the plot is the sum of the same motifs in the succession and the relations in which they are placed in the work."

Tomashevsky rightly observes that Veselovsky's motifs (particularly those of type 1, I would remark) are an entirely different matter: "not entities insusceptible of being further broken down but merely . . . those which historically were not so broken down, which have kept a unity of their own despite the fact that they move from one work to another."[13]

It might be observed that the term "motif" is better adapted to the use Veselovsky and other folklore specialists make of it than to Tomashevsky's purposes; but it is the substance that matters, the search for *segments not further analyzable*.

Tomashevsky indeed takes yet another step forward, distinguishing between motifs that are *tied*, "which cannot be omitted," and *free*, "which cannot be omitted without damaging the integrity of the causal-temporal connection of events"; and between those that are *dynamic*, "which transform a situation," and *static*, "which cause no change at all"; specifying that "for the fabula only tied motifs have any relevance; for the plot, however, it is at times the free motives themselves [the "digressions"] whose functions are the most important, determining the structure of the work." Also, "dynamic motifs are the central motor elements of the fabula, but in the organization of the plot, static motifs may come to the fore."[14] Tomashevsky thus saw that there exist mutually obligatory elements in the fabula, while in the case of elements which make up the plot, the network of relations is looser and more readily varied.

1.2. In this type of investigation Propp's contribution must be considered decisive. The motifs of Tomashevsky's formulation ("segments not susceptible of further analysis") are given a term which describes them more satisfactorily and defines them much more exactly: "By 'function' we mean the behavior of a character determined from the point of view of its meaning for the unfolding of the event,"[15] to which the following clarification should be added: "If we wish to call my schema a model, then it is a model which reproduces all the constructive (constant) elements of the folktale, leaving aside the nonconstructive (variable) elements."[16]

In Propp's system the characters form part of the variables. The same function is often filled by different characters, with different attributes. Thus we have not characters carrying out functions but functions *of* the characters. As for the function itself, it can only be defined in relation to "its collocation in the unfolding of the narrative": that is, "what must be considered is the meaning of a given function within the narrative event."[17]

Nothing, then, could be less empirical than Propp's technique. He first established a well-defined corpus (tales 50–150 of Afanas'ev's collection), a closed system; he then defined its elements, taking into account the system in its totality. The *meaning* of the functions is their paradigmatic and syntagmatic value. Paradigmatic value: in all the tales of the corpus certain obligatory moments are present (prohibition, transgression of the prohibition, test, acquisition of a magical aid, etc.). On the basis of this general observation, it becomes possible to leave out of consideration the various modes in which these functions are carried out, and by whom. Syntagmatic value: since there exists a causal-temporal direction of the functions, actions which are equivalent in appearance are susceptible of classification only in relation to contiguous functions: "The action cannot be determined without reference to its collocation in the unfolding of the narration." He continues, "We can always trust to the determination of a function in terms of its *consequences*. If the achievement of the task is followed by the acquisition of the magical aid, we have to do with a testing by the donor; if on the other hand we find winning the betrothed and marriage, we have the problematic task."[18]

From this standpoint, Propp not only found himself in a position to give a more accurate definition of relations between composition, or narrative pattern, and plot; he was also able to bring to light its semiotic substance: "We might call the structure of the folktale the sum of its plot and its composition. This has no real existence, in the sense in which in the world of things those general concepts found in the consciousness of man do not exist. But it is thanks to just such general concepts that we know the world, discover its laws, and learn how to govern it."[19]

Propp rigorously defines the limits of his analysis, with respect both to other kinds of folktale and, even more, to different diegetic production, e.g., literary production. Mere exigencies of publication, he tells us, determined the present title rather than the more appropriate *Morphology of the Magic Folktale*, and he adds, "The method is far-reaching;

the conclusions, however, are valid only for that particular type of folklore narrative to whose analysis they owe their origin."[20] In other words, he is the first to reject the idea that the thirty-one fundamental functions he identified, with their fixed order of succession, can be maintained as they stand in any field which lies beyond the limits of the corpus chosen (and deliberately chosen because it is coherent). It is enough to find in a more widely based corpus a single new function or a different arrangement of functions in order for the abandonment of Propp's scheme to become imperative. The paradigmatic and syntagmatic combination which fixes functions within a closed system must give way to a new combination system once the field has been extended. This is the first lesson to be learned from Propp, and to my mind it is a positive one.

The second lesson concerns literature. I would not give too much weight to the obviousness of sententiae like the following: "[Our methods] are possible and fruitful when we are faced with the possibility of repetition on a wide scale, such as is found in language or in folklore. But when art becomes the field of action of an inimitable genius, the use of exact methods will yield positive results only if the study of repeatable elements is accompanied by study of that peculiar uniqueness which up to the present time has always been regarded as the manifestation of an unknowable miracle."[21] Much more important, it seems to me, is what Propp says of motivations ("By motivations I mean as much motives as the aims which determine the different interventions of the characters. *At times they confer on the folktale a particular color and effectiveness*, but they represent nonetheless a most unstable and inconstant element and, moreover, one much less stable and well defined than the functions and linking elements") and the attributes of the characters ("By attributes we mean the sum of all the external characteristics of a character: age, sex, condition, appearance, peculiar traits, etc. *It is the attributes which confer on the folktale its vivacity, its beauty, and its fascination*").[22]

Propp deals differently with motivations and attributes. The former are indicated anecdotally and considered not determinant with respect to the functions. For the latter, however, Propp declares that he is able to draw up tables (that he has in fact done so); in other words, that he can arrange attributes to form a system even if it remains, with respect to the functions, a secondary one. Indeed, Propp states, "analysis of the attributes renders possible the scientific *interpretation* of the folktale."[23]

It is essential to note here how precisely Propp has distinguished functional elements, those which tie together the tale's construction, from those other elements which, though they may prove more important in other respects, are not pertinent to its definition. If this is valid for the folktale, it is infinitely more so for works of literature in which actions are often merely the illustration, or at most the consequence, of motivations and attributes on which the artistic fabulation concentrates. A rigorous definition of what a narrative pattern is seems to point up by contrast what it is not, what this *particular* type of analysis sacrifices, leaving its treatment to differently conceived analyses.

Whether nonfunctional elements are susceptible of endowment with functionality at some other level or whether they constitute elegant fringes which escape investigation is a problem which continues to be discussed. Propp himself is open to either the first kind of solution (that proposed for attributes) or the second (that proposed for motivations).

1.3. If at this point we try to sum up the seemingly convergent findings of Shklovsky and Tomashevsky on one hand and Propp on the other, we realize that the oppositive pairs they work with are identical only in appearance: the fabula which literary theorists oppose to the plot does not coincide with Propp's narrative model.

Let us take a given text and break it down into "content units" in such a way that nothing is left over. We obtain what all investigators agree in calling the plot. At this point, a second kind of analysis can be undertaken. This leaves in their original position those content units whose relations are consequential in logical or temporal terms, but when shifts or displacements are involved, the units are reorganized to accord with what might be called their "natural" order. The result of this second analysis is a paraphrase which summarizes the text at the same level of abstraction as the earlier analysis but which eliminates all displacements of logical-temporal order.

At this point again, a third operation can be effected. Its aim is to reduce narrative data to their pure functionality, at a much more rarefied level of abstraction. In conclusion, we have

I   Discourse
II   Sum of content units corresponding to discourse level
III   Content units reorganized into logical-temporal order
IV   Narrative model

It is clear that Shklovsky and Tomashevsky call II plot, while their concept of fabula oscillates between III and IV. They do not yet possess a clear-cut conception of function; Tomashevsky's behavior is typical when he tries to reach IV by eliminating from III elements which are not determinant in terms of the action, i.e., by simplifying III but not measuring its level of abstraction. Propp, on the other hand, compares II and IV directly, without making explicit use of phase III. This is natural enough, since in folk narration one seldom finds temporal displacements or, generally, content displacement with respect to the "natural" order. In other words, Propp does not need to pass through phase III, because in the texts he works with it coincides substantially with phase II.

I would propose the following terminology for this fourfold division:

I   Discourse
II   Plot
III   Fabula
IV   Narrative model

When the critic passes from II to III, the shift is primarily one of logical and chronological order. It is a question of putting the ante before the post, the causes before their effects. Since "natural" order is rarely found in narrative literature, this initial operation is decisive in bringing to light the techniques employed by the writer (a task the Formalists undertook enthusiastically; see sec. 3.1), both in the sense of explaining the artistic motivation of the "infractions" and in order to describe the expository devices that render them comprehensible.

The passage from III to IV is different in kind. It is a passage from the particular to the general, since the model is the most general form in which a tale can be expounded while still maintaining the order and nature of its connections.[24]

Plot and Discourse

2.1. If what we take into consideration is the surface aspect, the discourse of a narrative text, its temporal succession seems to encounter no obstacles. The text is made up of a series of lines of print which follow each other from the first letter of the first word to the last letter of the last (in an oral text it is a series of words which follow each other in time). This linear aspect (which some contemporary visual texts break up) is, however, no more than a first impression.

Let us take the first sentence of any book whatever. The eye runs over the different letters, and at exactly the same time the reader adds together the separate words or, rather, syntagms; at the end of the sentence the reader has grasped a coherent sense. There is thus a constant movement toward the end of the sentence, followed by a more or less immediate apprehension of its overall meaning. Then the eye moves on and repeats the process over and over again. But at the end of the second (or third or nth) sentence, what remains of the first in the mind of the reader? "No one knows how meaning is represented within memory, but there is no evidence to show that any form of syntactic structure is directly involved." This is Johnson-Laird, and he bases his conclusions on experiments anyone can verify in terms of his own experience. He goes on, "It is natural to wonder whether the sentence is the largest unit normally involved in the recall of language. It is possible that from the meanings of sentences in a connected discourse, the listener implicitly sets up a much abbreviated and not especially linguistic model of the narrative, and that recall is very much an active reconstruction based on what remains of this model."[25] In short, the reader of a book *at any given moment reads no more than a single sentence*; all those that preceded it have been built up into a memorial synthesis[26] (of subject matter, stylistic elements, allusions), while those which remain to be read form an area of potentiality in both linguistic and narrative terms. I propose the following schema:

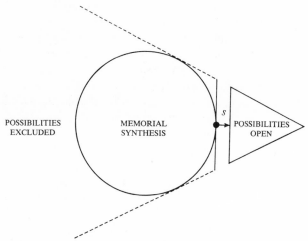

POSSIBILITIES
EXCLUDED

MEMORIAL
SYNTHESIS

s

POSSIBILITIES
OPEN

Here *s* is the sentence actually being read as such, while the preceding sentences have come to constitute a memorial synthesis from which possibilities the writer has not followed up have been excluded, while various other possibilities (from the reader's point of view) still remain open; they will be exhausted only when the closing sentence has been read, when *s* coincides with the apex of the triangle, and when the tale as a whole is transformed into a memorial synthesis.

The advantage of the schema proposed is that it shows the compresence of a linguistic reading of the text (its form of expression) and an assimilation of its content: at each point of a reading, linguistic experience is being brought to bear on the sentence being read, while what has gone before has already been assimilated as contentual and stylistic experience. In other words, along the time axis of a text, a purely linguistic reading is impossible.

Linguistic analysis and stylistic analysis are thus realizable only if reading order is left out of account; the elements of the analysis fall into classes or series which reveal at least in part the paradigm of the work, breaking down its syntagms, if the linear succession of the sentences of which it is composed is considered as such.[27] It would seem, then, that a (temporal) reading must be contrasted with an (achronic) stylistic-linguistic analysis.

The temporal succession of the act of reading, however, creates a sort of dialectic between the two processes. We have just remarked that once read, sentences are transferred to a synthesis in memory. Nonetheless, a careful reader will not register only subject matter; he will also pay attention to words, stylemes, constructions, etc.; these too he inserts into the pigeonholes of a formal memory. The reading of each new sentence thus becomes an act of recognition of a stylistic-linguistic system already partly discerned through what has been read so far, in particular, recognition of words, stylemes, and constructions, be they the same, similar, or opposed, or in some sense comparable with what has been met with earlier (recurrences); recognition and definition of connotative planes. It is the genetic integration of content and expression that makes it possible to carry through as a unity a reading apparently split up in this manner: in the overall complexity of a work, its formal elements play a fundamental role in defining content also.

If reading does indeed take place in the manner here briefly described, the inescapable conclusion is that a reading of linguistic elements is an *oriented* reading. A typical example is the repetition of identical sentences or lines. When it occurs at two points in a poem or prose work, a sentence remains unchanged only in its linguistic aspect. In fact its value changes not only, obviously, because it finds itself inserted into different parts of the text, susceptible of bringing to light different implications. The change in value I wish to stress springs from two separate causes, both related to reading order. A sentence which is found at two or more points of a progression (*a*) has been preceded by a greater or lesser degree of memorial synthesis and (*b*) occurs at different stages of extrinsication of the linguistic-stylistic system.

Manifold possibilities of artistic exploitation are thus offered. A sentence may change value in its various positions, may effect a climax or an anticlimax, after a number of puzzling appearances may present itself in a final semantic agnition. In short, we have a mirror-image version of parallelism: in parallelism, rhythmic or syntactic invariants are detected in the midst of linguistic variables; in this case, however, it is linguistic invariants that progressively give rise to semic variants.[28]

The linguistic-stylistic elements are thus analogous to content elements in that they work out a plot of their own. The reader follows not only the movements of action and character but those of stylemes and connotations as well. We must be capable of arriving at a "narrative" conception of the facts of language over and above their (more frequently effected) general consideration. For the facts of language, too, there exist moments of suspense, *coups de théâtre*, hints to be taken up and confirmed: phenomena often well spaced out. In consequence, chapters 3 and 8 of this book will offer two readings of linguistic phenomena, one achronic, the other temporal.

2.2. Since we are dealing with relations between the sentences which constitute the text, we might expect textual linguistics to make a significant contribution, and so it does.[29] The simplest outline of some of the points it deals with should suffice:

> *Coreference* (or *substitution*), by virtue of which the same entity is indicated by different words in successive sentences (pronominalization is a case in point);
>
> *Inclusion and logical implication*, which connect the elements of successive sentences of different conceptual capacity but of related object—a phenomenon similar to
>
> *Semantic contiguity*, i.e., a partial sharing of semic elements; the semantic line which links a number of sentences or all the sentences of a text is called "isotopy" (a term from Greimas);
>
> *Thema and rhema*,[30] in English "topic and comment," where topic is initial, fundamental information content, while comment is every addition or development;
>
> The *perspective of tense and aspect* (which I will discuss further on, at sec. 3.2.);
>
> The *system of the reader's linguistic expectations*, which involves precise norms for beginning, developing, and concluding a discourse, and so on.

But the suggestions of textual linguistics are useful primarily for their definition of "competence" (in Chomsky's sense): the competence of the writer, in the first place, but also that of the reader, for it is precisely because of sharing such competence that he is in a position to comprehend the text submitted to him; competence in forming and understanding not single sentences—the object of generative grammar—but coherent successions of sentences. There are two consequences of this program for us. (1) Textual linguistics is better suited to researches into everyday language than into literary languages; the latter often break many or all generally valid rules for the generation of texts. (2) Textual linguistics necessarily follows the order in which the sentences are formed, from the first to the second, down to the last. In this regard I would draw attention to the concept of semantic development and restriction[31] or to that of "disambiguation."[32] They imply (rightly) that a process of discourse is also a process of semantic recognition and definition.

In a literary text the same process is to be found, but with greatly altered value. Just as a narrator does not tell us at the outset who his characters are, what they are doing, and what they are going to do but leads us to discover these things gradually, involving us more and more in the story, so too a writer of prose or poetry, signposts the semantic and semiotic roads which we are then to travel along slowly and which we may well come to patrol. There is thus no cause to speak of initial ambiguity or indeterminacy; it is more a case of entering a semantic universe in the company of a capable guide. What look like initial ambiguities or indeterminacies are as fully determined as the precision and delimitation attained by the end, for what counts here is not the goal but the journey that leads to it. In sum, rather than the unidirectional orientation of textual linguistics, the literary study of a text must adopt a bidirectional orientation, one capable, in other words, of referring back from each sentence to the preceding one and of pausing at each sentence to check its necessity as expression. There is no progression from the more ambiguous to the less: literary reality exists in the space which lies between these two terms.

Plot and Fabula

3.1. In this chapter I do not intend to deal with style. Earlier sections (2.1, 2.2) have shown sufficiently that if we limit ourselves to the surface of the text, its discourse—the privileged domain, one would think, of temporal and linear succession—we find instead an intermittence, an alternating movement (reading of words or syntagms, adding together of sentences, integration of sentences into an earlier synthesis in memory). Three concomitant facts bring this about: (1) the inability of the mind to grasp more than one sentence at a time; (2) the translation of forms of expression into forms of content, in other words, the autonomy of content, narrative or not, as synthesized in its analytic (linguistic) formulation, whose coherence is maintained only during the reading of the single sentence; and (3) the breaking down of the syntagmatic elements of the text read so far into packages of paradigmatic elements.

The plot follows and sets forth the events narrated in the order in which they appear in the text; it is arrived at, moreover, by an act of synthesis (of summarizing paraphrase). Also, the description of any particular episode requires one to go behind its linguistic formulation and reformulate it in more simple terms.

Thus two types of summarizing paraphrase come face to face. One is by its very definition in chronological order (the fabula, subdivided into minimal elements); the other deliberately accepts all the temporal and spatial dislocations which the writer, with his particular ends in view, has put into effect (the plot). The fabula is thus seen to be a theoretical elaboration of fundamental importance for describing the plot by contrast, for it constitutes a touchstone, a means of measuring the dislocations there realized.

It is readily understandable that the Russian Formalists, in developing Veselovsky's insights, should have divided the field sharply, the literary critics taking the plot, the ethnographers the fabula and the narrative models. It should be noted, however, that a slight difference in publication dates, rather than dates of birth (Eikhenbaum 1886, Tomashevsky 1890, Shklovsky 1893, Propp 1895) resulted in the inability of the literary theorists to take into account the *Morphology of the Folktale*, for it appeared when the most productive period of Formalism was drawing to a close. Thus, even though they had formulated the concept of fabula as a working hypothesis, our theoreticians not only were unable to pass to the further and more basic phase of the model; they did not even fully exploit the fabula itself as a means for evaluating plot. Instead, they defined the different plots they dealt with by comparing them with each other. The astonishing critical discoveries of Shklovsky and the others thus reveal, in the last analysis, a fair measure of haphazardness.

After clearly expounding the reasons why the plot is not linear ("Art tends not to synthesis but to decomposition, since it is not a march to the sound of music but a *perceived* dance or promenade or, better, movement created to the sole end that we should hear it"),[33] Shklovsky nearly always arrives at such nonlinearity after comparison with analogous texts or with widely diffuse plot types ("For the birth of a particular tale what is necessary, therefore, is not just a plot but also a counterplot, a noncoincidence"; "Sterne works bearing in mind the adventure story, which, as everyone knows, has quite rigid forms and as a rule ends with marriage or betrothal. The forms of Sterne's novel are a deformation and a violation of traditional forms").[34]

The fact is that Shklovsky simultaneously set himself heterogeneous tasks: to trace a sort of history of plots, whose central thesis is the development of the tale into the novel, and to sketch out a typology of plots, to defend a particular antipsychological and antisociological poetic.

His *O teorii prozy* lists various types of construction technique systematically: circular construction, stepwise,[35] frame, brochette (*nanizy vanie*), and the rhetorical procedures which are built into them: parallelism and oxymoron. He takes account not only of relations between the materials but also of the effect they have on the reader: defamiliarization and above all retardation. Indeed Shklovsky tends to a too indiscriminate use of this kind of explanation, almost as if whole sections of a work had the exclusive aim of keeping the reader in doubt about future developments. This is a defect he subsequently corrects, giving a more complex explanation for the presence of apparently digressive pages: "Digressions fulfill three different functions . . . to permit the author to insert new material into the novel . . . to slow up the course of the action . . . to create contrasts."[36]

The dialectic between fabula and plot is sensed more clearly by Tomashevsky. The literary text is subjected to two technical procedures: first it is broken down into parts which constitute thematic unities; these parts are then rearranged and recombined "in their logical causal-temporal relationships." The first operation brings the plot to light, the second the fabula.[37]

These pages of Tomashevsky seem to me fundamental even in their defects. In particular I would remark a search for something that comes very near Propp's narrative model. This is seen most clearly when Tomashevsky declares that to arrive at the fabula, *free* and *static* motifs must be put aside (cf. sec. 1.1). He aims, in other words, at maintaining functional motifs alone in his fabula, even though he regards the others as decisive for the plot too: "It is enough to recapitulate the fabula of a work to realize at once what can be left aside while conserving the connections between the facts narrated and what cannot be left aside without breaking the causal link between them."[38]

But then Tomashevsky, either by making terminological distinctions ("theme" and motif") or by a double use of terms ("motif" for him is not only a minimal action like "evening came," "the hero died" but also a description of nature, place, setting, a character; he further contemplates the possibility of recurrent motifs, like musical leitmotifs), indicates that a different degree of conciseness may be involved in plot description and that as a consequence it is essential to show, according to the degree of synthesis, what role the motifs play.

By so doing we pass from theme as "a summarizing concept, which unifies the verbal material employed in the work," to the theme of each single part of a work, arrived at on the basis of its particular thematic unity,[39] to the fabula, to the plot with all the motifs which make it up, static and dynamic, bound and free. Tomashevsky shows that plot and fabula, clearly differentiated in terms of their relation to the chronological order, can also be arranged along a specific-generic line with numerous intermediate stages.

One of Tomashevsky's assertions should be kept in mind by all those who play on the chessboard of narrative: "The dynamic motifs are the central motor elements of the fabula; in the organization of the plot, on the other hand, static motifs may be brought to the fore."[40] This means, in substance, that there exist two orders of functionality, one of actions, the other of situations; or, if you prefer, that in a narration the weight of events does not correspond to their weight when manifested as concrete acts. Thus if the aim is to give a synthesis of plots, it is essential that what is sacrificed in a more advanced synthesis should be recovered in a different and complementary synthesis, to ensure that plot mechanism is not depicted inadequately.

3.2. The first operation to be carried out in discourse analysis is segmentation. Segmentation may set itself at least two main objectives: (1) to prepare sequences which, rearranged in terms of content chronology, will constitute the fabula and (2) to arrive at zones of convergence between various types of discourse function and various types of language. In other words, there is a linear segmentation and a segmentation into linguistic and functional classes.

In linear segmentation the demarcations may be thought of as determined by temporal dovetailing; those blocks constitute unities in which the succession of discourse coincides with succession in the narration. A segment ends as a rule either because it is followed by a digression (which leads to a different temporal moment, whether or not this is along the same line as the main narration) or because it is followed by a backward- or forward-looking segment. Obviously interruption exists only if we find a segment in another part of the text which carries forward the narration contained in the segment just defined. Almost as if they wished to stress this dovetailing, writers are not content with effecting such shifts with respect to the chronological order alone; they also nearly always create further phase differences between the external partitioning of the work (chapters, books, cantos) and content segments.[41]

The interest of linear segmentation lies in its impossibility. Linear segmentation brings us into contact with "cross-reference segments," those which assure the text's intelligibility over and above the temporal movement to and fro actuated within it. And it is not simply a matter of bracketing "cross-reference segments" in order to make possible a rearrangement of the fabula: backward- and forward-looking segments for the most part take on particular modes of exposition—speech, soliloquy, dream, presentiment, etc. (in the case of characters)—insertion, foreshadowing, etc. (in the technique of narrative discourse). This is why the fabula can be formulated only in summary form, which changes the way in which the events are formulated, a fact which confirms what has already been noted, that the fabula is primarily an instrument for measuring deviations from the order of narrative succession.

Even if attention is directed exclusively to the narrative aspect, it will be noted that the reader is offered a double itinerary for meaning. From the itinerary provided by the narrative discourse with its dislocations and its changes of route, the reader progressively discovers the temporal itinerary and is led to rearrange events that have been given him in terms of an *ordo artificialis* chosen by the writer. This constitutes the most general and most important form of defamiliarization. By its means the adventure entrusted to the narrative is supplemented by another: the adventure of reading. The order of the facts and the way they are brought to the reader's attention are such that their value is increased and polarized in a particular direction.[42]

If we go back to the schema put forward in section 2.1, the act of reading will now be seen to be even more complex, because while a "linguistic" reading faithfully follows the itinerary of the plot, a synthesis progressively added up in memory constantly tends to rearrange itself into fabula, in other words, to acquire and take into account each new clarification concerning the logical-temporal order of events. Each increase in information which reading furnishes constitutes a surprise and an elucidation as well. Even before serving as a theoretical hypothesis, the fabula is thus an absolutely essential moment in understanding a narrative text.[43]

The framing of norms for linguistic-functional segmentation is a less easy matter, despite the fact that in this case the discourse is more strictly adhered to and its articulations are more respected. In other words, it is *possible*. The term I employ shows the way I believe such segmentation can most usefully be put into effect. It is a matter of (1) arriving at compact discourse segments while taking into account eventual shifts in the way content is communicated; (2) distinguishing "action" segments from others that are descriptive, meditative, historical, etc.; and (3) defining the linguistic peculiarities of these segments.

This kind of segmentation paves the way for classifying the segments arrived at, a process which, at least from the point of view here adopted, comes down to an enumeration of *the ways content is communicated*. In effect, it is not merely temporal linearity which is broken up in narrative discourse; the very continuity of the discourse itself is interrupted as perspectives shift along the sender (narrator)–receiver (reader) line. I am thinking of the variety and variability of relations between narrator and reader on one hand and between the narrator and his characters on the other.

The narrator may identify himself with a character or with several characters in alternation, where use of the first person is appropriate; or he may see things through the eyes of a single character (his alter ego) and use the third person; or he may take up the differing points of view of characters involved. He may pretend to follow events, in other words, to be ignorant at each point in the story of what will happen next; or he may communicate events progressively though he knows them already, so that he can anticipate or recall them. He may address the reader directly, commenting on the narration and "conversing" with him, and he may expound impassively. He may even set up a fictitious play of three or more elements, presenting himself as no more than the editor of another writer's text or of a collection of letters.

Linguistic-functional segmentation allows the system of these perspectives of communication to be grasped[44] by isolating apostrophes to the reader or didascalic divagations; comments, anticipation, and recall; meta-narrative passages and feigned controversy between real and fictitious authors; patterning of present and past tenses, of first, second, and third persons, and so forth.[45]

Such segmentation, in other words, provides a general representation of narrative discourse in its proper sense: discourse of someone to someone else. And since this discourse, usually diegetic, nearly always contains parts in dialogue, i.e., mimetic parts, as well as monologues, indirect speech, and so on, segmentation brings to light their relationships and the reason that such various modes of communication alternate. We might say, paradoxically, that in more complex writers narration is often meta-narration, discourse meta-discourse; while the most complicated plot is that which concerns not events but their artistic extrinsication.

4.1. The two types of segmentation just described might be distinguished by the fact that one (linear segmentation) follows up links between referent (the tale told) and symbol (the narration itself)—from within the fiction, which the author initiates and the reader accepts, which considers reference as related to referent, though in a made-up tale it does not exist—the other (linguistic-functional segmentation) follows relationships between sender and receiver and possible mediations between one and the other.

This genetic bipartition of types of segmentation is, however, valid only in the first instance: the sender-receiver relation, when a literary work is transmitted, is almost exclusively communicative and unidirectional (the receiver does not in his turn become the sender or vice versa; there is no feedback); the object of communication is the narration itself, both signifying and signified. The peculiarities of narrative discourse thus depend totally on the reciprocal position of sender and receiver.

Segmentation thus allows us to investigate more thoroughly and systematically the problem of sender-receiver relations. This is a topic which lies outside the limits of my theme, but one on which much satisfactory work has already been done. A case in point is that of Genette: working on a concrete case, Proust's *Recherche*, he has brought together a series of analyses which systematize those of traditional poetics and those of the Russian Formalists while accepting a number of insights from German and American critical work.[46]

I shall but mention the problem of anisochronics or phase displacements between time narrated and the time of narration (i.e., in practice, the length of the text), or that of frequence (since the facts narrated can have a singulative, durative, or iterative aspect), inverse relations between diegetic (sender-controlled) or mimetic narration (where the characters and their words predominate),[47] tenses and moods in the narration.[48]

If we are emphasizing sender-receiver relationships, then we enter a different horizon from that of the utterance itself which is our theme (and where the act of communication is no more than a preestablished condition for the comprehensibility of a work which the author has furnished with meanings that, to a greater or lesser extent, the reader will recognize).[49] But if attention is turned to the forms these relationships produce, we find ourselves right inside the narrative text itself and, what is more, furnished with keys well adapted to unlocking it.

I have already noted, in fact,[50] that in the case of the literary work, the sender-receiver line breaks into two discontinuous parts: sender → message and message → receiver. Thus it is that the emergence of personal attitudes and direct intervention on the author's part are transformed into a formal datum, a part of the message. It is not the sender who addresses us; it is the message which contains, as one element of its artifice, the apostrophes or the meditations attributed to the sender, exactly as it contains the discourses and thoughts of the characters. And it is through the medium of this two-phase communication that the problems of tenses, moods, aspects, and so forth reveal their purely formal nature.

Indeed the analyses we have touched on constitute a complete program for the segmentation of a text. A case classification might be projected for grouping narrative texts in terms of the techniques adopted in them and, more importantly, the connections between them: for example, first-person texts with a certain kind of meta-narration and a prevalence of certain moods and tenses, and so on. Something of this kind has been attempted here (chap. 3); Genette provides a more sophisticated though not dissimilar example.

4.2. What is indispensable concerning the passage from segmentation to characterization of the fabula has been noted (secs. 3.1, 3.2). It represents a striving toward temporal linearity. At this point, however, I must add that temporal linearity is obtained by joining anew those segments into which a unified action (a unit of content) may have been divided. In other words, it is a matter of reconstructing units of sense. Each unit must have a completed sense and constitute a link in the chain of event units.[51] Integration can be effected within varying limits (corresponding to a more or less succinct summary, since such a summary will bring to light the type of connections arrived at). We are dealing with the scale of abstraction, of which more will be said later. But the segments can also be reconnected on a variety of ideal planes, still keeping the place they occupy in the text. In such a case, the segmentation brings to light other kinds of connection, from motivational to thematic.

Causal logic does not coincide with temporal logic, even if it implies it. Reconstructing a succession of events (the fabula) does not mean reconstructing their motivations, for these are often impalpable, remote, oblique. So true is this that the fabula is always a summary; but the sum of the motivations is so complex that only the text in its entirety can indicate it. The text remains impregnable to our attacks; our most striking success can be only to make it speak to us.

Thus segmentation distinguishes, but without particular privilege, those parts of the text which contain acts and direct causes, separating them from others which present broader motivations, more refined characterization of the characters, right down to environmental data and unconscious drives.[52] Such case classification, for the moment but roughly sketched out, will stand revealed in its various implications when we go on to deal with attempts to provide functional descriptions of the tale.

But the literary work is characterized precisely by the fact that it does not limit itself to explicit motivations. The narrator hardly ever says that a character performs an action for a certain reason; he gives us instead a series of clues which will set us on the right track to discover the reason for ourselves and to understand its complexity. This is an indirect enunciation which constitutes a correlative to the tangle, the frequently ungraspable nature of the forces that act on mankind.

A segmented text reveals to scrutiny a series of segments referable to a given system of motivations. These comply with the necessity, which modern linguistics has brought to light, of recursivity (in this sphere, semantic and lexemic affinities witness the connections, indeed the continuity, between segments even at a distance). And thus they are connected over a distance by means of the same techniques that rhetoric studies for continuous segments (anaphora, correlation, contraposition, etc.).

But recursivity has a double function: denotative and connotative. It is denotative in the way it brings to light chains of connections, in the way it progressively defines motivations; it is connotative in the measure in which insistence produces, more than an increase in facts, an increase in expressive effect. It is for this reason that two segments of a series are at one and the same time connected and separated: they are connected with regard to denotation and separated with regard to connotation. What characterizes these linked chains is, however, the musical nature of their execution, which is like that of an orchestral score; they give a particular rhythmical character to narrative discourse:

> In the first attempts he made to formulate a theory of prose, Shklovsky postulated a close correspondence between the artifices of composition and those of style. He maintained that "the techniques used in plot construction (*syuzhetoslozhenye*) were similar to, indeed basically identical with, those used in verbal orchestration." An analogy is thus established between seemingly disparate phenomena like "architectonic tautology," the recurrence of the same event in an epic poem, and verbal repetition.[53]

In other words, it is at this point that we verify in its macroscopic aspect (the most important for narrative discourse) my earlier observation (sec. 2.1) that every reading is *oriented*. Each segment, in fact, can be superimposed on a related segment and give rise to what Shklovsky calls the "transcurrent image": "The subject [plot] is constituted, via connections between the various parts, by the repetition of the same passages, and these become transcurrent images. . . . When we read a passage, we perceive it against the background of another. We have been given an orientation toward a connection, and we try to interpret it. This modifies our perception of the passage."[54]

We may say, then, that not only does the writer prefer to give us clues to motivations rather than the motivations themselves; he often drags us into the area (or aura) of these motivations by the use of techniques not so far removed from those of "hidden persuasion."[55] The reader's inductive activity is polarized by means of suggestions.

We know well enough—traditional stylistics have taught us this— that recursivity is not to be sought at the level of content alone. What I have said so far concerning thematic values holds equally for words or sentences which recur along a text. It would be important to find a point of convergence between contenutistic and stylistic recurrences. That this is possible is beyond question, since a theme often brings in its wake a whole lexical or semantic constellation, or even definite modes of enunciation.

I have tried to provide an example of this divergence in chapter 3, where segments of monologue, apostrophe, dialogue, prevalently direct or memorial narrative, and other elements which are introverted or segments of meta-narration all correspond to quite definite partitions of the tale, each with its own tone color, while at the same time they alternate according to specific symmetries.

To this end the notion of *register* should prove most useful. It is drawn by metaphor from music, where it indicates a device for variation of sonority and timbre. A whole text is "performed," alternating registers whose functions are evidently coloristic, though other functions serve to distribute the matter narrated as well. Unfortunately the meaning of the term is not as yet definitely established. One goes from register as "the sum of lexical and rhetorical motivations and techniques," involving "a definite expressive tone,"[56] to its definition as "a sum of communicative conventions whose existence one is obliged to postulate to account for the transmission of a particular kind of message. As such, it might be termed code. . . . As an inventory of selective affinities, oppositions, and similarities aspiring to become linked together in the contiguity of a text, register fulfills the function of rules of combination in the constitution of a text,"[57] or "a network of preestablished relationships between elements of different levels of formalization, as well as between the levels themselves"; while others consider as registers the writer's linguistic means, according to whether the referential aspect (descriptive discourse), the literary aspect (abstract discourse, figured discourse, direct discourse) or the process of enunciation itself (personal discourse, evaluative discourse) prevails.[58]

This final definition gives precedence to modes of enunciation which it is perhaps pointless to call registers. Zumthor's definition (particularly "network of preestablished relationships between elements of different levels of formalization, as well as between the levels themselves") is operatively most useful, even if, in view of his historiographical intentions, Zumthor stresses the traditional nature ("preestablished relationships") of the registers; what matters more to us is the complex and structuring character of a notion whose constituent elements ask to be defined anew for each text investigated.

I hold to my proposal to read a whole text—especially if it is stylistically elaborated and varied—as an orchestral score of registers which at times accompany, at times may even overwhelm the narration itself, replacing a plot of events with a plot of artistic tonalities.[59]

Functions and Fabula

5.1. For reasons that have to do with the political and cultural history of Europe during 1930–60, Propp's proposals came clearly and forcefully to the fore only during the 1960s, first in the field of folklore and ethnography and then in the field of literature.[60] I shall begin with this revival in literary theory, though some mention will be made later of the ethnologists' contribution.

No one has advocated Propp's approach more insistently than Bremond. At the beginning of one of his first contributions he gives an excellent definition of how Propp's analyses can be transferred to the literary domain (and within what limits). "What Propp studies in the Russian folktale . . . is a layer of autonomous meaning endowed with a structure which can be isolated from the sum of the message: the *récit*. As a consequence, any kind of narrative message, irrespective of the expression technique it employs, reveals the same approach at this same level. It is necessary and sufficient that it tell a tale. The structure of this tale is independent of the techniques that take charge of it."[61] Here the semiotic value of the narrative model is reconfirmed and its independence of expressive means and techniques stated. But Bremond further realizes that Propp's closed system will not retain its validity once attention has been directed to other texts. What Bremond seeks to accommodate at this point is the possibility of options: any given action will be followed up or it will not; if it is, the result will be propitious or it will not. Analysis of the *récit* must thus be binary ("It is essential never to postulate a function without postulating at the same time the possibility of a contradictory option").[62]

The fixed succession of functions which Propp presents is thus called into question (at least in abstract terms) by a different exigency: a series of open alternatives for each separate function. It is then exposed to even more damaging criticism by a further observation; between certain functions there exists a relationship of presupposition and consequently a fixed order, while others occupy a preferential position that is no more than probable. This allows us to perceive the possibility of free-standing functions.

I shall not go into such details, however important they may be, as Bremond's suggestion that the functions should not be made to follow each other along a unified chain, but homogeneous, correlated classes of functions within a *récit* should be looked for and then placed in position, respectively, along parallel lines in such a way as to constitute connected but not consecutive sequences of the narration (susceptible, however, of being broken down into smaller units [the functions] and larger units [the sequences]).

What should be underlined at once, however, is the necessity for dichotomy, which as Bremond himself points out,[63] allows connections to be established with archetypal behavior patterns and cultural stereotypes to which the listener (or reader) relates the *récit*, recognizing narrative meanings or noting infractions should the narrator (or writer) effect them. For Bremond, the functions are in fact "sense unities."[64] They may constitute models of greater or lesser complexity: "It is undoubtedly possible, in combining a limited number of easily arrived at elements (the functions grouped in triads), to construct models of situation and behavior of indefinitely increasing complexity, capable of constituting the 'simulacra' of events and characters (dramatis personae, actants, roles, whatever one calls them) which semiotic plot analysis requires."[65]

Moving on to constructive proposals, Bremond explains his program as a description of the "logical constraints which every series of events arranged in the form of a story must respect if it does not want to run the risk of being unintelligible."[66] Thus we are dealing with a design which is deductive in character and for which Propp's formulations constitute no more than a typical inventory of exemplifications. Here, meanwhile, is his definition of *récit*: "Every story consists of a discourse which integrates a succession of events of human interest into the unity of a single action."[67]

Bremond holds fast, naturally, to the aforementioned points: no function is obligatorily followed by another, because each time a binary possibility is opened up which admits passage or nonpassage from the potential to the actual.

What concerns us here is the language employed to describe the functions. We have seen that Propp made his classification while taking into account the system as a whole. At a certain point of his *Morphology* we find this outline of a generalization: "From a morphological point of view, we may define as folktale any development from an injury (X) or a failure (x) through intermediate functions to a marriage (N) or to other functions employed as dénouement. . . . We have called this development *movement*; each new injury, each new failure, gives rise to a new movement."[68]

Bremond's procedure is the opposite. Given that the point of departure for an action can only be a human project that events either favor or hinder, all narration can be reduced to two types:

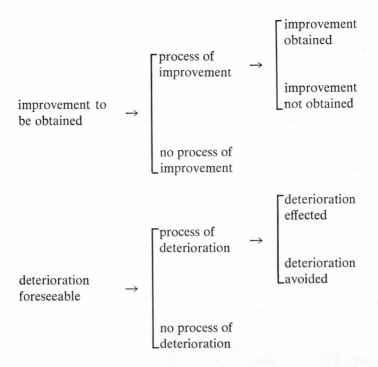

Into these general patterns (in part using Propp's terminology) the main intermediate events are inserted: *obstacle to eliminate, task to*

perform, problem to solve, negotiation, aggression, etc. In this case classification the characters (*ally* and *beneficiary of aid, adversary* and *person attacked, seducer* and *seduced*) serve to distinguish the sequences, i.e., the series of functions in which they are involved. Bremond informs us that every sequence has a parallel marked with its opposite sign, since the victory of one character is the defeat of the other; the success of one, the failure of the other; and so forth. It might be objected or at least pointed out that such doubling is hardly ever used in the fabula, since every event is set in relation to the protagonist(s) and judged from that viewpoint.

We might at this point ask ourselves what kind of actions Bremond counts as functions and how he passes from the general to the specific. For the first point, Bremond affirms that "to elementary narrative types there correspond . . . the most elementary forms of human behavior. The promise, the contract, the mistake, the trap, etc., are all universal categories." The passage from the general to the particular is then actuated by the piling up of sequences within the great triad-matrix: in other words, it is a matter of listing the obstacles that intervene to block *improvement,* the *aids* that are furnished the protagonist, the means for *eliminating the adversary,* and so on, "in a hierarchy of sequences, always the same, which determine exhaustively the field of what can be narrated"; "construing, by starting out from the simplest forms of the narratable, sequences and roles, concatenations of situations ever more complex and differentiated, we lay the foundations for a classification of story types. . . ."[69]

The advantage of this project of Bremond's is thus, it seems to me, that the passage from the general to the particular is always actuated on the same plane of abstraction.[70] Improvement, obstacle, means for its elimination, and so on are all terms which maintain a generality open to a whole range of subarticulations. Nonetheless, the choice of this plane is arbitrary, and one may well question its validity.

There is little doubt that in a lexicon of functions like that used by Bremond any kind of narration can be entered. But there exists a point beyond which a description becomes falsification. Can I describe as "seduction" in the same way the behavior of both a dishonest adviser and an ardent lover or place under the same heading the deception of a swindler and of an adulterer? And if I begin to distinguish the functions even in lexical terms, do I not find myself moving on a slope which will take me far afield?

Let us take a classic example, that of Propp. We are given these five initial situations:

1. The king sends Ivan to look for the princess. Ivan sets out.
2. The king sends Ivan to look for a rare object. Ivan sets out.
3. A sister sends her brother to look for a medicine. The brother sets out.
4. A stepmother sends her stepdaughter to look for fire. The stepdaughter sets out.
5. A blacksmith sends his help to look for a cow. His help sets out.[71]

For Propp the five segments are functionally identical. They constitute the *sending* and the *setting out on the search*. Within the system of the magic folktales these initial situations are typical, and their unification is not open to challenge. Precisely because the system is so rigid, it might be held that if at any time event 4 should not present the development it *ought* to have but constitute a merely anecdotal episode, then it should not be considered as a function but should be taken up into another function or simply disregarded. On the other hand, other systems may be imagined in which fundamental importance is attributed to the difference between an animate search object (1, 5) and an inanimate one (2–4), a pleasant (1, 2) or a useful object (3–5), etc.

The degree of generalization in delimiting functions is thus conditioned by the system. In its turn, a system can be provided with boundaries which are either more or less confined in accordance with the aims of the critic. The text under examination (i.e., its fabula) can itself be given the status of a system, as can all the related works of a writer or all related works of a single or several epochs. A necessary consequence of this is that functions should be defined against a variable scale of generalization. In other words, the passage from the general to the particular should not be effected merely within a two-dimensional framework whose internal divisions are of greater and greater density (which is what Bremond proposes); it should be, rather, a passage from generic to specific, which will have as its opposite extremes maximum generalization and maximum specification. In any case, there is a limit beyond which we cannot go: that of the semantic identity of the text under examination. Plot and fabula naturally preserve a mass of particulars and specifications which the narrative model must leave aside. But I would not consider of much use a narrative model in terms of which the text would be unrecognizable. There is an antinomy between individuality and generalization which is of fundamental importance in the case of narrative models. The models must allow for a description in uniform terms of texts of varied nature and of different date; in other words, it must define invariants. But the moment these invariants are found to be of no significance when the text is totally unrecognizable in the model, then the model itself has been shown to be useless. What is needed is a biunial relationship, however general, between text and model.

It might be noted, on the other hand, that the triads dear to Bremond are made up of homogeneous elements on the logical plane, but this is not the case on the narrative plane. In terms of narrative, the initial element (virtuality) and the final element (goal attained) may have a purely minimal consistency. The first may very well not be expressed at all but taken up entirely into the middle element (actualization). I would suggest, then, that Bremond's matrix scheme should be transformed as follows: (virtuality) → actualization → (goal attained), to show that the *récit*, in the most abstract form possible, is to be identified with its middle element, even though the other two elements are a necessary condition of its subsistence.[72]

A tendency toward tripartition is, however, congenital, we might say, and it has been very accurately stated by Aristotle: "A whole is that which has a beginning, a middle, and an end. A beginning is that which does not itself follow anything by causal necessity, but after which something naturally is or comes to be. An end, on the contrary, is that which itself naturally follows some other thing, either by necessity, or as a rule, but has nothing following it. A middle is that which follows something as some other thing follows it.[73] Here the initiating and moving function of the first element and the conclusive function of the last are well evidenced. And this suggests that Bremond's "virtuality" should be replaced with real functions which already belong to diegesis like, e.g. (at a much reduced level of abstraction), "falling in love," "promise of marriage," or such.

Let us take, for example, this triad: promise of marriage → delaying misfortunes (obstacles to overcome → means of overcoming the obstacles → obstacles overcome) → marriage. It will fit hundreds of texts, from Alexandrian romances to *I promessi sposi* to sentimental love stories. Or again, depending on the type of "contract" the promise of marriage constitutes and the type of obstacles encountered, progressively narrower groupings can be established which will bring to light, case by case, the specific elements which must be included in the generality of the basic formula.

A narration which starts out from the function "falling in love" will be even richer in developments. A first distinguishing feature (at least in a monogamous society) will be the preexistence of a marriage or its absence, the second such feature the intention of consummating the affair or not, etc. Hence the presence or absence of a function "adultery," which may then be considered as conclusive (as a goal reached) or interlocutory with respect to subsequent developments. Within this framework, stratagems directed against the legitimate husband can be looked at only in relation to their scope (overcoming the obstacle) or else compared with all stratagems to whatever end, defined as "deception" or even more closely specified when the narrative turns on their modality, the means employed (the *beffa*; see chap. 4), which add to the deception itself a desire to humiliate the other party.

In the second instance, functions can be paired or united in wider groupings. Where there is a promise of marriage, the obligation, explicit or not, to preserve chastity may be considered concomitant or not, and this entails a series of developments parallel to that of the basic formula in terms ever more complex. It is naturally on the basis of these patterns (because they are stereotypes) that any infractions will achieve effects of surprise, comedy, etc. (see chap. 5).

In my opinion, therefore, the network which defines the *récit* should not only offer possibilities of closer meshing, i.e., of enrichment of its particulars; it must allow further measurings of greater or lesser precision against a generic-specific scale, so that the focal point of the analysis can be placed at different distances from the object, associating it, as occasion shall serve, with larger or smaller classes of objects described respectively by the same scale.

5.2. Propp defines characters by setting out from functions, not vice versa. Having found seven principal types of character (antagonist, donor, helper, princess or king, sender, hero, false hero),[74] he characterizes them on the basis of the functions they fulfill, defining the spheres of action that pertain to them and stressing the likelihood that a single person might embrace several spheres of action or that a single sphere might be divided up among several characters.

This extremely original theoretical decision, which in substance deprives the character of any separate individual physiognomy *prior to the action* and transforms it into a role *in the course of the action*, involves a precise conception of the magic folktale, which I shall not discuss here (and which, moreover, Propp leaves implicit): a conception in which subjects are subordinated to their acts, since the acts themselves are simple formal variants of an event which is already predisposed as immutable. This impossibility of a function having alternative outcomes empties of significance the figure of the person who fulfills it.

Propp says that "all the *predicates* give us the composition of the folktale; all the *subjects*, the *complements*, and the other parts of the sentence determine the narrative plot."[75] It is clear that in extending Propp's account to literary activity in general an attempt has been made to take into account not only the predicates (i.e., the actions) but also subjects (i.e., characters) and modalities (i.e., complements).

It is probably this statement of Propp's which gave rise to Todorov's 1969 attempt at analysis of the tale. His basic principle (which aims at a great deal more than just describing the novelle of the *Decameron*) is that a possibility must exist of synthesizing the content of a tale by making use of the principal categories of grammar: the characters will be subjects or objects of the action, in other words, agents or sufferers; their actions will be verbs; their properties adjectives or nouns; and so on. Nor are other grammatical categories lacking—negation, comparison, mood—even though their use is more metaphorical than that of the basic terms.

There is no point in providing a summary of the ingenious way in which Todorov synthesizes Boccaccio's novelle, reducing them to formulae. I might merely mention his thorough examination of the relationship between character and function; his distinction (though arguable in many details) between a syntactic and a semantic plane, the first of which institutes the *sense* of the functions in relational terms (along the lines of Propp), while the second, leaving aside the tale itself, supplies its meaning; and his setting up of special signs to distinguish between a chronological and a causal succession.

Todorov, however, maintains the preeminence of function over character. The agent is qualified by the predicate attached to it: "The agent is someone, but it is also no one"; it is "like an empty form which the different predicates (verbs or attributes) come to fill."[76] This is a decision which, if one wishes to reduce the tale to a pure succession of functions, is perfectly justified. As for Todorov in particular, it should be emphasized that he then recovers the personality traits of the character by inserting its attributes into the sequences; but they are no more than qualifying elements involved in the tale.

The main advantage of Todorov's attempt is that it suggests a formalized and linear representation of the sequences which constitute the tale, a representation which identifies not only functions but also characters, with their determining attributes and volitions. Its main defect, without going into details already amply discussed by others,[77] is the way it classifies the verbs in three categories, "to modify," "to sin," "to punish."[78] These are not located at a single level of generalization; they do not constitute a single coherent semantic system and are not capable of grouping together under their aegis even the actions which really are described in the *Decameron*.

It is, however, an extremely instructive defeat. Let us leave aside "to modify," whose range is naturally enormously vast, and take instead "to sin." Under *pécher*, Todorov registers *acte sexuel, voler, tuer, manger, se saoûler, manquer de respect, blasphémer, trahir une promesse, avoir le cœur dur, faire partie d'un peuple ennemi, être riche* (naturally in particular situations). The verbs registered are described at the level of fabula. The verb from which they derive can embrace them all only from within a particular conception of life, that which Todorov attributes to Boccaccio. In seeking to unify all these verbs under no more than three headings, Todorov has shown implicitly that every category is necessarily tied to an ideology, that of the historical period to which the text belongs or that of the historical period in which the analysis is carried out. The adequacy of Todorov's patterns subsists, therefore, only in the adequacy of his categorizations in their turn, i.e., in his having effected an adequate historical-ideological interpretation. Extreme abstraction does not lead, in this particular case, to extreme applicability. The model is a historical one (cf. sec. 5.4).

5.3. Bremond has recently come back to the problem of the *récit*, with the greater part of his latest work, under the title "Les rôles narratifs principaux."[79] At the beginning he seems to revert to his earlier position, repeating his triadic scheme (*éventualité* → *passage à l'acte* → *achèvement*) and also his insistence on binary possibilities. But one senses immediately that the emphasis is different, and this is confirmed by the absence of the earlier article itself from a book which brings together writings from as far back as 1964.

In effect, this new proposal turns Propp's approach upside down, even on a point where Bremond had previously accepted it: the character now prevails over the function:

> The function of an action can only be defined from the standpoint of the interests or initiatives of the character who is either its sufferer or its agent. Several functions do not link up together unless one supposes that they concern the history of the same character (thus *victory* does not follow *struggle* unless one admits that one and the same character is first fighting, then victorious). Thus we define function not merely by means of an action (which we call *processus*) but by establishing a relationship between a character-subject and a processus-predicate; or again, to adopt an even clearer terminology, we might say that the structure of a *récit* depends not on a sequence of actions but on the connecting [*agencement*] of roles.[80]

Such an innovation makes redefinition obligatory. Function is defined no longer in terms of its incidence in the overall movement of the *récit* but from the relationship of an agent and a predicate; the *récit* is no longer made up of a succession of actions but of a concatenation of roles.

If we compare the earlier and later Bremonds, we note that the schematizations of the first present processes of improvement (or deterioration), obstacles to be overcome, aid to be received, services to be offered, all arranged in columns under the role of beneficiary or victim of the processes in question, identified with the perspective of the tale. Now it is the character itself which is involved in or carries out the process, which brings about the modification or is its object, and so on. Furthermore, reflexive functions, those in which the agent is identified with the sufferer, are also stressed.

All of Bremond's work thus centers on definition of possible roles. There are two main categories: sufferer and agent. The sufferer may be the object of influences that provide him with or deprive him of information, that give or eliminate satisfaction or dissatisfaction, hopes, and fears; he may be the object of actions which modify his destiny (by improvement or deterioration) or maintain him in his former state (by protection or frustration). Correlatively, the agent may appear as the one who influences, improves, or deteriorates, as protector or frustrater. There also exist numerous subdivisions and subspecies: the agent may act voluntarily or involuntarily, and so on.

One sees at once that, though their terminology may seem to correspond in part to that of Propp, the roles are in fact markedly different, because their validity is much greater (it is indeed total, at least in intention). To Propp's antagonist, for example, was reserved a series of limited functions whose outcome is foreseeable, whereas Bremond's degrader and frustrater may present themselves in any kind of tale and have as many possibilities of success as of failure; Propp's king and princess disappear not so much because their presence in narrative literature as a whole is minimal but because, in a given tale, the qualification of king or princess is only one among an infinite number of possible qualifications, while its bearer may be agent or sufferer, protector or frustrater, etc.

As distinct from his earlier writing, the Bremond of 1973 thus insists much more on roles than on the *récit* itself; but it turns out that it is only a question of the direction his researches have taken if his conclusions are based on the passage "from precoding of roles to encoding of the *récit*."[81] In the conclusions indeed it is the process which predominates with respect to the roles in a series of six-column tables which list syntactic connection, process, process phase, volition, persons (agent and sufferer). Reading the columns from right to left we thus find agent and sufferer of the process, voluntary or involuntary nature of the process, phase of the process (potential, in action, completed), process (the types foreseen are some fifty), types of relation between one phase and another (cause and effect, means and result, obstacle and goal).

The contrivance assembled by Bremond 1973 is much more compact and complex than that of the earlier Bremond. It should be stressed too that now Bremond refers (however summarily) to concrete examples—folktales, stories, theatrical scenes, *exempla ficta*, etc.; in other words, he checks his deductions against an inventory. His final tables appear to take into account the double perspective of every narration, an aspect which is already present in his earlier work. Processes and their voluntary nature are always defined in relation to agent and sufferer: a pairing which, however, makes it difficult to take into account the eventuality that two independent actions might collide, bringing about for their agents and sufferers consequences neither had bargained for. The logic of the function which is inevitably a human action, even in Propp, continues to dominate, whether the characters are absorbed (Propp) or are the initiators (Bremond).

And it dominates too in the exploitation of motifs and attributes. See how Bremond distinguishes between purely descriptive static and dynamic attributes "by whose means he [the character] undergoes or provokes an evolution" and takes account only of the latter.[82] Or note how the passage from a state A to a state B is always seen as a process of modification, not as an effect of a force produced by the state itself (poverty, dissatisfaction, etc.). Brought to the center of the tale, in other words, the character continues to be qualified by the actions he performs or is subjected to, by the movements he sets in motion or by which he is swept along.

In my opinion (and especially when there are in question texts with a marked degree of literary responsibility) these relationships ought, rather, to be inverted: an action interests in the measure in which it reflects the intentions and will of a character: indeed a character who for the most part has a name and surname, is enrolled in however fictitious a parish register, and constitutes a cluster of aptitudes and character traits (hence the appropriateness of the English term "character") which, whether he is an atypical individual or a traditional type or "mask"— according to the poetics or literary genres involved—constitute ipso facto the explanation of his motives and encompass the likelihood of internal development. The character, finally, effects a unification of the functions, since these make sense because they are carried out by him, fanning out from him: "A common technique for grouping and linking up the motifs as series is the introduction of characters who constitute their living carriers."[83]

5.4. Todorov's and Bremond's are the most ambitious attempts so far made to analyze the tale. Rather than carry out detailed criticism of them, it will be helpful to put them to the test in concrete terms, perhaps attempting their unification.[84] But the discourse I wish to touch on here concerns the very foundations of the method. All these analyses of the tale make use of a meta-language which they apply to the language text (the literary work, the folktale, etc.). This meta-language may lead to formalizations, but it will do so only by way of the humble technique of paraphrase, for the most part in the form of a summary.

This deserves a whole history; but I shall do no more than touch on its two extremes. Plato, contrasting mimetic and diegetic discourse and recasting in narrative form the discourses of Chryses and Agamemnon's reply, produces a reduction and a banalization of the Homeric text:

Iliad:

"Ye sons of Atreus, and ye other well-greaved Achaeans,
To you may the gods who have homes upon Olympus
Grant that ye sack the city of Priam, and return safe to your homes;
But my dear child do ye set free for me,
And accept the ransom out of awe for the son of Zeus, Apollo, that
    smiteth afar."
Then all the rest of the Achaeans shouted assent,
Bidding reverence the priest and accept the glorious ransom,
Yet the thing pleased not the heart of Agamemnon, son of Atreus,
But he sent him away harshly, and laid upon him a stern command:
"Let me not find thee, old man, by the hollow ships,
Either tarrying now or coming back hereafter,
Lest thy staff and the fillet of the god protect thee not.
But her will I not set free: ere that shall old age come upon her
In our house, in Argos, far from her country,
As she walks to and fro before the loom and tends my couch.
Nay, get thee gone; anger me not, that so thou mayest go the safer."
So he spake, and the old man was seized with fear and hearkened to
    his word.
Forth he went in silence along the shore of the loud-resounding sea,
And earnestly thereafter, when he had gone apart, did the old man
Pray to the prince, Apollo, whom fair-haired Leto bare:
"Hear me, thou of the silver bow, who dost stand over Chryse,
And holy Cilla, and dost rule mightily over Tenedos, thou Sminthian,
If ever I roofed over a shrine to thy pleasing,

Or if ever I burned to thee fat thigh-pieces of bulls or goats,
Fulfill thou for me this prayer:
Let the Danaans pay for my tears by thy shafts."

Republic:

The priest came and prayed the gods on behalf of the Greeks that
they might capture Troy and return safely home, but begged that they
would give him back his daughter, and take the ransom which he
brought, and respect the God. Thus he spoke, and the other Greeks
revered the priest and assented. But Agamemnon was wroth, and bade
him depart and not come again, lest the staff and chaplets of the God
should be of no avail to him—the daughter of Chryses should not be
released, he said—she should grow old with him in Argos. And then
he told him to go away and not to provoke him, if he intended to get
home unscathed. And the old man went away in fear and silence,
and, when he had left the camp, he called upon Apollo by his many
names, reminding him of everything which he had done pleasing to
him, whether in building his temples, or in offering sacrifice, and
praying that his good deeds might be returned to him, and that the
Achaeans might expiate his tears by the arrows of the God.[85]

Naturally a further reduction would also be possible, not only in the
form "Chryses asks to have his daughter ransomed; Agamemnon refuses
and sends Chryses away" (as Genette proposes)[86] but also as "Request
for ransom; refusal" (considering the dismissal of Chryses as nonfunctional).

Hendricks finds himself faced with the same problem when, fully
aware of the gap that exists between linguistic and narrative meanings,[87] he proposes a series of phases for a passage from one group to
the other which is intended to be as unsubjective as possible.[88] What he
calls the "normalization" of a text is very similar to the simplification
carried out by Plato (see the "normalized" Faulkner passage in his
"Methodology," p. 173); but a series of successive normalizations leads,
in any case, to a "summarization" that is inevitably a summarizing paraphrase.[89] Hendricks concludes correctly that "summarization is a more
powerful operation than normalization, but it is also more subjective in
that it is not closely tied to grammatical form."[90]

Hendricks does not realize, however (and this would weigh even
more heavily on the subjective side of the scale), that the summary of
a work which the critic proposes serves not only to indicate what he has
considered most significant (pertinent) in it but also to prepare his own
interpretation, for this adapts itself naturally to the choices and the em-

phasis which the summary synthesizes. Thus unless one takes the summary as the equivalent of the work (and no one suggests that we should), it can be maintained that it is a critical act of the first importance; while its inevitably subjective nature is an indicator of the impossibility of an incontrovertible definition of narrative meanings.

Let us further exclude the case of inaccurate summary, in which narrative events are expressed which are absent from the text or different from those contained in it; the fact remains that the choice of events, and even more their concatenation, interpret what the text says more diffusely and with a greater degree of complexity precisely because the concatenation is not, in the narrator's intention, as simple as the paraphrase makes it seem. There thus exists an infinite number of possible "honest" (i.e., perfectly faithful) paraphrases of any given text.[91] No measure of objectivity exists, because paraphrases are by their very nature not objective.

That functions are formulated by means of a summarizing technique is well known. Propp has said as much, indicating in the summary a preliminary phase of the operation: "The content of the folktale can be entirely expounded in short sentences of this kind: the parents go into the wood, they tell the children not to go into the road, a dragon carries off the little girl, etc."[92] Propp is glossed by Meletinsky, who talks of "condensation of content in a series of short sentences."[93] And it might be remarked that the whole *Morphology of the Folktale* is based not on the tales themselves but on their summaries effected within the framework of Propp's own theoretical discourse.

In an even more thorough fashion, Todorov points out the existence of a scale of generalization of summaries:

> The basic syntactic unit will be called *proposition*. It corresponds to an action which cannot be further broken down; for example, "John steals money," "The king kills his grandson," etc. Nonetheless, such action is not susceptible of division at a certain level of generality only; at a more concrete level, such a proposition will be represented by a series of propositions. In other words, the same story can be provided with summaries that are more or less succinct. Thus one such will contain the proposition "The king courts the marquise," whereas the other will have "The king decides to set out," "The king travels," "The king arrives at the house of the marquise," etc.[94]

Thus Todorov reaches the point of confessing quite openly that "we deal with résumés of stories rather than the stories themselves,"[95] giving rise to scandal that would be justified only if the summaries were not "honest" or not the work of the critic himself.[96] The technique of summary is an indispensable step.

One should add that the telescopic series of greater or lesser summarizing generalizations acts principally on the totality of the motivations:

> A historian may summarize a reign by writing, "He set about consolidating his throne"; he may provide a first qualification by adding, "He set about consolidating his throne and breaking the power of the great feudal houses" and then a second by writing, "He set about consolidating his throne, relying on the middle classes to break the power of the great feudal houses." Within such telescoping [emboîtement] of means, consolidating the throne may be designated by the récit as the means for a monarch to do his duty, in other words, to satisfy an ethical motive, the ultimate scope of his conduct; bringing down the feudal lords is the means of consolidating the throne; i.e., it is the means to the means; relying on the middle classes is the means of bringing down the feudal lords, i.e., it is a means three times removed.[97]

One example will suffice to show all the responsibility a summary eventually takes upon itself. Folktale 113 in Afanas'ev is quoted and commented upon by Propp to show the method he has adopted to arrive at his functions;[98] Bremond counterproposes an analysis of his own which brings to the fore moments of the tale Propp neglects and represents its narrative logic quite differently.[99] The disagreement between the two scholars is no more than a clash between two summaries.

Even if we aim at a formalization of the récit, this formalization cannot avoid passing through the phase (by its very nature subjective) of paraphrase.[100] One cannot very well avoid the schema récit → paraphrase → formalization. Here lies the difference with respect to scientific formalizations. A chemical or mathematical formula *can* be stated in a natural language, but almost always to the detriment of its clarity and universality: chemical equation or transformation → formula → paraphrase; the formulation of the récit, however, *has its basis* in a summary carried out in a natural language, and it does no more than express this in a synthetic and symbolic way. In other words, it is not a true formalization.

There is still more. Functions as a rule are indicated by means not of paraphrases but of generic terms, which I shall call "labels." In this new passage there is a further subjective intervention on the critic's part. Thus in Propp the following function is defined as connivance: "The victim falls into a trap and by so doing involuntarily helps his enemy," while this function is *lack*: "One of the members of the family lacks or desires something," not to speak of functions which no longer describe events but classify them in relation to their collocation in the tale: thus *moments of connection*, which stands for the following: "The disaster or lack is made known; recourse is had to the hero with a prayer or an order; he is sent or allowed to go."[101]

Propp's technique is unexceptionable. In fact both his paraphrases and his "labels" are formulated on the basis of a knowledge of the corpus considered as a closed system. By comparing all narrative segments which are analogous in (1) their content and (2) their meaning in the unfolding of the plot (the first analogy holds only where the second subsists), Propp arrived at a "normalized" formulation which constitutes, we might say, an average of all the paraphrases of analogous segments drawn from single stories.

What we have shown for Propp holds good for any kind of attempt to arrive at and *name* functions. Of course the actions of the text can be analyzed in relation to the unfolding of the plot, but to what corpus must they may be related in order for us to be able to label them? A statement of principle seems indispensable: a general model of narrativity seems to me impossible because it is events themselves which, according to times and places, are enucleated differently from reality and take on different meanings. Narrative functions reflect this slow but continuous change. I cannot analyze a medieval epic text without making use of the feudal code and its relative violations, without giving to family rivalry, to the insult, to betrayal, to the heroic deed[102] a value totally different—and different in extension—from that possessed by such terms as "breaking the contract," "struggle," "moral injury," or others like them. And above all, the logical connection between the actions is different, because each historical period has a different conception of merits and defects, enjoyment and suffering, gratification and punishment and imagines in a totally different manner the way they are interconnected in the life of a man. The logic of a tale (on the basis of which actions can be defined as functions and labeled) is the logic of a particular culture, the reflection of a society or of its earlier historical phases.

Thus it seems to me pointless to try to generalize Propp's kind of model, perhaps by simplifying it further. For even if we could force into it absolutely any tale of any period at all (and this is not the case), this would only be done at the cost of total falsification not simply of the "label" but of the connections which exist between one function and another. It has been said that Propp has provided, in a certain sense, a general schema for all Russian magic folktales. Well and good. But such a schema is not that of all extant narratives, and if this is true for the succession of the functions, it will hardly be less true for the functions themselves, for they are defined on the basis of this very succession.

The same thing might be said for any other closed model. Open models (Bremond, Todorov) are more readily utilizable because they can more readily reflect the ethical conceptions expressed in the texts, but they present difficulties in their lexical and semantic definition. In the infinite variety of the actions that a subject can perform and that the dictionary of a given language registers as verbs, which terms (verbs) are we to adopt in order to group in a satisfactory and sufficiently general manner all actions capable of being realized and the verbs that designate them? Once again we are faced with the problem of generalization, and the difficulties in our case arise from the necessity that the various actions narrated in the texts should be labeled not with terms which are not generic enough or which are too generic, given the relationships established between them (and which legitimize the term "function") but with terms which will be valid for a possibly comprehensive number of texts (cf. sec. 5.1).

What is called for, in short, is a preliminary operation: to determine the intertextual logic of the actions in a given corpus, endowed with a precise historical status which may be checked against the context. It is only when this has been done for any given text that three different orders of operation can begin: (1) a choice of the degree of simplification of the fabula into nuclear actions; (2) a choice of the level of abstraction on which to determine nuclear actions; and (3) a choice, from within the totality of the terms which designate such actions, of those most apt to act as "labels" in relation to both contextual and intertextual logic.

Diachrony and Achrony in the Fabula

6.1. As has already been seen (sec. 1.1), what characterizes the fabula is by definition its chronological and causal ordering of events. Any paraphrase which falls short of this arrangement can be replaced by a paraphrase which respects the chronology. (A separate problem, negligible from a theoretical point of view, is a possible series of contemporary events.) Propp holds firm to this principle, defining function in relation to the unfolding of events (cf. sec. 1.2), i.e., on causal and positional bases. "The structure of the folktale, as Propp outlines it, appears as a *chronological* succession of qualitatively distinct functions, each one of which constitutes an independent 'genre.' "[103]

In Lévi-Strauss the break with Propp's approach is decisive, right from his 1955 address,[104] where Propp's ideas are present only very indirectly, probably filtered through the teaching of Jakobson.[105] Mention is made, in fact, of a "twofold structure of myth, at one and the same time *historical* and *ahistorical*," by virtue of which it "can simultaneously belong to the sphere of the *parole* (and be analyzed as such) and to that of the *langue* (in which it is formulated), while at the same time offering on a third level a character of its own as absolute object."[106] As *parole* myth is realized syntactically in elements lined up in a spacial-temporal succession; as *langue*, it is analyzable into elements (mythems)[107] which can permutate and be arranged according to achronic meaningful groupings.

A myth's constituent mythems should be arranged (as in an orchestral score) in such a way that their order of succession will be maintained horizontally at the same time as vertical columns are constituted and labeled as semantic relationships. The horizontal reading of the mythems is that of the tale itself (chronological); the vertical reading is that of the *sense* (achronic). This conception was naturally enough reaffirmed after the publication in America of *Morphology of the Folktale* (1948), as it happens in discussion with Propp himself: "If our conception is adopted, the order of chronological succession is taken up into a structure whose matrix is atemporal, whose form, in fact, is constant, while shifts in its functions will be no more than one of their modes of permutation (vertically by columns or fractions of columns)."[108]

This affirmation of the significance of mythems has borne fruit in the successive history of Propp's method. It has become possible to escape from his closed system, which was conditioned by his type of folktale to which all magic folktales could be reduced, and to put forward the feasibility of systems which their own semantic coherence in each separate case holds together. The possibility has been shown that when folktales are made up of different movements, they do no more than present and reaffirm from different anecdotal points of view one and the same schema, establishing equivalences between functions at first view extraneous to each other. On the other hand, it can hardly be held that Lévi-Strauss is aiming to capture in the geometry of his cages narration of all kinds if he admits that "the folktale offers greater possibilities of play; in it permutations become relatively free and acquire progressively a certain arbitrariness."[109] It is easy to deduce that the fabula of a tale or novel will be even more free and more arbitrary.

If there is some uncertainty in Lévi-Strauss, it regards the techniques to adopt for arriving at and defining atemporal matrices. At times he speaks of permutations, at times of transformations, at times of bundles of relationships (as if he were striving to grasp something not easily definable—hence his resort to metaphors and analogies). In effect, Lévi-Strauss has touched on a problem which is vital to the semiotics of narrative models. On one hand functions are minimal elements of the model, not further reducible; on the other, affinities subsist between certain functions such that, even in a model, their appearance at successive points establishes a form of partial recursivity. Clearly the functions, even if irreducible, can be taken apart, as is logical if one remembers that functions are elements a great deal more complex than semantemes, which can easily be broken down into their lesser semic elements. Lévi-Strauss's terminological variety opens up two possible lines of inquiry for analysis of the functions: one is logical in emphasis, looking exclusively toward the model (e.g., *infraction* would be the inverse of *prohibition*, and this a negative transformation of *order*; *setting out* and *returning* would be a single function, *separation*, expressed negatively and positively);[110] the other is semantic in emphasis—two functions would be cognate by having one or more semes in common. Naturally the second type lends itself to use at a lesser level of abstraction, unquestionably at the level of fabula.

And it is at just this level of fabula that Lévi-Strauss analyzes the myth of Oedipus,[111] reading it according to his statements just quoted, as a "score." We might dwell for a moment on his vertical reading. The legend is distributed over four vertical columns. In the third column we find

Cadmus kills the dragon
Oedipus sacrifices the Sphinx

and in the fourth

Labdacus (father of Laius) = "lame" (?)
Laius (father of Oedipus) = "crooked" (?)
Oedipus = "swell foot" (?)

The meanings of the two columns are, respectively, *negation of the autochthonous nature of man* and *persistence of human autochthony*. Without entering into the mythological comparisons from which it results that the sons of the earth are frequently represented as walking with difficulty, I would remark that (1) the fourth column, unlike the other three, has no narrative content and so has no place in a horizontal reading of mythems and (2) the fourth column clearly shows that it has been composed in symmetry with the third, while this in turn has been given a label derived from deductions of an ethnological kind and thus quite heterogeneous with respect to the functions.

A third observation is decisive for our purposes: the titles given the columns do not constitute their generalization; they are not homogeneous with the myths inscribed under them (the third column, for instance, could only be unified as "slaying of chthonic monsters"). They are labels, in short, which do not lie along the same paraphrastic axis as the mythems; they are *interpretations* of the myths, labels which reduce the myths by force to non-coextensive categories.

We are not discussing here the validity of Lévi-Strauss's method (of which later and more highly elaborated applications exist, although it is these first attempts which function as paradigm). It should further be specified that in dealing with myths the inmost meaning itself is the primitive basic datum, which is a vastly different matter from the meanings of other narrations, whether literary or not. The stress Lévi-Strauss lays on "vertical" coordinates thus corresponds to precise exigencies of the object, and his techniques of elucidation must be judged solely in terms of the validity of his findings. In our case, on the contrary, since we are not dealing with myths, it is important to define the implications of this "breaking up of linearity." It is effected not merely at the cost of a different evaluation of the mythems—considered horizontally as narrative abridgments and vertically as semic complexes—but it also means imposing an interpretive pattern formulated a posteriori by means of comparisons with a mythological system put together quite outside the text. This is what Propp (in a tone of resentment which does not involve us) remarks: "The difference between my mode of reasoning and that of my critic lies in the fact that I derive generalizations from my material, while Professor Lévi-Strauss elaborates my generalizations in abtract terms."[112]

As for violations of the chronological order, however, we can hardly make Propp's fears our own: "The forcible removal of functions from their temporal succession destroys the fragile web of the narration, which like a finely elegant tissue falls apart at the slightest touch."[113] For we shall see how paradigmatic reconstruction serves to throw even more light on the logic of the tale which the search for functions is intended to reveal. Besides, I showed at the beginning of this chapter (sec. 2.1) that the linear nature of reading or listening is totally illusory: contents are added up progressively, arranging themselves to form an achronic grid. Lévi-Strauss's own grid (or any others that may be offered) should be considered its improved version. It is this framework which guarantees both the memorability and rationality of what is narrated.

Subsequent ethnographic studies along Formalist lines all develop out of or further investigate the approaches of Propp and Lévi-Strauss.[114] I shall give a brief account of them here,[115] since it is in this field that the most heated discussions have taken place about the problems of the logical relations between functions, the antinomy of syntagma and paradigm, and the overall structure of the tale. The fact that I have made an attempt at defining the nature of the function as propositional paraphrase will be of considerable help in what follows. Here, then, are the main problems on the agenda:

Logical relations between the functions. Every function, whether represented by "labels" or discursive definitions, is the statement of an action. Within the logic of the tale there can hardly fail to exist relations of succession and connection among such actions as they are lined up one behind the other.

Propp himself noted that many functions always appear in pairs: "prohibition and infraction, seeking and obtaining information, deception (snare) on the part of the antagonist and the hero's reaction to it, combat and victory, marking and identification."[116] Quite clearly these elements are linked in a relationship of implication (and this must be read backward, since the second element of the pair implies the first).[117]

This same path has been followed, though with some modification of the inventory of the functions (rather unfortunately called "motifemes"), by Dundes,[118] who systematizes the binary arrangement of the functions, keeping in mind the scale of generalization involved (motifemes are realized within the limits of an arc of allomotifs). The fundamental pair, into whose limits almost all folktales fall, is deficiency–removal of deficiency (an idea Bremond further develops). From within, every tale (or at least all the Amerindian tales analyzed by Dundes) can be schematized either as a succession of oppositive series, as a series of motifemes followed by their second elements in reverse order, or as plots whose complexity is greater but which are always nonetheless based on the original dichotomies. This point of view was followed up by Pop[119] more satisfactorily than by others; see, e.g., the symmetrical arrangement of the opening and closing movements of the Rumanian folktale entitled *The Girl Soldier*, as Pop analyzes it:

I *Deficiency*
  II *Deception*
    III *Test*
      IV *Violence*
      Elimination of the violence
    Elimination of the test
  Elimination of the deception
Elimination of the deficiency

There is little to be gained by reproducing here Bremond's discussion of Dundes's thesis,[120] because the principal difference between the functional representations of the two scholars lies only in a preference for a binary formula of opposite movements (Dundes) or a triad which stresses the moment of mediation (Bremond). It is merely a matter of conventional choices, not of contradiction in substance. As I suggested earlier (sec. 4.3), the middle moment might equally well be considered the vital one, since it effects the passage between the two extremes, which are intellectual in nature and not necessarily worked out concretely.

Very similar to Dundes's is the initial approach of Meletinsky, who states, "The tale of marvels appears . . . at a more abstract level as a hierarchical structure of binary groups, within which a final group (paired member) obligatorily bears a positive sign."[121]

But then Meletinsky structures the elements of behavioral characteristics paradigmatically: "The rules of conduct, the structure of behavior in the tale, constitute a complete semantic system within which the functions reveal complementary logical relationships independent of their syntagmatic links."[122] Thus the folktale's syntagmatic development is conditioned by the different combination of both positive and negative behavioral elements. Last, there exist basic oppositional relationships (e.g., for the character of the test the hero undergoes, familiar or unfamiliar, philanthropic or egoistic, mythical or not): depending on the presence of a positive or negative variant of the elements of each of these pairs, general categories of folktales are established and allow of precise classification.

The experience of this Soviet semiotician is important, in my opinion, not only because it is a thorough investigation of the possibilities of syntagmatic or paradigmatic analysis of the folktale but also because it introduces the concept of *value*, obviously limited to the sphere of the conceptions on which the folktales are based. But it is important above all because it records in its formalizations those behavioral and institutional data which insert the folktale into time and history.

The overall structure of the tale. The subdivision of the syntagm into *movements* which contain several functions is specified: "The principal movement of the folktale (as Propp has shown) is interpreted as a movement from deficiency (damage) toward the elimination of the deficiency and toward further conquests; in the second place [not in a second moment but, rather, within the movement itself], this movement is realized by means of the tests which the hero of the tale must pass."[123] These movements too can be formulated by way of abstraction or, in purely formal terms, by means of "empty" expressions. For the first, see the proposals of Bremond et al. discussed herein; for the second, I should cite the schema of Labov and Waletzky:[124]

I   Orientation
II   Complication
III   Evaluation
IV   Resolution
V   Coda

This may also be compared with Greimas's schema and even with certain divisions of classical rhetoric.[125]

The paradigm. Segal has an interesting reelaboration of Lévi-Strauss's schema: a horizontal arrangement of syntagmatic elements so carried out that equivalent unities are arranged vertically to form columns. The unities Segal arrives at on the level of fabula are "predicates (narrative relationships to which a precise value is attributed)."[126] He analyzes three variants of the same Amerindian tale, arriving at the meaning of all three versions by both analyzing the succession of the "predicates" and breaking down these "predicates" into their lesser semic components, observing the presence or absence of each in all three versions. This breakdown of "predicates" into semic components is beyond question one of the most promising proposals so far put forward for a concrete analysis of the fabula.

6.2. It is Greimas who has most radically reelaborated the lessons of Propp and Lévi-Strauss, attempting a bold synthesis. One aspect of his researches can be briefly recalled here, that which deals with the functions. Starting out from the same functions which Propp had brought to light, Greimas operates a numerical reduction (from thirty-one to twenty) and does so—this is the most significant point—by arranging them into contrary pairs. He thus gives geometrical form to Propp's empiricism.[127] Greimas then goes on to group the functions into three large classes of syntagms: performantial syntagms (tests), contractual syntagms (the establishing or breaking of contracts), and disjunctive syntagms (setting out or coming back).[128] He then unifies the greater part of the movements which the actions effect into a large quadripartite block, which has at its extreme points the breaking of the contract and its reestablishment (or the setting up of a new one); in its two central sections are alienation and reintegration of the hero through his performance or test or else, in more recent formulations, "the setting up of a *conjunctive* contractual relationship between a *destinateur* and a *destinataire-subject*, followed by a spatial *disjunction* between the two actants. The achievement of the *récit* will be marked, on the contrary, by spatial conjunction and a final transfer of values, which will establish a new contract through a new distribution of values, no less objective and modal."[129]

The phases of the narration are linked to relationships between characters much more uncompromisingly than in Propp. Thus it is that the contract constitutes a link between sender and receiver (communication); struggle expresses the type of link that exists between the helper and the antagonist. And Propp's characters, now reduced to six, take up a predetermined stance with respect to each other:

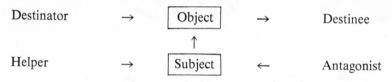

But one sees at once in the greater degree of abstraction with which the characters are designated that Greimas, despite the fact that Propp's analyses are his starting point, is aiming at schemata whose validity is to be general. Furthermore, his degree of abstraction shows that, much more than Propp, Greimas subordinates the consistency of the characters to the functions they perform. This explains why he takes over the term "actant" from Tesnière, for it ties a character to his acts, stripping him at the same time of all contingent qualification: "actant" is related to *acteur* as phoneme is related to sound; and it is as likely that we shall find a single *acteur* who takes upon himself the role of a number of actants as that we should be faced with several actors who constitute a single actant. Actants are subordinated not only to functions but also to values: "The actants are no longer conceived of as operators but as places where value objects can be located, places to which they can be referred or from which they can be withdrawn."[130]

The most interesting aspect of this actantial schema is the way it realizes modalities: *knowing* on the destinator-destinee line, *ability* on the helper-antagonist line, *desire* on the subject-object line. As the plot develops, *desire* will then become *action*.

The inherent difficulties and complexities of Greimas's thought are rendered even more difficult by the fact that it is in continual development, hardly pausing for even temporary arrangement. For our present purposes we may not unreasonably concentrate on two texts, of 1966 and 1969.[131] In the first Greimas (in the wake of Lévi-Strauss) distinguishes three structural components of myth: framework, code, message. The framework is "the structural statute of myth insofar as it is narration."[132] It is thus a unity of discourse possessed of a temporal dimension. The kinds of behavior described set up reciprocal relationships of earlier as opposed to later. The message is "the particular meaning of the myth occurrence," which can be read equally on the discursive or the structural plane (on the hypothesis that the first is a manifestation of the second). Thus we are in a phase of passage from the achronic to the temporal. On the discursive plane, actors and events have the value of incarnations, so to speak, of semic unities organized syntactically into statements. On the structural plane, the semic unities themselves are arranged in terms no longer of the moves of those who realize them (actors and actions) but of their conceptual relationships, and these are given from the outset.

Last comes the code: "The *code* is a formal structure (1) made up of a small number of semic categories (2) whose mode of combination is susceptible, as it produces sememes, of accounting for the sum of the contents invested which form part of the dimension of the mythological universe that has been selected."[133] The order in which the components of the myth are indicated does not imply priority of one over other but, rather, an alternative praxis with regard to messages, framework, and code such that our understanding of the message and our knowledge of the code are progressively increased.[134]

But another, more recent article by Greimas uncompromisingly expresses an order of priority of code over message and message over framework. According to Greimas, every narration has an apparent level (subject to the specific exigencies of the linguistic substances through which it expresses itself) and an immanent level on which the narrativity is organized prior to its manifestation. In other words, "the meaning is unaffected by the modes of its manifestation." Thus it is necessary

> to imagine *ab quo* instances of generation of meaning such that
> setting out from sense agglomerations as unelaborated as possible
> one may obtain, descending through successive stages, meaningful

articulations or progressively greater refinement, until one arrives simultaneously at the two goals at which sense aims in manifesting itself: to appear as *articulated sense*, i.e., meaning, and as *discourse about sense*, i.e., a vast paraphrase which envelops in its own fashion all the earlier articulations of sense. To put it another way, *the generation of meaning does not pass in the first instance through the production of statements and their combination into discourse; it is relayed in its passage by narrative structures, and it is these which give rise to intelligible discourse articulated into statements.*[135]

At the outset, then, we have what Greimas considers the elementary structure of meaning, the logical development of a binary semantic category which embraces two contraries (e.g., black and white) and two subcontraries (e.g., not black and not white) in an intersecting relationship of contradiction (white vs. not white, black vs. not black) and in a direct relationship of implication (not black vs. white). Each of these structures can be set up as a *constitutional semiotic model* and take into itself a more extensive field of signification, subordinating to itself, in the form of articulations, yet other binary categories.[136]

This obviously static semiotic model forms a kind of morphology which is nonetheless susceptible of dynamic (syntactic) representation when its meaning is considered "as an apprehension [*saisie*] or as the production of sense by the subject."[137] In such a case, the model's constituent *relationships* are projected as *operations*. Since these syntactic operations are brought to bear on categories whose terms are contrary or contradictory, they are clearly *oriented*, from the positive to the negative term or vice versa, or from a contrary to a subcontrary, etc.

The moment conceptual elements are set in motion, they are rendered anthropomorphic: even abstract or inanimate subjects are considered in their operations as if they were persons; the operation becomes an action (*faire*), and since it involves at least two contradictory actions, in terms of performance it embodies a polemical antagonism (with respect to the two subjects, which take on the attributes of *negation* and *domination*). The performance is, moreover, "the most characteristic unity of narrative syntax."[138] Thus from the outset functions and actants are constituent elements of narrative grammar; we then have narrative utterances, elementary syntactic forms, and finally narrative unities (performance is the typical example) which are syntagmatic successions of narrative statements.[139]

All this is expressed in terms of "grammar." The fundamental grammar is conceptual, that of constitutional semiotic models (in the first model, code); then comes an intermediary semiotic level, on which this grammar is given an anthropomorphic representation which is not yet figurative (message); and, finally the *récit* (framework), which is expressed in figurative form (with human actors or personifications who carry out tasks, undergo tests, reach goals). Since Greimas is interested only in the first two levels, he calls the second "superficial narrative grammar."[140] leaving no possible qualification for figurative grammar which, if Chomsky's now inadequate image is to be retained, must be defined as *outright superficial*, the merest *veneer*.

6.3. The analyses of the *récit* carried out by Todorov and Bremond derive not only from Propp but also from Greimas's reelaboration. I have dealt with Greimas last (without thereby upsetting chronology, for his theory is constantly being reformulated) in order to stress exigencies which he is the one to feel most strongly. They are such indeed, it seems to me, as cannot lightly be set aside.

In itself, Greimas's forceful attempt to remodel the proposals of Propp and Lévi-Strauss theoretically cannot be accepted without reserve. Hjelmslev himself, whom Greimas refers to above all others when there is a question of institutional affirmations, denied (faithful here to Saussure) any kind of preeminence or priority between form and substance, either when dealing with the linguistic sign[141] or for grammar as a whole:

> The construction of grammar on speculative ontological systems and the construction of a given grammar on the grammar of another language are necessarily foredoomed to miscarry. . . .
> The old dream of a universal phonetic system and a universal content system (system of concepts) cannot therefore be realized or in any case will remain without any possible contact with linguistic reality. It is not superfluous, in the face of certain offshoots of medieval philosophy that have appeared even in recent times, to point out the fact that generally valid phonetic types or an eternal scheme of ideas cannot be erected empirically with any validity for language.[142]

Direct experience of texts also, whether literary or not, does not permit one to identify actants with key concepts or leading ideas. Key concepts (which might be called existential vectors) are drives, motivations, objectives which the characters must come to terms with but which constitute an intricate network, not mere triggers in a univocal relationship with each of the single actants.

Often these leading ideas are more closely related to the action than to the characters: in other words, they constitute poles between which the characters move, modifying (or not) their own mental makeup.[143]

Even if we admit the usefulness of this advance on the part of the critic toward the conceptual wellsprings of the text, it is still not possible to deduce from it the axiom that a writer (or teller of folktales, or rhapsode) has advanced in the opposite direction, moving from his conceptual sources to their anthropomorphization and so to their figuring forth in characters and actions. The relative weight in the relationships between characteriological elements and evenemential and ideological elements is so variable from one narration to another that it effectively blocks any attempt we may make to hypothesize a level on which the latter exclusively function as motors. Now the edifice erected by Greimas is founded on a belief in just this axiom; otherwise the *constitutional semiotic model* would be transformed, less ambitiously, into an attempt to schematize leading ideas.

For the concept of surface narrative grammar, too (which would not, however, be surface in Chomsky's sense), further clarification would be useful. The examples of anthropomorphization Greimas gives—like "Le crayon écrit"[144]—obviously belong on the level of the characters, not on that of the actants, so that one is led to ask whether *two* surfaces are not perhaps too many.

Finally, the logical rectangle often turns out to be, in terms of any given narration, a redundant tool. A narrative may oppose goodness to evil or, as Bremond would prefer,[145] goodness to lack of goodness; a development of the logical rectangle can of course be met with in particularly captious authors, but in general narrative (with its conceptual correlations) proceeds through a series of contraries (or contradictories).

Despite these reservations, I consider Greimas's work a milestone in research on the *récit*, because it points out the need to reintegrate into analysis what Propp had more or less drastically excluded (characters, motifs, modalities) to the exclusive advantage of the functions (see sec. 1.2).

This is a need pointed out by many—for example, by Barthes,[146] who offers an analysis of narrative unities which is much more detailed than that effected by Propp and by those who integrate him. Barthes resolves the problem of the greater or lesser functional importance of the unities by means of a terminological hierarchy: from functions one passes to clues, which refer not to a complementary and successive act but to a concept more or less widely diffused, but still necessary to the sense of the history,[147] and then to the *informants* "which serve to identify, to locate in time and space";[148] from the cardinal functions or *nuclei*, which offer or exclude an alternative, to the *catalysts*, which "cluster around one or another nucleus, without modifying its alternative nature."[149]

Barthes, however, maintains a degree of abstraction at a much lower level than that of the narrative models: on the surface of the discourse, even where this is understood in its paraphrastic synthesis and not in its verbal aspect. And it is natural that on this level more or less functional elements should be met with, or even ones which at first sight are not functional at all.

In my opinion, the more one is obliged at a given level of abstraction to leave out of account notions, qualifications, and even events, the more it should be possible to reorganize what has been deleted at a less abstract level. It must be possible to schematize in a functional manner relationships between key ideas, between sentiments and themes which an enunciation of the plot necessarily leaves out of account. It must be possible to schematize these relationships between persons whose transformations the tale or novel narrates (and then the various configurations of these relationships will come at the end of these groups of actions by which their relationships have been changed), or even just the consequences (and then the schema will constitute the motivation of the actions narrated). It should be possible to schematize relationships between the discriptive elements of a text, once these have been sacrificed to the schematic nature of the narrative model. This is no gratuitous exercise. An analysis of a tale presents itself as a striving toward rationality, and thus no less toward the singling out of causes. It is clear that the logic of the functions does not exhaust all the causal drives, for if it did the extrafunctional elements would be no more than pointless filling up.

The technique of elimination and recovery, deleting in order to functionalize and functionalizing what has been deleted, allows us to concentrate on a search for narrative invariants (models abstract to the utmost degree with respect to the physical nature of every work of art), managing at the same time to save what gives the single work its character and qualifies it (at least on the content plane). Thus we safeguard two seemingly antinomic exigencies: that of the generalized nature of the model and that of an adequate description of the literary object.

Should the forthright monogenetic projection of Greimas be found inapplicable, an attempt might be made to represent relationships (of opposition, alliance, commutability, etc.) between the characters, observed first of all in their individuality, which is already a synthesis of characterizing data (age, marital status, social class, temperament), and then to observe the permanence or modification of these relationships in concomitance with the phases of the story.[150] Thus too, polygons of forces between leading ideas can be sketched out in such a way as to define the ideological space within which the action unfolds. It is not difficult to integrate these polygons of leading ideas with the characters themselves.[151] Thus one initiates a unification of those elements which have been rejected from a table of the functions.

Such polygons, of persons, concepts, or both, may at times schematize situations which remain unchanged in the course of the tale (delimiting the space in which the functions are inscribed); but at other times they may synthesize dynamics whose functions are the development of the narration.[152] In other words (and here we come back to the problem of time), such schemata may have an achronic status (like Greimas's logical rectangle), but they can appear as a series of successive phases as well, deriving from the succession of the actions.

It thus becomes evident that it is essential that there should exist a contrast between the radically temporal nature of the fabula and the achronism or the slow movement of personal and conceptual polygons. In an action which is not overcomplex (e.g., in a short story), relationships between persons or ideas may be the key to the actions of the characters who do not exercise any influence over such relationships; or again, they may quite possibly have a before and after which result from the action itself. Thus a clear distinction must be made between static schemata and others which are subject to phases: the former have a univocal relationship to the action, the latter a bivocal one.

The separation of these schemata from the functional chain cancels the illusion of a unicentral interpretation, but in exchange it emphasizes, with its infinite possibilities of combination between schemata and chain, the breadth of the inventive space set aside for narration: a space for actions and for their motivations.

7. Narratology is one of the youngest branches of the theory of literature, for even if we wish to attribute its paternity to Russian Formalism, we must take into account the nearly three decades of hibernation which followed the years 1928–30. It has cut itself free, in any case, only in the last decade; and it now occupies so many researchers that one is obliged, even in a panorama like the present one, to make choices that our demonstrative discourse will, I hope, have sufficiently motivated.

If we remain at the levels of plot and fabula, the results of critical inquiry are abundant and beyond discussion. Nor should it be forgotten that many *analyses du récit* do not go beyond the level of fabula, despite their use of formalizations. But the distance between fabula and narrative model is not easily measured: it seems to expand or shrink with the kind of research undertaken.

The elasticity of the measures adopted is particularly evident when analysis of the tale is carried out from within or in the service of comparative study. The comparison between two analogous texts in fact often leads to the discovery of common content segments more complex and detailed than those a functional study would deal with, and this undoubtedly favors the comparison itself.

See, for example, the analyses of the *canto di Ulisse* (*Inferno*, 26) carried out by Avalle.[153] He arrives at the following four functions:

I.   The hero *decides to set out* on a dangerous search (*departure*).

II.   The hero *communicates* this decision to his companions in a discourse in which he lists the motives which drive him to this heroic undertaking (*allocution*).

III. The hero and his companions *overstep* the borders of the "unknown country," which from the particulars which follow is found to be the country from which no traveler returns alive (*infraction*).

IV.   The hero and his companions *die* as a result of this foolhardy undertaking (*punishment*).

In truth, the paraphrastic formulae ("The hero decides to set out," etc.) expound the fabula, while the narrative model is constituted by the terms in parentheses (departure, etc.).

Now the extremely interesting relations between this episode and other parallel medieval texts, from the Arthurian romances to the *Alexandreis* of Gautier de Châtillon, are all based on resemblances or identity at the level of fabula; elements of the plot are indicated as particularizing or characterizing (motivations, character functions, etc.). At the level of the narrative model, it would be possible to place side by side—but no longer to compare—the most heterogeneous texts. In comparison, therefore, invariants are defined subtractively and remain (if the comparison is adequately oriented) common elements of notable consistency.

Naturally it would hardly be legitimate to aim at reaching the model by means of reiterated comparisons, i.e., inductively. The model, on the other hand, cannot leave out of account objects for whose interpretations it is being employed. It must owe its birth to a direct experience of the texts, and the task is to find the best type of generalizing semic relationship among the functions and the real, or possible, narrative segments. Thus the text is the necessary basis for arriving at the functions, as the attempts already made in fact show (when one does not set out from the texts explicitly, one sets out from Propp, who in turn based his work on the texts).

Without going back over what has already been expounded here and there at the end of my various sections, I wish at this point to touch on the main motifs which, in my view, do not allow the creation of a general narrative model, i.e., a closed catalog of functions with the rules for their combination: the inevitable mediation of the summary—whose nature is inescapably subjective—for the passage from any kind of fabula at all to a functional structure; the lack of any all-embracing narrative system which will allow one to arrive at minimal unities by means of commutation—the researcher must on each occasion take as his system the text itself or a corpus of texts linked by some kind of affinity, chronological, contenutistic, thematic, etc.; the impossibility of establishing a uniform distance of generalization between the vocabulary of this inventory and the very receptive series of real actions which each item of the inventory must embrace.

These motifs depend on a basic fact: that the literary work can be considered if we wish as an object only insofar as it is analyzed in its verbal manifestation. The moment meanings are taken into account, it enters into a communications circuit: it exists only insofar as it is read and emits contents which are the result of contact between reader and text; the result, that is, of interpretation.

Interpretation leads us, beyond question, along the slippery path of the subjective (with all the defenses philological and hermeneutic scruple will wish to erect); in exchange, however, it opens up a dialectic between reader and text with possibilities for analysis which are closed to any consideration of the text as an immobile object, an absolute which, for the reasons outlined, would also lie beyond our reach. It is up to the wisdom of the interpreter to ensure that his functional summary should be if not unassailable, at least honest; and also in his hands is the scale of the degree of abstraction he will try to employ in the most profitable manner, defining the corpus in relation to the objectives of his research.

But there is more than the reader-text relationship; there is also text-context relationship. I have already pointed out that the logic of the functions is homologous, however indirectly (i.e., through literary conventions and their viscosity), with the logic of real behavior in definite times and places.

When any action at all is labeled (and even more so when it is a class of actions so labeled) and considered as a function, it cannot be left out of account that (1) the capacity of the class and its label are in a definite relationship with a given conception of the world (that of a text or corpus, that of the context, or that of the analyst); (2) if it is advisable to strive after closed inventories of functions so as to set up systems with definite internal relationships, once they abandon synchrony such inventories cannot avoid changing in their internal relationships and their components; (3) relationships of implication, opposition, causality between the functions are themselves valid (or invalid) only within the framework of norms immanent within the texts (and deriving from the context), never of norms fixed from the outset and unchangeable; and (4) further, combination rules for the functions are themselves subject to spatial and temporal changes.

I believe that the definition of narrative models must be arrived at from within a study of cultural modeling systems.[154] The "logic of the tale" falls under the "logic" of codes of behavior and ideologies; the mode of naming the functions forms part of that very meta-language with which the leading ideas of a given civilization are expressed.

If this is true, the loss of a (for me utopian) general model of narration will be amply made up for by the achievement of a type of fundamental contact between the literary work and society. These two systems, which in an astronomical image one tends to imagine as concentric, are really lines of force which coincide for considerable stretches and which have the same points of convergence.

Then it is that the models put forward (and even better models yet to be constructed), which threatened to stand revealed as instruments of doubtful validity, can be recovered, for they will prove to be of extreme utility if they are employed not as models of narration but as models for the reading of narrative texts. The reality of discourse, of plot, of fabula, of functional structure is that of moments, separated by descriptive convention, in the understanding of a text; it is the reality of semiotic operations, i.e., of operations that are human, experienced, and subject to history. Logic, like mathematics or any other artificial system, determines impossibilities but does not determine real occurrences. Semiotic models are historical models.

Two

Deconstruction and Reconstruction of a Tale: From *La mort le roi Artu* to the *Novellino*

Sections 70–71 of *La mort le roi Artu* constitute a strongly unified episode, almost a tale within the romance.[1] The mysterious aspects of the opening (the elegant little ship which suddenly appears under the tower of King Arthur) soon shift the reader's attention to Arthur and Gawain, who go on board to explore; a touch of ecstatic pathos is introduced when the two come upon a fair maiden dead in a splendidly adorned bed. At the heart of the tale there is yet another compelling element: a short, passionate letter which, while following a barely perceptible pattern of epistolographic norms, expresses the love and despair of the woman, victim of a rejection by the noblest of knights, Lancelot himself. (Later on, in the obligatory conclusion to this kind of tragic tale, a tomb will receive the body, its stone summing up her fate).

The following narrative elements can be singled out (I shall call them *actions* since, for reasons which will become clear, I stop at a level of schematization less advanced than that at which we might appropriately speak of functions):

1. A mysterious little ship arrives.
2. Arthur and Gawain go on board.
3. On a bed they discover the body of a maiden.
4. Gawain finds a letter and hands it to the king.
5. The letter is read and the mystery resolved.

Yet the episode not only is linked to the romance; it constitutes its nodal point. In fact, the maiden who has arrived at Arthur's court—on her last journey—is the Lady of Escalot (Shalott), who has died for love on being rejected by Lancelot (as Guinevere's faithful lover he was unable to accept her offers, attractive though they were). But Guinevere has judged Lancelot unfaithful: in the first place because, constrained by an ill-considered promise, he had worn the colors of the lady in the lists and second because his love for the lady was affirmed by Gawain. Hence the unjust condemnation of Lancelot, obliged by the queen's anger to abandon the court. As a consequence of his absence, Guinevere has been deprived of the only valiant champion who could defend her against Mador when he accuses her of killing her own brother. Thus the ship's arrival throws light on a number of things and opens the way for subsequent developments.

The episode has a more subtle function, however. The letter of the Lady of Escalot, while it shows Lancelot's innocence (with respect to the queen), indirectly confirms Guinevere's guilt to Arthur, a fact he has only recently been made aware of, thanks to Morgan and the pictures made by Lancelot himself when a prisoner of the sorceress (in the Salle aux images). Thus what Morgan had brutally represented as adultery now takes on a heroic, courtly aspect for Arthur: it becomes more noble, but also more serious and inevitable. This is surely the reason why the author has Arthur himself rather than Gawain read the dead maiden's message.

Links with the plot as a whole are effected by means of a series of circumstantial disclosures and comments. When the little ship arrives, the preoccupied king is looking toward the river, concerned over the threat to the queen that Mador represents. Once the maiden is found, Gawain recognizes her as the Lady of Escalot and reminds the king of their conversation with Guinevere in which Gawain had said that she was the lover of Lancelot. The king, who had shown his disbelief at Gawain's revelations, meditates (we may well imagine) on the bitter implications of having been correct.

Within this framework, our first analysis of the actions is seen to be incomplete. Others must be singled out, and then all together must be arranged as phases of a progressive clarification: in 1–3 the atmosphere is still adventurous[2] and abstract. After 3, an action (3a: Gawain's recognition of the lady) becomes fundamental, as it inserts the episode into the plot as a whole. As a result the other actions are situated on the same narrative plane as the romance, and this is particularly the case with action 5, which demonstrates to the queen and to everyone else the absolute loyalty of Lancelot, and which brings about a further action, 5a (the queen's repentance), presented, in fact, in this episode.

When we review the actors, we observe that their number and their relationships change when we move from the single episode to the romance as a whole. In the episode there are three actors actually present (Arthur, Gawain, and the lady, who speaks through her letter) and one who is absent (Lancelot), of whose action the results remain (the lady's death). In terms of internal chronology the actors are grouped in pairs: Lancelot and the lady (their relations and the dire consequences of them), and Arthur and Gawain, who act as posthumous witnesses. But in the larger plot the lady is no more than a secondary actor, functioning as a catalyst (an unrequited lover) with respect to the triangle of Lancelot and Guinevere (reciprocal lovers) and Arthur (betrayed husband). Unlike Gawain, Arthur passes from the role of witness to that of discoverer of his own dishonor.

These successive exercises in schematization are not gratuitous. In fact the unified nature of the episode has been perceived by another writer and cut free from the particulars of tone and the actions (3a and 5a) which connect it with the romance. I allude to the compiler responsible for novella 82 of the *Novellino*.[3]

The connections between the novella and *La mort le roi Artu* are well known,[4] but no study has ever been undertaken of the method used by the compiler in adapting his source. A schematization of the novella gives these elements (or actions):

1' The Lady of Escalot's unrequited love for Lancelot
2' Instructions for the preparation of the bier/bed, for the ship, and for arraying the body
3' Composition of the letter
4' Death of the lady
5' Putting her commands into effect
6' Voyage to Arthur's court
7' Arthur's arrival on board
8' Discovery of the bed with the body
9' Discovery of the letter
10' Text of the letter as clarification of events

It is immediately evident that actions 6'–10' of the novella correspond to actions 1–5 of the episode in *Artu*. But it is instructive to define more closely the narrative technique in the novella which has led to actions 1'–5'.

The episode in *Artu*, as we have seen, offers a stage-by-stage solution of its mysteries: the ship is entirely mysterious; then the dead woman is identified as the Lady of Escalot; finally, the letter explains why she has died, and it is made clear that she had herself put on board in order to bring her message, indeed her complaint, to Arthur and his knights. This technique is made possible because of the links which exist with parts outside the episode itself. At sections 38–39 the lady's passion for Lancelot and his refusal have been described, with this conclusion: "Tout en ceste maniere devisa la damoisele sa mort; si l'en avint tout issi comme ele dist; car ele morut sanz faille por l'amour de Lancelot, si com li contes le devisera ça en avant" ("And this was the way in which the damsel planned her death; and it was done exactly as she had commanded; for she undoubtedly died for love of Lancelot, as the tale will tell further on"). At section 57 other, more moving particulars are added, concluding thus: "Lors se parti la damoisele . . . et s'en vint a son lit et se cocha a tel eür que onques puis n'en leva, se morte non, si com l'estoire le devisera apertement" ("Then the damsel departed . . . and went to her bed, and lay upon it in such a manner that she never more left it save in death, as the history will fully unfold").

The reader of *Artu* thus retains in memory empty valencies which this episode fills: the expectation aroused by the formulae "si com li contes [l'estoire] le devisera ça en avant [tout apertement]" is satisfied by reading the episode. It should be noted, however, that the order of events, chronological in the extra-episodic premises, becomes retrogressive within the episode: first the ship arrives, then the lady's death is discovered, and finally its causes are revealed. Add to this the fact that of the extra-episodic actions (disappointed love [a] and death [e]) and those of the episode itself, three are implicit and are only made clear upon full revelation of the facts: the composition of the letter (b), the lady's command that she be placed on board the ship (c), and the execution of this command (d).

All the changes made in the novella derive from a perfectly natural decision: to explain to the reader who the Lady of Escalot is. In other words, the compiler understood that in order to arrive at a novella he had to eliminate references to the romance which for his purposes were superfluous; but he was also obliged in his new context to embrace those elements which in *Artu* are its preparation. However, by the act of declaring from the outset the identity of the lady, the possibility of a stage-by-stage solution is eliminated, as is strictly retrogressive presentation of the facts, as offered in *Artu*.

Thus once the compiler of the novella has stated action a, he finds himself on a slippery chronological slope and feels obliged to render explicit the implied actions of b–d before narrating action e, after which he goes on following the original order. Thus we find ourselves with actions 1'–5' of the novella corresponding to a–e of *Artu* and actions 6'–10' of the novella corresponding to 1–5 of *Artu*. The two series of the novella are mirror images of each other, the second (6'–10') limiting itself to presenting anew but in reverse order what the first (1'–5') had given us in chronological order.

This is no hypothesis but facts we are describing. And it is undoubtedly to the level of facts (in particular, to a certain inexperience on the part of the compiler) that we must refer in noting that the connection between actions 1'–5' and 6'–10' remains imperfectly realized, unequivocally proclaiming the difficulty of effecting the suture. I refer to these sentences: "E in questa borsa avea una lettera, ch'era de lo 'nfrascritto tenore. Ma imprima diciamo de ciò che va innanzi la lettera" ("And in this purse there was a letter, which was in these terms. But first we should tell of what happens before the letter"). "Ma imprima diciamo" and "de lo 'nfrascritto tenore," satisfied only at the end of the tale, show forth the uncertainties of the restructuring, as does the imperfect "avea una lettera" (i.e., action 3′) situated in an indeterminate ambiguous time (and tense) between the moment of imparting instructions and the moment of effective discovery (action 3′ might well precede 2′).

The consequences as regards the actors are even more striking. The Lancelot-Guinevere-(Arthur) "system," with the lady as catalyst, gives way to a Lancelot-lady "system," where it is Guinevere who has the secondary function of unwittingly impeding the love between the two, and where Arthur is allotted the function of mere witness (discovering the lady and the letter). Arthur's lack of involvement in the action is clearly indicated by two facts: (1) he absorbs into his own person Gawain's merely mediative functions; and (2) it is not Arthur who finds the missive, nor is it he who reads it in trepidation: unperturbed, he has others read it ("fecela leggere") ("he had it read").

Nonetheless, even as elaborated, the tale serves the compiler's purposes perfectly. It was the letter which attracted his attention, for it recalled on one hand the letter-writing models then in vogue and on the other the love lyric tradition itself, two currents which had already coalesced in the erotic *dictamina*.[5] The final part of the letter scans like the stanza of a canzone: "Già nol seppi tanto pregare d'amore / ch'elli avesse di me mercede. / E così, lassa! sono morta / per ben amare, / come voi potete vedere" ("I knew not sufficiently well how to solicit him to love / and to make him have pity upon me. / And so, unhappy as I was, I am dead / as a result of loving well, / as you can see").

But courtly love in the *Novellino* is generally "distanced" in a romantic or aristocratic perspective. Here a romantic distancing is rendered even more effective by the tone adopted, which is that of the folktale (and it replaces the adventurous tone of the source). The folktale tone is reinforced by the emphasis laid on the exquisiteness of the decor:

E comandò che quando sua anima fosse partita dal corpo, che fusse aredata una *ricca* navicella coperta d'un vermiglio sciamito, con un *ricco* letto ivi entro, con *ricche* e nobili coverture di seta, ornato di *ricche* pietre preziose; e fosse il suo corpo messo in questo letto, ves-

tita di suoi piue nobili vestimenti e con bella corona in capo, *ricca*
di molto oro e di molte pietre preziose, e con *ricca* cintura e borsa.

The little ship covered with its bright red drape is rich, rich the bed,
with its rich and noble silken coverings, rich the precious stones which
adorn it, rich with much gold and many precious stones the beautiful
crown which the lady has placed on her head, rich the belt and the
purse. The fantasy of the folktale appears more than anywhere else in
the ("senza vele") sail-less voyage of the tiny ship which the water
bears toward Camelot.

That these elements are pertinent appears from a comparison with
Artu. Here the adjective "riche" is used more sparingly and in more
widely separated phrases, so that it produces at most a particular atmosphere at the level of the setting. On the other hand, statements regarding the beauty of the lady are numerous: "Moult avoit esté bele . . .
si bele damoisele . . . trop bele riens . . . la grant biauté . . . la bele
damoisele . . . la bele damoisele . . . une des plus beles damoiseles del
monde ("Very beautiful she was . . . so beautiful a damsel . . . too
beautiful a creature . . . the great beauty . . . the beautiful damsel . . .
the beautiful damsel . . . one of the most beautiful damsels in the world").
Of this nothing remains in the *Novellino*. In fact the beauty of the damsel
has in *Artu* the function of rendering more heroic Lancelot's refusal of
her. This is of considerable importance for the plot of *Artu*, while it is
irrelevant in the *Novellino*, where the center of the stage is held by the
damsel, who dies of longing for love ("mal d'amore"), and by her desperate posthumous message.

This example of analysis, facilitated by the simplicity of the stylistic
and structural means employed by the two authors, suggests several deductions and generalizations. At the same time, we have been provided
with an eloquent demonstration of the difference between the structural
laws which sustain romance and novella: even the unsophisticated compiler of the novella shows that he is aware of them. In their turn, these
structural laws are put into effect in terms of preconceptions of taste and
literary strategies, so that substantially identical subject matter is subjected to radical transformations. Full weight must be given to this in
studying the relations between a text and its sources: the degree of the
text's faithfulness to its sources is strongly conditioned by forces of this
kind.

Deductions of even greater validity have also, I believe, emerged from
these analyses. The actions have come to identify themselves with the

shaping patterns of the tale. But (1) the actions have been formulated somewhat broadly (further simplification would have been easy but would have involved the elimination of characterizing differences in the schema: differential elements are at the base of all analysis, whether linguistic or literary); (2) the existence of implied actions has come to light, where the likelihood of their being made explicit directly influences narrative status; and (3) a clear-cut difference has appeared in the results obtainable with substantially similar subject matter by means of a different sequence of actions (effects of surprise used or eliminated, effects of expectancy stimulated or neutralized).

It has become perfectly clear, I believe, that there exists a "measurable" importance of elements definable at first sight as connotative. The theme of beauty is an important element in the episode of *Artu*, where it is related to Lancelot's adamant fidelity. The *Novellino*, concentrating exclusively on the unrequited love of the damsel, has eliminated it, while rendering functional what before had been merely accidental: references (connotative in *Artu*) to the richness of fine clothes and array.

Finally, the complexity of the system of the actors has come to light: perhaps it is here that the differences between episode and novella have proved to be most clear-cut. It seems obvious to me that the actors cannot be defined merely by investigating them as persons: their status derives from a paradigm of relationships and from the changes which may take place in it during narration time. Thus while in the short time span of the novella the actors fall into a simple, static schema, in the episode of *Artu* they feel the repercussions of their earlier involvements in events and in particular of their earlier interactions.

The "model" which emerges, even on the basis of quite simple data of the kind our example offers us, thus shows that it is not enough to reconstruct the interaction among the systems of the actors, the actions narrated, and stylistic constants. A fundamental role is also played by time itself, not as duration but as the dimension of changes within the system of interactions itself. Every change effected is brought, by the characters as well as the reader, into relation to or contrast with the memory of preceding phases: a memory which becomes an indispensable requirement for the total intelligibility of the diegesis.

Three

Structures and Registers in the *Fiammetta*

1. It would seem obvious that a work like the *Fiammetta*,[1] the lengthy monologue of a woman abandoned who recalls the season of her love and runs through the whole spectrum of melancholy, not excluding despair, should adapt itself to a "syntonized" critical approach. But the results of such criticism have been merely negative.[2] Within its rhetorical framework Fiammetta's lament forms a single compact block, and any search for genuine expression of feeling is anachronistic and limiting when the writer has staked everything on the specifically literary character of his work.

Here my aim will be, as I work over the text several times, following out different descriptive "programs," to isolate some of its underlying structures and grasp the functionality of its literary techniques. I will conclude with suggestions for reassembling the parts separated out so that they become operative in a "reading" at once comprehensive and more subtly sensitive.[3]

2. It is by setting out from the envoi (*commiato*, 9), wherein Fiammetta tells the book to address itself only to those who can sympathize with her experiences, that the effectiveness of one of the structuring inventions of the *Fiammetta* becomes evident: its pseudo-autobiographical discourse. The insistence with which Boccaccio located his works within an autobiography, rearranging and readjusting in continuation, prior to this work had primarily affected their prologues with dedications to the woman loved, whether disdainful or kind, and their internal allusions, extraneous to the content. We had, in short, on one hand Boccaccio with his personal affairs (to what extent fictitious is of no account) and on the other the themes of his works juxtaposed by virtue of their affinity with these affairs. The *Fiammetta* gives us two important innovations: first-person discourse and a first person who is not the author.

"Fiammetta," it is true, is the *senhal* of Boccaccio's Neapolitan mistress, while "Panfilo" is the name under which he had disguised himself on other occasions. Autobiographical fiction is thus not abandoned but turned upside down, to be taken up again in a more ambiguously allusive fashion. This change, this identification with another's "I," creates a wide open field for invention and allows the author, in talking of love, to address himself directly to women (as he will do in the *Decameron*) on a level of solidarity and in a confidential tone, to which only a female character like the one he creates could aspire.

Among many such precedents, we know the one on which Boccaccio is most dependent, since it is his source: Ovid's *Heroides*.[4] From Ovid he derives the invention of a monologue of a woman who recalls her love in melancholy or despair.[5] Choice of model is also choice of genre. The *Heroides* have a double claim to be called elegies: their meter is the elegiac distich, and their argument is a melancholy one. Horace's definition of elegy underlines precisely these two points: "Versibus imparibus iunctis querimonia primum / post etiam inclusa est voto sententia compos: / quis tamen exiguos elegos emiserit auctor / grammatici certant et adhuc sub iudice lis est" ("Verses yoked unequally [the elegiac distich] first embraced lamentation [the melancholic argument], later also the sentiment of granted prayer: yet who first put forth humble elegiacs scholars dispute, and the case is still before the court": *Ars poetica* 75–78). During the Middle Ages it was the second point which was especially insisted upon, from Papias (*"Elegi*, versus miserorum") to Uguccione ("Item ab *Eli*, quod est Deus, dicitur quoddam verbum grecum *eleyson*, idest miserere. . . . Et ab *eleyson*, *elegus*, *-a*, *-um*, id est miser, *-a*, *-um*. Unde versus facti de miseria dicuntur *elegi*. Unde *elegia*, *-e*, id est miseria, et hinc *elegiacus*, *-a*, *-um*, id est miser"); from John of Genoa (*"Elegus*, *-ga*, *-gum*, idest miser, misera, miserum. Et dicitur ab *eleyson*, quod est miserere. Unde versus facti de miseria dicuntur *elegi*. Unde *elegia*, *-gie*, idest miseria") to John of Garland, who adds the erotic note ("[Carmen] elegiacum, idest miserabile carmen quod continet et recitat dolores amantium," *Poetria*, p. 926), as had Eberhard of Béthune before him in the *Graecismus* ("Castigat satira, sed elegia cantat amores," 10.245, and "Est *eleis* miserans, elegia comprobat illud," 8.129).

Dante repeats Papias's definition, "Per elegiam stilum intelligimus miserorum" ("By elegy we mean the style of the unhappy," *De vulg. el.* 2.4.5), and seems to allude to a thematic qualification when, in speaking of Guido Ghisilieri and Fabruzzo, both of Bologna, he states that "si ad sensum subtiliter intrare velimus, non sine quodam elegie umbraculo hec tragedia processisse videbitur" ("but if we wish to go more deeply into their feeling, it will be observed that this tragic poetry was not written without some slight trace of elegy," ibid., 2.12.6). Nonetheless, he includes the elegy (together with tragedy and comedy) in his scale of stylistic levels, assigning it to the lowest position: "Si autem [canenda videntur] elegiace, solum humile [vulgare] oportet nos sumere" ("If one wishes to sing in elegiac style, he must choose only the humble vernacular," ibid., 2.4.6). Here is a definition in terms of tone, by no means immune to challenge[6] and remote indeed from the *Fiammetta*.

It is true that Boccaccio himself seems to accept it, when in chapter 9 he writes, "E se forse alcuna donna delle tue parole rozzamente composte si maraviglia, di' che quelle ne mandi via, però che li parlari ornati richieggiono gli animi chiari e li tempi sereni e tranquilli. E però piuttosto dirai che prenda ammirazione come a quel poco che narri disordinato, bastò lo 'ntelletto e la mano" ("And should any woman perhaps show surprise at your roughly arranged words, tell her that you send them abroad nonetheless, since ornate expression requires that the mind should be clear and moment calm and untroubled. Tell her, rather, to marvel at how, when so little is disordered in the recounting, mind and hand could suffice.")[7]

But the solemnity of the invocation (" . . . Priego, se alcuna deità è nel cielo la cui santa mente per me sia da pietà tocca, che la dolente memoria aiuti, e sostenga la tremante mano alla presente opera, e così le faccia possenti, che quali nella mente io ho sentite e sento l'angoscie, cotali l'una profferi le parole, l'altra, più a tale oficio volonterosa che forte, le scriva": "I pray any divinity there may be in heaven whose sacred mind is touched with pity for me to assist my distressed memory and sustain my trembling hand in the present work, rendering them strong and able, so that exactly as in my mind I experienced and still do experience anguish, so may the memory provide the words, and the hand, in such an office more willing than able, set them down") and the confident expectation of eternal fame in the conclusion ("Vivi adunque: nullo ti può di questo privare; ed essempio etterno a' felici e a' miseri dimora dell'angoscie della tua donna": "Live, therefore: nothing can deprive you of this; and remain as a lasting example to both the happy and the unhappy of the torments of your mistress") make it clear that the author's stylistic ambitions were far from modest. Nor should the noble status of the protagonist and of those she addresses be lost sight of ("O nobili donne, ne' cuori del quali amore più che nel mio forse felicemente dimora": "O noble women, in whose hearts love lives, more happily perhaps than in my own"), since another axiom of medieval rhetoric was the obligatory relationship between the level of the characters and the level of the style. Finally, the prose of the *Fiammetta* itself decides the case with authority; but with this prose I shall deal at greater length further on.

As a matter of fact, Boccaccio was well acquainted with Latin elegies written in anything but "humble" style: we need only to cite the last of them, composed in Florence by Arrigo da Settimello (1193), the *Elegia de diversitate fortunae* (or, in one manuscript, *Elegia sive miseria*— once again the medieval definition of elegy), which arrives at manneristic paroxysms in its elaboration of language and style; it is, or strives to be, sublime. Boccaccio situates his work in this exact literary genre with its very title (*Elegia di madonna Fiammetta*), while Horace's definition is echoed in its prologue: "Con lagrimevole stilo seguirò come io posso . . ." ("With sorrowful pen and style I shall follow as I may . . .").[8]

Here it is important to define how Boccaccio uses the term *elegia*, the value he gives to it, and what it is based on, precisely because we know the attention he paid (though without concerning himself with theoretical implications) to literary genres as such.[9] It is in relation to them that nearly all his works have an inaugurative or innovative function, from the epic poem in *ottave*: "Tu, o libro, primo a lor cantare / di Marte fai gli affanni sostenuti, / nel volgar lazio più mai non veduti" ("You, my book, have them [the Muses] sing / the labors borne by Mars / as yet unknown in our Tuscan speech") to the allegorical pastoral romance in prose and in tercets, the *Commedia delle ninfe fiorentine*; from the bucolic "metamorphosis," the *Ninfale fiesolano*, to the collection of "framed" tales, the *Decameron*. Add to this the further fact that the use of the *cantare in ottave* is in all probability his invention.[10] In the final analysis, it is this stance of disguised revolutionary which characterizes all Boccaccio's activity, and not only on the formal plane. The *Decameron* is as medieval in the evidence of its sources, themes, and cultural allusions as it is pre-Renaissance in the naturalistic and anthropocentric lack of inhibition of its attitude to life.

We thus have a work defined as an *elegia* and its Ovidian model, the elegies of the *Heroides*. The use of prose is a bridge between these two facts, not an obstacle to them. Entire pages of the *Fiammetta* are directly translated from Ovid, and we know that the *Heroides* were particularly dear to professional *volgarizzatori* before and after Boccaccio. The whole history of these translations into the vernacular serves to demonstrate that up to Boccaccio's time prose alone was used for all translations from the Latin. Thus for writing an extensive "heroid" in the vulgar tongue the prose offered itself as the most appropriate mode. And it was also the most convenient, if we remember that prose alone could adapt itself to the manifold complexities of classical rhetoric, to its hairsplitting oratory of interrogation and exclamation, its unfolding of adjective and noun more in terms of emphasis than of rules, its elaborate periphrases. Prose indeed had served for the most characteristic work of Boccaccio's Latin-oriented apprenticeship, the *Filocolo*. Be it added, *ad abundantiam*, that the most sought-after pattern for Boccaccio *rhétoriqueur* was the *Metamorphoses* of Apuleius and that even Dante, in proposing paradigms for supreme stylistic construction, had set beside Vergil, Ovid, Statius, and Lucan, the authors of "altissimas prosas," Livy, Pliny, Frontinus, and Orosius (*De vulg. el.* 2.6.7).

3. But once the *Fiammetta* has been defined as *elegia*, and even more precisely as "heroid,"[11] attention must be given to the other elements which constitute a new literary genre, of which this would remain the unique example in Italy. The adoption of prose form and thereby the opening out of its measures allows Boccaccio to divide it into chapters (absent from the *Heroides*), and this, together with the content headings, gives the text the appearance of a romance.[12] This is in agreement with the arguments, i.e., with events which unfold, their narrative character unhampered by the invocational concentration of the *Heroides*. Furthermore, Boccaccio abandons the epistolary fiction of the *Heroides*, substituting for the communication circuit of lover and beloved a different circuit, one of emotional complicity, of empathy, between Fiammetta and those to whom the "piccolo libretto" is addressed: a circuit in which the didactic element—for medieval writers so commonly a justification for erotic subject matter—is barely alluded to: "Io non vi conforto tanto a questo affanno perché voi più di me divegniate pietose, quanto perché più la nequizia di colui per cui ciò m'avviene conoscendo divegniate più caute in non commettervi ad ogni giovine" ("I do not point out this grief to you to make you more conscious of my position, but the more you know of the wickedness of the man through whom this befell me, the more careful you will be in entrusting yourselves to young men," 5.1). The *Fiammetta* is didactic in a descriptive sense, if at all, in terms of the detailed phenomenology of the love it proposes[13] and, in a humanistic sense, the totality of the classical references it elaborates, as well as the new model which it comes to constitute in itself.

Finally, the relationship between Fiammetta and the recipients of her complaints suggests recourse to the device of the envoi or *commiato*. This unquestionably derives from lyric poetry, but here the intention is, I believe, more ambitious. Yet another model for the *Fiammetta* is, as we know, the *Vita nuova*. There Dante creates for himself an ideal audience of women "che sono gentili, e che non sono pure femmine" ("who are high-minded and who are not only women"), those whom he addresses in the canzone *Donne ch'avete intelletto d'amore*. Just as these are chosen because they alone are worthy to hear Beatrice's praise, so the women, noble and in love, to whom Fiammetta addresses her book are those whose disposition will best dispose them to share her sufferings.

And pleas for the sympathy and understanding of these women form the connectives between the various parts of the *Fiammetta*, from the invocation of the proem, which begins the very first chapter, to the beginnings of the various chapters, with the exception of 7 and, of course, the *commiato* which is addressed to the book (9):

> Mentre che io, o carissime donne, in così lieta e graziosa vita, sì come di sopra è descritta, menava i giorni miei, poco alle cose future pensando, la nemica Fortuna a me di nascosto temperava li suoi veleni. . . .

> [While I, O my dear women, passed my days in a life so happy and gentle, as I described above, paying but little heed to what the future would bring, unbeknownst to me Fortune the enemy mixed me her poisons . . . , 2.1]

> Quale voi avete di sopra udito, o donne, cotale, dipartito il mio Panfilo, rimasi. . . .

> [My Panfilo once departed, in the state I have told you of, O women, did I remain . . . , 3.1]

> Così, o pietose donne, sollecita, come udito avete, non solamente al molto disiderato e con fatica aspettato termine pervenni, ma ancora di molti dì il passai. . . .

> [Thus, O compassionate women, preoccupied just as you have heard, did I not come merely to the date so long desired and so painfully awaited, but I went many days beyond it . . . , 4.1]

> Lievi sono state infino a qui le mie lagrime, o pietose donne, e i miei sospiri piacevoli a rispetto a quelli, i quali la dolente penna, più pigra a scrivere che il cuore a sentire, s'apparecchia di dimostrarvi.

> [But light have been my tears until now, O most compassionate women, and my sighs pleasant compared with those which my sorrowful pen, more slow to write than the heart to feel, now makes ready to show you, 5.1]

> Quale voi avete potuto comprendere, pietosissime donne, per le cose davanti dette, è stata nelle battaglie d'amore la mia vita, e ancora assai piggiore. . . .

> [In the state which you will by now have understood, O most compassionate women, from the things that have so far been said, in the battles of love my life has been passed, and worse yet . . . , 6.1]

Sono, adunque, o pietosissime donne, rimasa in cotale vita, quale voi potete nelle cose udite presumere. . . .

[Thus was I, O most compassionate women, abandoned in this situation, as from the things you have heard, you may well imagine . . . , 8.1]

These cross-references link up the chapter, and their recapitulation is clearly marked with phrases like "si come di sopra è descritta," "quale voi avete di sopra udito," "come udito avete," "infino a qui," "per le cose avanti dette," etc.

Such connectives do not merely unite the chapters horizontally; vertically they also form a sort of grid inside which various prose segments (narrative, meditative, deprecative, etc.) of the first five chapters are arranged. Here is a specimen, drawn exclusively from chapter 1:

Questi adunque, o pietosissime donne, fu colui il quale il mio cuore con folle estimazione fra tanti nobili, belli e valorosi giovani . . . elesse per signore della mia vita.

[He it was then, O most compassionate women, whom my heart, judging foolishly amongst so many noble, handsome, and valiant young men . . . chose as lord of my life, 8]

Deh, pietose donne, chi crederà possibile in un punto uno cuore così alterarsi.

[Alas, O compassionate women, who would believe that in one instant a heart could so change, 9]

Deh, donne pietose, se Amore felicemente adempia i vostri disii, che doveva io, e che potea rispondere a tante e tali parole, e di tale dea, se non: "Sia come ti piace"?

[Alas, compassionate women, may Love with all good fortune meet your desires, what should I, what could I have replied to such and so many words, and from so great a goddess, if not "As you will, so be it"? 18]

O pietosissime donne, che non insegna Amore a' suoi suggetti, e a che non li fa egli abili a imparare?

[O most compassionate women, what is there that Love cannot teach his subjects, and what does he not render them capable of learning? 23]

Se io, o donne, non erro imaginando, egli non fu piccola la fermezza degli animi nostri. . . .

[If I, O women, do not err in what I imagine, no light matter was our strength of mind . . . , 24]

Ma in prima che io a ciò pervenga, quanto più supplicemente posso
la vostra pietà invoco. . . .

[But before I come to this particular point, in as suppliant a style as
I can master I call upon your compassion . . . , 24]

. . . Sì come voi medesime, le quali forse forza cercate a ciò che più
vi sarebbe a grado, sapete che sogliono le donne amate fare.

[. . . Exactly as you yourselves, who perhaps hope that force will
achieve what most you desire, well know what women are accustomed
to do when loved, 25]

What is immediately evident here is the diversity of tone: in the first
instance (horizontal connective), the women are primarily attentive
listeners; in the second (vertical connective), they are the confidantes
whose experiences and aspirations can be called to witness or invoked
for approbation. Both types of connective follow well-defined rules: the
vertical involve the horizontal, but not vice versa. In chapters 6 and 8
we find an exordium addressed to the women readers, while in 8 there
is a conclusion as well, without internal dialogue; in chapters 1–5, however, there is as much dialogue in exordium (or perhaps in conclusion)
as there is internal dialogue. For a possible explanation, see section 10
below.

4. Let us now attempt to deal with the text by working from the
outside in. There are nine chapters, preceded by a prologue. The formula 1 + 9 immediately brings to mind the *Decameron*, with its groups
of ten tales, nine of which are devoted to set themes, while the tenth is
a free choice. As for the number 9, it is one of the most heavily loaded
numerals in symbolic and religious terms: we need only refer to one of
the *Fiammetta's* own sources, the *Vita nuova*. Boccaccio devotes careful attention to the numerical aspects of his divisions. We move from
the twelve books of the *Teseida* (whose archetype is the *Aeneid*) to the
fifty cantos of the *Amorosa visione*, to the 100 tales (10 × 10) of the
Decameron,[14] equal to the number of cantos in the *Commedia*. But for
the schema of the *Fiammetta*, the most rewarding comparison is with
the *Filostrato* of only a few years earlier.

The *Filostrato* also is divided into nine parts, of unequal length, and
preceded by a proem. Furthermore, in the *Filostrato* part 9 also has the
function of *commiato* ("nella quale l'autore parla all'opera sua a im-
ponli a cui e con cui deggia andare e quello deggia fare, e fine": "in
which the author addresses his work, laying down to whom it should go
and with whom consort and what it should do, and concludes"; cf. the
Fiammetta, "nel quale madonna Fiammetta parla al libro suo, impo-

nendogli in che abito, e quando e a cui egli debba andare, e da cui guardarsi; e la fine": "in which madonna Fiammetta addresses her book, laying down in what style, and when, and to whom it should go, and whom to avoid, and concludes").[15] Here too, as in chapter 9 of the *Fiammetta*, echoes of Cavalcanti's *ballata* from exile are found. Part 9 of the *Filostrato* and chapter 9 of the *Fiammetta*, in other words, have the function of envois: it is the more original in the *Fiammetta*, in that here the rhythm and the linguistic conventions of poetry have been abandoned.

The nine chapters of the *Fiammetta* are of distinctly uneven length (as is clear from the diagram below). The longest chapter (5) falls exactly at the midpoint. The sum of the pages that precede it (forty-five plus two for the prologue) is almost equal to the sum of the pages that follow (fifty). And exactly in the center of chapter 5—and thus of the

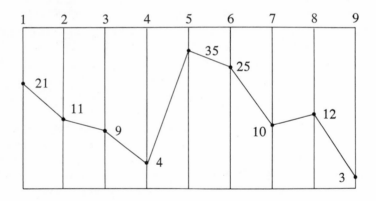

book—comes the prayer to Fortune, which is, in terms of a popular conception particularly dear to Boccaccio, the dea ex machina of events: "La nemica Fortuna a me di nascoso temperava li suoi veleni" ("Unbeknownst to me, Fortune the enemy mixed me her poisons," 2.1); "Quando la Fortuna, non contenta de' danni miei, mi volle mostrare ch'ancora più amari veleni aveva che darmi" ("When Fortune, not content with the harm done me, wanted to show that she had poisons more bitter yet to give me," 6.2); "Ma mentre che in questa disposizione mi tenevano dispettosa gl'iddii, la Fortuna ingannevole . . . non contenta de' dati mali, apparecchiandomi peggio, con falsa letizia indietro trasse le cose avverse e il suo corruccio" ("But while in this state of mind the gods kept me downcast, treacherous Fortune, . . . not content with the evil done and preparing still worse for me, with a false show of joy withdrew adverse events and her displeasure," 7.1). Fortune is actually defined as such in the conclusion to chapter 8: "Ecco adunque, o donne, che per gli antichi inganni della Fortuna io sono misera" ("Thus it is, O women, that by the inveterate treacheries of Fortune I am unhappy," 18).

Another characteristic element of chapter 5 is a sort of prologue-transition; it is placed as a watershed between the first part of the elegy (chaps. 1–4) and that which follows (5–8, given that 9 is merely envoi):

> Lievi sono state infino a qui le mie lagrime, o pietose donne, e i miei sospiri piacevoli a rispetto di quelli, i quali la dolente penna, più pigra a scrivere che il cuore a sentire, s'apparecchia di dimostrarvi. . . . Adunque fermate gli animi, né vi spaventino sì le mie promesse, che, le cose passate parendovi gravi, voi non vogliate ancora vedere le seguenti gravissime. . . .

> [But light have been my tears until now, O most compassionate women, and my sighs pleasant compared with those which my sorrowful pen, more slow to write than the heart to feel, now makes ready to show you. . . . Therefore steel your spirits, and do not let what I promise so frighten you that, when what is past seemed so heavy, you will not desire to go on and see what follows, which is heavier yet, 5.1]

This is an internal prologue which itself has a precedent in the *Filostrato*,[16] where the invocation that opens part 3 divides the ninefold succession into $2 + 7$ (and 7 is another magic number). Chapter 5 is, in other words, the keystone of the *Fiammetta*. This is also true from the point of view of subject matter, as we shall soon see.

In the opinion of various critics (I shall use the words of De Robertis), the *Fiammetta* "is a love romance narrated in the first person, wholly inward, slow moving. It might be thought of as a variation on a single theme, and it is nothing less, at times embellished with fleeting modulations, something akin to the speech of the soul." This judgment, the soul apart, is substantially correct. And yet the text is neither uniform nor static (De Robertis goes on: "And at certain moments [it is] enriched with contrasts, curiously linked, deliberately sought out").[17] The alternation of narrative modulation and tone, the varied use of dialogue and monologue, the use of different "tenses" all enrich Fiammetta's long discourse with precious veinings. My aim is to sketch out an analysis which will give due weight to these internal differentiations: if we were to seek for mere narrative functions, in the manner of Propp, the book would break down into a very limited number of elementary propositions.

5. The *Fiammetta* is, however, a narration; and the first technical device we should observe is the combination of the most elementary narrative time and tense, the progressive, with other kinds of time, directly related to verbal tenses. The following table might be hazarded:

	Narrative Time	Verbal Tense
1	progressive	perfect
2	progressive	perfect
3	mental	imperfect
4	mental	imperfect
5	progressive × mental	perfect × imperfect
6	progressive	perfect
7	progressive	perfect
8	presentative	present
9	desiderative	imperative

Chapters 8 and 9 are nearly or even completely uncoupled from the narration, which comes to a close with chapter 7. Chapter 8 is a procession of literary characters, mostly classical, whose sufferings Fiammetta calls up, concluding the short series of exclamations and considerations each inspires with the affirmation that in her case suffering is greater than in the case of all others. The procession makes use of fairly uniform formulae of presentation: "con meco penso" ("I consider with myself," 2); "mi si para [davanti]" ("there appears [before me]," 3, 6, 9, 12); "considero, veggio" ("I consider, I see," 3); "mi viene la pietà di" ("pity comes to me for," 4); "viemmi poi innanzi" ("there then presents itself to me," 5); "ricordami" ("reminds me," 7); "aggiugne ancora il mio pensiero" ("my thought adds further," 8); "con costei accompagno la doglia" ("in her company I place the grief," 8); "appresso vegnente nella mia mente" ("next coming into my mind," 10); "m'apparisce" ("appears to me," 11); "m'occorrono" ("comes before me," 13); "mi vengono innanzi" ("present themselves to me," 14); "vengonmi ancora nella mente" ("return again to my mind," 15); "mostranmisi" ("show themselves to me," 16); "mi si fanno sentire" ("make themselves felt," 17). The precise function of these phases is to align no small number of figures before the protagonist, who then compares herself with them. Memory progressively draws out these names from the learned repertoire of Fiammetta (Boccaccio) and pronounces them in the present tense, which is that of the selecting out which actualizes them.

As for chapter 9, with its envoi character, it is quite extraneous to the whole pseudo-autobiographical narration: Fiammetta now turns to the book itself, telling it to whom it must present itself and what it must say.

Hence the series of imperatives, which among other things introduce the second person into a book where the first necessarily predominates. After dwelling so long on her own acts and words and thoughts, Fiammetta now turns her attention to the acts and words of her book, conferring the status of message, directed to well-defined recipients, upon her introspective confession-apology.

Even more significant, given its limited range, is the tense alternation of the first seven chapters. The shift from the progressive tense of the first two to the mental tense of the second two is a consequence of a determining fact at the level of subject matter: all the action involving Panfilo and Fiammetta is over and done with by the end of the first two chapters; for the rest Fiammetta remains alone on the stage, her attitudes changing in accord with the news, true or false, which she hears of Panfilo, and with her imaginings.[18] When both lovers are present, events are narrated in their real succession, from falling in love to abandonment, in a narrative to which the perfect tense is perfectly adapted in a clearly singulative aspect. In contrast, in the two succeeding chapters (3–4) nothing happens. Fiammetta, trusting in Panfilo's promises, passes her period of waiting in solitude. Her only interlocutor is heavenly time, whose movement through the sky infallibly measures out the day. It is Fiammetta herself who, in an exhausting subjective cross-examination, calls up the arguments for and against Panfilo: "a me opponendo, e rispondendo, e solvendo" ("objecting, and replying, and resolving to myself," 3.5); "Quasi tutti i preteriti pensieri del dì mi venivano nella mente, e mal mio grado con molti più argomenti e pro e contra mi si faceano ripetere" ("Almost all the past thoughts of that day came back to my mind and, adding against my will further arguments for and against, obliged me to repeat them," 3.12). In this restricted meditative space not only is there no order of the succession; the possibilities of repetition are infinite, whence the prevalence of a particular tense (the imperfect), whose iterative aspect is further reinforced by the adverbs: "io alcuna volta diceva" ("I at times would say," 3.5); "o quante volte già mi ricorda che" ("oh, how many times already I recall that," 3.4); "e così molte volte gran parte del dì trapassava con poca noia" ("and many times I would pass the greater part of the day without pain," 3.8); "egli mi pareva alcuna volta . . . altre mi pareva" ("it seemed to me at times . . . at other times it seemed," 3.12); "mi sospingevano sovente i pensieri ad imaginare" ("often my thoughts drove me to imagine," 4.2); "alcuna volta pensava" ("at times I would think," 4.2); etc.

With chapters 5–7 things are again set in motion, at least in the sense that news regarding Panfilo provokes reactions on Fiammetta's part—

on the level of thought but also on that of action (attempted suicide in chap. 6). And so there is a move back to the time axis, to follow out a succession of events which can be summed up as news of Panfilo's marriage; news of Panfilo's imminent arrival; Panfilo's arrival—but it is merely someone of the same name. These are events, then, of very little weight, and this is underlined by the negation which frequently follows them (marriage → no marriage; arrival → failure to arrive); but they are of sufficient substance to produce, in their exhausting alternation of hope and its frustration, the inward tempests which form the elegy's main argument.

Thus we return to a progressive time and to use of the perfect tense: most particularly, however, in chapters 6 and 7. Chapter 5, on the other hand, presents an alternation of narrative and mental tenses, quite natural given its variation in subject matter and tone, but for which a preeminently technical motivation can be found. In fact at this point the husband, whose wife has provided plausible but false motives to account for the state to which she is reduced, persuades her to frequent places of amusement and relaxation which earlier had formed the backdrop for her love of Panfilo. Thus in Fiammetta's memory are revived (and appear before the reader for the first time) other moments of her previous happiness. This entails an overlapping of tenses; the past recalled and the unhappy present, where the present follows the real order of events, while the past appears in inserts, subject to no more than the laws of an ever changing memory.

6. If we are to get inside the articulations of the tale, a census of the characters and their functions is called for. The way they are distributed over the chapters is symptomatic in itself:

1	Fiammetta, Panfilo, nurse, Venus
2	Fiammetta, Panfilo
3	Fiammetta
4	Fiammetta
5	Fiammetta, husband, merchant
6	Fiammetta, husband, nurse, servant, Tisiphone
7	Fiammetta, nurse
8	Fiammetta

The only really active characters are Fiammetta and Panfilo. The nurse is no more than a psychological helper, in the sense that it is she who first seeks to dissuade Fiammetta from an illicit love and then tries various ways of comforting her and of limiting her self-destructive fury. In chapter 7, however, the nurse has the function of messenger (first she announces the imminent arrival of Panfilo, then acquires and produces the proofs that the news was false). Other messengers are the merchant (5) and the servant (6), by whose means Fiammetta is informed of Panfilo's supposed marriage and then of his new love affair. The husband is a psychological helper like the nurse, with this difference: first, he is ignorant of Fiammetta's motives for desperation, and second, he is in a position to influence her actions to a greater degree (undertaking to amuse her between Baiae and Naples). Finally, there are two divine apparitions at the most decisive moments for Fiammetta: Venus, who sweeps aside all her scruples and exalts the inexorability of love (1.17), and Tisiphone, who provides the final stimulus to suicide (6.20), a suicide which of course fails.[19]

It all adds up easily enough: the chapters through which Fiammetta moves alone (3, 4, 8) are also those in which time has only mental developments, of personal or cultural memory (see sec. 5 above). Since they close the two parts of the tale (1–4, 5–8; it will be recalled that 5 has a new prologue), they represent the inward echoes of a drama previously lived through in terms of passionate participation. On the other hand, Panfilo and the husband, who are also placed symmetrically (1–2, 5–6), push the action forward decisively: the former because he is the constituent element of the love affair, the latter because, with his tender interference, he lacerates his wife's wounds at the very moment in which she has given up hope, quickening her long delayed remorse.

7. The abundant use made of classical texts from which lengthy passages are translated, even though they are developed independently or contaminated, is fundamental to the system of stylistic levels. A work in which the nurse, dissuading her mistress from love, perorates in sentences from Seneca's *Phaedra*[20] and in which Venus herself sustains the opposite point of view, also plagiarizing *Phaedra*; in which the most violent recriminations of an abandoned woman come from the second *Heroid*, while her desire for sleep is expressed in a mélange of the *Metamorphoses* and the *Hercules furens*,[21] inevitably draws upward all the stylistic levels that are brought into play. This ennoblement of the whole should undoubtedly be brought into relation to the almost completely classical adornment of fourteenth-century geography and custom: a church is a "sacro tempio" ("sacred temple," 1.4); a religious service is "il solenne oficio debito a quel giorno" ("the solemn office set down for that day," 1.4); Neapolitan aristocrats are "gli onorevoli prencipi del nostro Ausonico Regno" ("the worthy princes of our Ausonian realm," 5.27); and Tuscany is "Etruria" (7.2).

There is no need for surprise. Similar observations might be made in abundance for early *volgarizzamenti*. And it would be equally easy to cite, from the *duecento* down to Humanism itself, further examples of deliberate obscuring of the Christian religion (however, rarely so systematic). Here Fiammetta makes invocation to Venus, Jupiter, and Tisiphone with the other Furies, but never, or hardly ever, to the Christian God ("Iddio" at 5.32 and "grandissimo rettore," "great ruler," at 5.35 could refer equally well to Jupiter). What we are faced with, however, is an institutional fact[22] which is also reflected in structures. The classical world as literary texts present it is for Boccaccio in the *Fiammetta*, and thus for Fiammetta herself, a firmament of archetypes. If, as she proceeds to church in all the splendor of her elegance and beauty, Fiammetta feels herself "simile alle dèe vedute da Paris nella valle d'Ida" ("like the goddesses seen by Paris in the Vale of Ida," 1.4) and is then naturally enough observed by the faithful "non altramente che se Venere o Minerva . . . fossero in quello luogo . . . nuovamente discese" ("not otherwise than if Venus or Minerva . . . had in that place . . . descended anew," 1.5), we may be justified in thinking of embellishment. But when it is Panfilo who finds himself in the midst of knights "de' quali per autorità alcuno Scevola simigliava, e alcuno altro . . . si saria detto il censorino Catone, o l'Uticense" ("of whom in point of authority one resembled Scaevola, and another . . . might have been called Cato the Censor, or the Utican"), while others remind him of "il magno Pompeo" or "Scipione Africano o Cincinnato"; when Panfilo himself compares the princes in tournament "allo arcadio Partenopeo" or "al piacevole Ascanio" or "a Deifebo . . . a Ganimede" (5.28), it becomes evident that this classical dress is the most satisfactory outcome of a drive toward confrontation and comparison.[23]

Thus there stands revealed in its full importance the bridge that begins with the speech of Venus—who, in order to break down any remaining resistance, unfolds before a Fiammetta already in love a goodly list of gods, demigods, and heroes (1.17)—and leads to the procession of characters, again mythological and literary, victims for the most part of misfortune in love, which fills chapter 8. This bridge rests on several intermediate points, e.g., when Fiammetta's comparison of her sufferings with those of Tityos, Tantalus, Ixion, and the Danaids (6.14) or, on the other hand, the group of betrayed women and demigoddesses which the nurse offers for the consolation of her desperate mistress (6.15). If we were to find, prosaically, a disproportion between Fiammetta's fairly banal story and the classical fables with which it is compared, we would (if we refrained from passing judgment) seize on one of the work's constituent elements; for it carries out a detailed, refined, psychological analysis within parameters derived from classical literature. Boccaccio's game must be accepted on its own terms (and these are not without a touch of irony): the comparisons are made officially not by the author but by the "I" character, and all exaggeration can be charged to her (learned) desperation.[24]

All the stylistic levels thus aspire upward. There is no reason then to complain of the scarcity of scenes of refined naturalism, though such scenes are not lacking in the *Fiammetta* (e.g., that in which a merchant, while he displays and sells his jewels to the Neapolitan noblewomen, gives news of Panfilo to a young lady who is so insistent in her questions and so visibly disturbed by the answers that Fiammetta, although she hides the fact, understands that her lover had not been faithful to her even in Naples). Indeed it might be observed that rapid, lively dialogue is kept to a bare minimum and is reserved for those points at which it will serve to drive the narrative forward: in particular the opening of chapters 5 and 6. Elsewhere exchanges are harmoniously turned and elaborated or are made the occasion of little perorations which alternate in micro-tournaments of oratory.[25] It might be added that these verbal expressions, in which figures of thought and figures of speech alternate, find their most satisfactory formulation when there is no addressee—in the monologues. In this case, there is no question of a prevalence of emotive and poetic over referential and conative functions; the former is in unchallenged predominance.

A considerable part of the *Fiammetta*, which is itself a message to the women who read it and as such an extended peroration, is interwoven with dialogues and monologues; and these at times may contain still further dialogues, at two removes from the reader (an example is the nurse's speech at the beginning of chap. 7). But after reference has been made to the predominant stylistic types, our survey should take in other kinds as well, particularly those which pertain to the narration. They can be classified in relation to their models, which now are in the vernacular. One is the *Vita nuova*, which with its ecstatic, almost visionary tone can hardly be held to be anything other than the most elevated style. A great many of the *Vita nuova*'s situations[26] become part of the concentrated prose solution of the *Fiammetta*, from the incidence of falling in love in a church (1.6), a profane and worldly version of *Vita nuova* 1.3–6, to the scene of the compassionate women at the bedside of the unconscious Fiammetta (6.3), which should be compared with *Vita nuova* 23.11–14. Even expository formulae are involved, such as the "mi pareva" series, to indicate different stages of a dream (3.12; *Vita nuova* 23.5–10).[27] Indeed the *Vita nuova* is present in the whole structure of the *Fiammetta*, not only because it too narrates the birth and the growth of a love, different though it is, but also because of the considerable role already played in it by elements of imagination, by monologues, dreams, apparitions, and even by imaginary verbal contests (*tenzoni*) between the protagonist and a variety of personifications (Love, etc.).

But if the *Vita nuova* is a model particularly as regards happenings at a subjective level, for his descriptions of landscape and of courtly life Boccaccio makes use of his own experience as a lyric poet. Those parts of chapter 5 which might serve as a guide to the amusements of medieval Campania are full of personal reminiscence.[28] One example will suffice:

> Egli avveniva spesse volte che, essendo, sì come la stagione richiedeva, il tempo caldissimo, molte altre donne e io, acciò che più agevolmente quello trapassassimo, sopra velocissima barca, armata di molti remi, solcando le marine onde, cantando e sonando, li rimoti scogli, e le caverne ne' monti dalla natura medesima fatte, essendo esse e per ombra e per li venti recentissime, cercavamo. . . .
>
> Niuno lito, niuno scoglio, niuna grotta da me non cercata vi rimaneva, né ancora alcuna brigata.
>
> [It would often happen that, since the weather was hot, given the season, many other women and I, in the hope of spending it more pleasantly, on a swift, many-oared ship plowing the waves of the sea, singing and playing the while, would seek out distant rocks, and caves in the mountains made by nature herself, when these were cool, thanks to the shade and the breeze. . . .
>
> There was no shore, no rock, no grotto which remained unexplored by me, nor any company unfrequented, 5.26]

Sulla poppa sedea d'una barchetta,
che 'l mar segando presta era tirata,
la donna mia con altre accompagnata,
cantando or una or altra canzonetta.
Or questo lito ed or quest'isoletta,
ed ora questa ed or quella brigata
di donne visitando, era mirata
qual discesa dal cielo una angioletta. . . .

[At the stern of a little boat,
which swiftly drove on cutting through the sea,
sat my lady with other women in company,
singing now one, now another song.
Visiting now this shore and now this island,
now this and now that group
of women, she was looked upon
as if she were an angel come down from heaven . . . , *Rime* 6]

And we might go on, pointing out, for example, borrowings from the *Commedia*[29] or the *Filocolo*;[30] but our purpose here is merely to show the various stylistic elements which are amalgamated into a prose that is substantially and ostentatiously classical.

8. We are in the domain of the word and of argumentation, where a census of narrative functions would prove disappointing; techniques at the level of discourse and the uses they are put to (i.e., their function, for here too it is function we are dealing with) may well prove to have more weight. I shall start out, then, from a census of discourse techniques, with the intention of then going on to see the way they interact within the chapters of the *Fiammetta*, about whose clear-cut characterization few doubts can by now remain.

The slightness of the narrative element in the *Fiammetta* has a genetic motivation and structural repercussions: the motivation is in its matrix of those first-person laments that are the *Heroides*; the repercussions are the abundance of dialogues and monologues, whose range is vast indeed. Communicative dialogue is, as we have seen, reduced to a minimum; much more common is persuasive dialogue, in which each of the participants develops his own arguments, balancing out in a variety of ways both rational and rhetorical elements. Monologue too has different aspects: there is monologue that is actually spoken and internal monologue, and there is the apostrophe-oration. Given a strictly "Fiammetta-centric" point of view, all the monologues are Fiammetta's, and in the dialogues Fiammetta always intervenes (or is at least present).

On the basis of this presence of dialogues, monologues, and apostrophes, the chapters of the *Fiammetta* are no less well defined:

1	dialogues
2	dialogues
3	monologues
4	monologues
5	dialogues, monologues, apostrophes
6	dialogues, monologues, apostrophes
7	dialogues, monologues, apostrophes
8	

In her first two chapters, which are narrative, the protagonist, who in her contacts with others (Panfilo, the nurse) uses dialogues as her natural vehicle, does not pause for soliloquy—her reflections are more likely to be contained within the discourse she addresses to her readers. The primarily meditative and introverted nature of chapters 3–4 is marked, however, by a wealth of monologues: indeed the chapters are divided evenly into exposition and monologue; when she is quite alone, Fiammetta can no longer indulge in dialogue. In chapters 5–7 dialogues, monologues, and apostrophes alternate within the exposition. Finally, chapter 8 shows a complete absence of dialogues, monologues, and apostrophes. The protagonist, her hopes and even her passionate outbursts exhausted, gives her readers an account of the learned excursions which confirm her intellectually in the proud incommensurability of her misfortune. Once more, the final chapters of the two groups (3–4 and 8) are clearly marked off from those which precede them; but there is clearly a much greater diversity of discourse techniques in chapters 5–7 (in particular, as we shall see at once, in the central and principal chapter, the fifth).

The affinity between monologue and apostrophe (in talking to oneself it is easy enough to imagine a dialogue with one who is absent) comes out most clearly in the fact that the apostrophes—with the exception of one timid apparition (3.10)—are met with only in the chapters which also contain monologues, even indeed and more subtly in the immediate interchanges which are effected between one and the other. In chapters 3 and 4 Panfilo is always introduced into the monologues in the third person: "Or come potrebbe Panfilo . . . ricevere nel cuore . . . un altro amore?" ("Now how could Panfilo . . . take into his heart . . . another love?" 3.6); "Ora al mio Panfilo rincresce l'essere a me stato lontano" ("Now my Panfilo is displeased to have been away from me," 3.14). In chapters 5–8, apostrophes to the gods or to a variety of hypostases[31] alternate with apostrophes to the absent Panfilo: "O Panfilo, ora la ragione della tua dimora conosco" ("O Panfilo, now I understand the reason for your delay," 5.5); "Deh, perché, o Panfilo, mi dolgo io del tuo essere lontano . . . ?" ("Alas, why, O Panfilo, do I lament your absence . . . ?" 5.6); or even to the distant and unknown Florentine rival. In short the monologue of chapters 3–4 is meditative and reflective in character, while chapters 5–7 become more extraverted and argumentative in relation to a polarization toward the apostrophe. To this may be seen to correspond, though here supporting evidence is more limited, a polarization toward the dream of the first chapters. It is a fact, however, that Fiammetta's only dreams are found in chapters 1 and 3; one of them (1.3) is a warning dream whose function is to discourage her from consummating her love, a function similar to that of the nurse's speeches; the other (3.12) is a recurrent dream of consolation, brought about by the final illusions of a woman in love. Further on, Fiammetta dreams no more: decision, fear, and rage all have been burned up in her vigil.

9. By soundings within the context as a whole, at various depths and from a variety of angles, we have brought to light a series of structures, each of which is provided with a symmetry of its own. But the totality of the text which results from them (even in the purely theoretical event of an analysis of *all* the structures) is not given by the sum of the structures arrived at, and not even by their combination. It is, rather, the result of an interaction, which can only come about and be perceived within a temporal space—i.e., the succession of words, sentences, sequences, and chapters (of which the text consists by virtue of the fact that it is a linguistic product); these are transformed from straightforward (spatial) graphic signs into meaningful signs by means of a reading which can only unfold in time. This interrelation throws the different symmetries into relief and establishes among them relationships of concomitance or oppositional or complementary relationships, etc. It is by means of these that a fairly restricted number of techniques gives rise to a vast series of configurations.

Let us begin by observing, within the extremely limited range imposed by our particular method of breaking down the *Fiammetta*, some examples of combinations of structures which we can bring to light extratemporally, i.e., within the conventional time of analytical juxtaposition. Chapters 3–4, with their alternation of exposition and monologues and their mental narrative time, contrast with chapters 1–2, where exposition alternates with dialogues and the tense/time is progressive; chapters 5–7, where tense/time is primarily progressive, are thus parallel to chapters 1–2, and chapter 8 is parallel to chapters 3–4; but the exposition of chapters 5–7 contains dialogues, monologues, and apostrophes, whereas chapter 8 has no monologues at all, unless we decide to consider it as a single monologue in itself. Chapters 3–4 and 8 correspond again by virtue of the fact that Fiammetta alone is present in them.

There is an obvious parallelism between chapters 1–2 and 5–6: both pairs work to a dramatic climax which ends in the first with Panfilo's departure and in the second with Fiammetta's attempted suicide. The increase in dramatic tension corresponds to more concise treatment (eleven pages in 2 versus twenty-one in 1, twenty-five pages in 6 versus thirty-five in 5). Chapters 3–4 and 7–8, in contrast, constitute an anticlimax: in the first two the stylistic approach is homogeneous, in the second two there is sharp contrast. It is as if the persistence in 7 of a strong tide of feeling needed to be counteracted in 8 by enumeration and erudition.

On the other hand, between chapters 1–2 and 5–6 there further exists a chiastic parallelism. The couples Fiammetta-Panfilo and Fiammetta-husband (3 and 5) are contemporaneously flanked by the nurse and a mythological apparition (Venus, Tisiphone) in 1 and 6. In each case there is an antagonistic relationship between the nurse and the divinity who makes incarnate on each occasion the instinct which is uppermost in Fiammetta's mind: first the erotic, then the death instinct. The clear parallelism between the presence of Panfilo (1–2) and that of the husband (5–6) falls into a more complex pattern: since in chapters 5–6 Panfilo is in some measure present in the action through the mediation of the messengers who bring news of him (the merchant in 5, the servant in 6), chapter 7, where the husband is no longer active, opens and closes with more news of Panfilo, brought this time by the nurse in the capacity at once of messenger and helper.

10. If we now take up a slightly larger point of view, we will be in a position to segment the text of the *Fiammetta* and leave nothing over. Taken as a whole, the work is the discourse of "the 'I' character," and it is addressed to the women who are her readers and confidantes. This discourse is primarily expository in tone, but it is interspersed with allocutive sentences—addressed directly to the women readers—which function as a distributive and tonal grid. The allocutive sentences, in fact, either link chapters or mark passages and peaks in the chain of events, almost as if they were invoking understanding and help (cf. sec. 3 above). The second element of the allocution/exposition pair branches out into a further pair: narration/speech inserted into narration. These speeches may be dialogues, apostrophes, or monologues (as illustrated here under sec. 8). The various stylistic types and the connotations they are likely to derive from their models (cf. sec. 7) are made to realize those parts of the overall discourse which we have just listed and give rise to tonalities (ingratiating or apologetic in the allocutions, descriptive or dramatic or elegiac in the narrations, eloquent or logical or moving in the speeches inserted into the narration, and so on—the spectrum is susceptible of a variety of subdivisions). Once they are actualized, these tonalities may be termed registers.

The use here proposed for the term "register" allows observations on stylistic levels and on the tonality of the prose to be referred to clearly defined articulations of the sentence, while it endows with functional characteristics observations which otherwise might remain excessively analytical or impressionistic. Registers are in fact characterized by a play of alternation and contraposition, of successions and implications. In their totality they constitute a whole range of potential orchestration of expressive techniques. In the *Fiammetta* the whole complex of the structures in play has been predisposed to allow this alternation of registers. In a plot emptied of events very early on and carried forward instead on the plane of the meditations and variations of mood of the first-person narrator, it is this extremely able play which establishes a new order of movement, a diagram full of carefully regulated agitation (a diagram clearly planned by the author, who has Fiammetta promise her readers, "Davanti agli occhi vostri appariranno le misere lagrime, gl'impetuosi sospiri, le dolenti voci e li tempestosi pensieri, li quali, con istimolo continuo molestandomi, insieme il cibo, il sonno, i lieti tempi e l'amata bellezza hanno da me tolta via": "Before your eyes will appear the sorrowful tears, the heaving sighs, the mournful expressions, and the tempestuous thoughts which, tormenting me with ceaseless goading, deprived me at once of food, sleep, past happiness, and my own beauty," prologue). Between the disappointment of those who do not find enough adventure in the *Fiammetta* and a misguided admiration for "the first modern psychological novel" (Koerting), comparable perhaps to Proust's *Recherche* (Battaglia), there stands this consciously controlled alternation of registers, the stylistic correlative— not the representation—of a typical emotional experience and the range of states of mind which may lead to its variation.

A first alternation of registers is a constituent element of virtually the whole work: a dense intertwining of the allocutions to the women readers (see sec. 3)—which already set out from an area which lies behind events, an area of reflection, of comment, of recrimination, of self-defense—with exposition in which the readers are considered or called upon not as accomplices or judges but merely as recipients of information. This alternation takes place over more or less short stretches, but it is inexorable, beginning with the very first paragraph, where details of the noble birth, refined education, beauty, and early social success of the protagonist are shot through with exclamations and considerations on the register of one who has arrived at the ultimate gulf of misery.

The function of this allocutive register with respect to the rest of the exposition is further accentuated by contrast, on its sudden cessation in chapter 6 (which contains only an initial allocution) and 7 (where even this is lacking). It should be noted at once that the chapters where allocutions abound—though they are at least present in each of the first five—are 1 and 5. In these the protagonist is torn by contending forces (resistance and surrender to love, discouragement and reverie, touched with what hope remains), while in chapters 6 and 7 Fiammetta relives, with no extraneous elements, the feelings she narrates, whether she gives herself up to the demon of self-destruction or follows out the parabola of a final illusion. The framework of allocutive sentences, which are used to mark passages between various mental states and to predispose the consolation of comprehension and of justification during critical moments of her love, thus serves to stress the possibility of doubling narrator and protagonist, paralleling the persistence of doubts and contrasts within the protagonist herself. These doubts and contrasts are replaced in the final chapters (once Panfilo's betrayal has been registered) by clear-cut attitudes in which there are no hesitations: despair counseling suicide, the betrayal of remaining hope, isolation without illusions in the midst of symbols. The narrator is identified with the protagonist without the distance of memory.

It must be added that the interruption of the allocutive register exactly coincides with the beginning of a theme which, announced at the end of chapter 6, reappears at the end of 7 and the beginning of 8, where it combines with the allocutive register taken up there again: the project of a journey which will allow Fiammetta to see Panfilo once more. We might deduce that up to chapter 6 the narrator has turned back toward the past, with its moral and sentimental values, while from 6 onward she has begun to project herself forward into a problematic future. But the two attitudes do not have the same weight. If up to chapter 6 Fiammetta mixes events and reflections on them, in 6 and 7 events themselves, the thoughts and words evoked, totally dominate her discourse: her occasional references to a future journey are no more than wishful thinking.

The alternation of the registers of allocution and exposition implies a character who integrates (with the aim of constituting the romance-elegy) the technique of the "first-person narrator": in other words, the repeated foreshadowing of the unhappy ending (which programmatically plays down the factual consistency of events in favor of an account of attitudes and states of mind). Hence, on a larger scale, a further alternation of registers, on which the whole first chapter rests: if the woman's internal conflict, externalized and crystallized in the two great perorations of the nurse (against love) and of Venus (on the relentlessness of love), attains the stylistic level of the sublime by virtue of its loftiness of tone and the nobility of its historical-mythological comparisons, the register of tragedy is insinuated and made predominant by means of inauspicious supernatural signs ("aperta visione," 2; "segnale . . . manifesto," 4): the premonitory dream, the flower from the garland caught up in the hangings of the bed. Thus we have on one hand the dramatic quality of a dilemma whose solution cannot be delayed and on the other an anticipated awareness of failure.

A consequence of the level to which this construction of forces and counterforces has been raised (far removed as it is from a steady, detailed narration, from the abandonment to time and the pleasures of that love which, however, still dominates: see the break, indeed the paraleipsis, which foreshadows paragraph 25, the passage from courting to complete fulfillment) is the fact that the dialogues between the two lovers are given only at the moment of their final meetings, i.e., in chapter 2. Here the dialogue between Fiammetta and readers is the merest counterpoint, as well as a separate comment, to the lengthy phrasing of a debate between Fiammetta and Panfilo, in which Panfilo's justification for his departure and her pleas that he should not abandon her are developed into veritable demonstrative-persuasive harangues whose force is drawn no longer (as in the case of the perorations of the nurse and Venus in chap. 1) from the nobility of classical references (and sources) but from the intrinsic value of the argumentation itself. As a consequence, there are two registers: the first, impassioned but clear, is that of a discussion between the lovers; the second, more abandoned and melancholy, that of the discourse to the readers.

The analogous chapters 3–4 have already been defined in their meditative aspect (see sec. 5 above). Fiammetta is alone with her thoughts, whence the unchallenged use of interior monologue. Recalling now those drawn-out days, in the act of narrating, she establishes as exclusive recipients of her dialogue the women to whom the book is addressed, in whose company—sustained, as it were, by their unfailing solidarity— she works over in their finest shadings the feelings she experienced in all those days of waiting. Here, where the substance of events is lacking, the character of the work as monologue becomes evident. It is a monologue which embraces the interior monologues of Fiammetta, her conjectures concerning Panfilo's life, and her justification of his delay (the second register, different from that of the perorations of chap. 1 and the harangues of chap. 2). The dreams too (happy and distressing) are an imaginative extension of this solitary daydreaming (3.12).

The intonation of chapters 3–4, more elegiac than dramatic, to which correspond a reduction in the distance between the registers and thus their convergence, is brusquely turned upside down in chapter 5. Fiammetta is now between Scylla and Charybdis: she now knows she waits in vain for Panfilo after the news of his marriage (exasperation transforms the interior monologues into apostrophes—to Panfilo himself, to the gods, called on as witnesses and helpers); her husband, inappropriately compassionate, strives to arrest the physical and moral decline of his wife, urging her on to amusements and excursions which only serve to provoke the painful comparison of the carefree attitude of others with her own unhappiness, of the moments of joy once known in these same places with the desolation of the present.

With the exception of the initial dialogue with the merchant, rapid and full of subtle touches (a type of narrative-evocative function which will also open chaps. 6 and 7), this chapter represents the most striking innovations with regard to the address to the readers. The ingratiating-apologetic register moves on to a descriptive-elegiac note (amusements at the seaside and on the shore at Baiae, hunting scenes, dances, tournaments, marriage feasts) only to move back, through memories of happiness enjoyed at other times and with other inclinations, through the irrational expectation that Panfilo will appear, called up by the sounds and the beauty, to a totally different psychological attitude: heartsick reevocation. The life of the two lovers in the phase of their reciprocal passion is described to us only now, in terms of intermittencies of memory stimulated not only by the landscape but by solitude in the midst of happy companions. These are the most lyrical moments of the romance (and, not surprisingly, those in which the Boccaccio of the *Rime* appears most markedly). But while the discourse with the women readers at times may open out in this concomitant evocation of an immediate and a remote past ("quelli tempi con questi altri misurando": "comparing that time with this other," 23), it reaches the point of embracing, in terms of a technique already described, Fiammetta's own monologues, which this time are nearly always apostrophes in form and often too in substance. They represent the registers of eloquence in alternation with those of lyrical memory. These registers also effect calculated variations: the group of apostrophes to Panfilo, of self-apostrophes or monologues (3–12), first mix with and then are entirely replaced by apostrophes and invocations to gods, abstract entities, and epochs of the past ("iddii," 4; Venus, 11; Sleep, 13; Fortune, 25; the Golden Age, 30; God, 32; Beauty, 34; God, 35), following a parabola which moves from a call for vengeance in the first instance to a prayer in the last to have Panfilo once again. These invocations alternate a desire to participate positively in life again (invocations to Venus, Fortune, God) and a desire for escape and oblivion (invocations to Sleep, the Golden Age, Beauty). The classical sources of these latter, compared with the relatively greater and dialectical connection of the former with events themselves, determine their marked difference of timbre.

But in chapter 6 there is no longer scope for nostalgic abandonment or escape into the past or into oblivion; even the dialogue with the women readers is almost interrupted. Reality (Panfilo has another lover;

it is not true that he has married) presents itself, as usual, through rapid dialogue. And reality drives acts and words along a much more direct, headlong path. First, some two pages of narrative, a fainting fit, recovery from it, in a register that subtly stylizes astonishment and discouragement. Then the first lengthy apostrophe, to Panfilo, to the gods, takes place from what is now an unbridgeable distance; in that space is situated, through dialogue with the pathetically affectionate spouse ("caro marito," as he is always called), a feeling (at first imperceptible), remorse, expressed in an agitated monologue; but jealousy of the unknown rival breaks out too, apostrophized in her absence and proffered to all the torments of the invoked Furies. Externally, then, the affair seems ended, and such an ending is reaffirmed by the nurse, who strives to place it on a plane of meditative resignation; but in the mind of Fiammetta it is an ending which comes to coincide with death itself, and she chooses the kind of death which involves a decision, a final act, with no appeal.

This drift toward suicide is prepared for by verbal contrasts, direct or indirect, between a proposed acceptance and a helpless refusal of fate; but even more by increasingly frequent reference to the powers and pains of hell in Fiammetta's discourse until Tisiphone, earlier aroused against the rival, appears to provide a final encouragement toward the abyss, just as Venus had earlier done toward passion. The calmly rationalizing register of the nurse exacerbates the register of Fiammetta's apostrophes to acute notes of ire and rage, which then suddenly quiet in a melancholy farewell to her house, her husband, and her relatives before suicide. Her rush to self-destruction, the obstacle, the struggle with the servants who have now hastened to her aid are all represented with fully mastered syntactic mimesis. Thus even her will to resist slackens ("Niuna ira è sì focosa che per passamento di tempo freddissima non divenga": "No anger so blazes that with the passage of time will not become quite cold," 22), and the chapter closes in subdued tones.

Even more rapid, and much more simple, is the movement of chapter 7, which follows out a parabola from hope reborn to hope forever sunk in night. Its exposition is rapid: narration, discourses, and nothing more. And as in chapter 1, the unhappy outcome is announced at once: "La Fortuna ingannevole . . . con falsa letizia indietro trasse le cose avverse e il suo corruccio, acciò che, più movendosi di lontano . . . più m'offendesse" ("Treacherous Fortune . . . with a false show of joy withdrew adverse events and her displeasure so that, by lengthening her stride, . . . she might strike me the more effectively," 1). The two rapid dialogues with the nurse are situated symmetrically, at the beginning and the end: the first incites Fiammetta to illusion, the second sets the seal on misery. In between comes the account of a short, happy period of waiting, with monologues and apostrophes to the gods, revealed as benevolent—not, however, to Panfilo, as if in presentiment of estrangement.

The monotony of chapter 8 is so obstinately ostentatious that it can only be attributed to deliberate intention. Expectation of a future journey, of an ultimate meeting with Panfilo, serve Fiammetta only as a justification for outliving so many proposals of death; for the author, they serve to mute the excited tones of the final chapters. Moreover, it is a theme present only in the opening and closing allocutions which bring to an end the discourse of which the book consists. What dominates chapter 8 is a feeling of adjournment *sine die*: "Sono adunque, o pietosissime donne, *rimasa* in cotale vita, qual voi potete nelle cose udite presumere . . . ; in cotale guisa come udirete *il tempo* malinconosa *trapasso*" ("Thus was I, O most compassionate women, *abandoned* in this situation, as from the things you have heard you may well imagine . . . ; and in such fashion as you will hear, miserably *I pass the time*," 1). The wave of exclamation and interrogation which terminates every comparison with the famous and unhappy in literature (and the chapter does no more than pass characters in review, each of which is compared with the unfortunate protagonist) shows a weariness which resembles despair. Fiammetta seems to move about inside a cold gallery of sculptures. The persons from whom, in the intensity of her drama, she had sought words, attitudes, example, have turned back to marble, dusty and silent.

Four

Functions, Oppositions, and Symmetries in Day VII of the *Decameron*

Day VII of the *Decameron* is beyond question its most self-contained section, whether taken as a whole or in comparison with other groups of stories.[1] The tales it brings together, with the exception of X (which, in accordance with a license the author allows himself for each day, is on a freely chosen subject), all develop a single theme (even VI does not go beyond its bounds; it merely gives a more complex variant). Moreover, it is a theme which in this precise form will appear nowhere else in the *Decameron*. It is to be found in folklore the world over (and needless to say, not in folklore alone): a triangle of lovers of the type H-W-L (husband–wife–wife's lover); and its unfolding follows a fixed pattern: the wife, by contriving a trick to her husband's discomfort (*beffa*), manages to put into effect, disguise, and in one way or another carry on her betrayal. It is no accident that the narration is set in the Valley of Women, the *Valle delle Donne*.

Day VII thus seems to have been created expressly for formalist-semiotic analysis. It is no less structurally homogeneous than a carefully selected group of folktales; indeed, it is the more securely so, given the existence of a single author, for this entails a unified outlook which the stories exemplify and unified symbols to express it. The fact that we are dealing with works that are "signed" (and with such a signature) is an invitation to experiment with types of schematization and formalization which will embrace the largest possible number of "values" a text contains. In other words, we are no longer extrapolating for a literary text symbolic functions or symbolic representations which have been arrived at deductively by analyzing texts of low stylistic quotient (folktales, detective stories, adventure stories, etc.); what we are doing is recognizing these functions in the literary text itself, following the mirage—how remote it is we shall see—of touching from time to time on properties peculiar to its nature as literature.

For example, it has been asked whether narrative functions can absorb the characters (the actants)[2] into themselves; attempts have been made to distinguish between the basic moments of the action and any other collateral (and thus secondary?) forces there may be. We shall see that it is impossible, at least in our case, to leave out of account the qualities and, I would go so far as to say, the social status of the characters and that the material importance of the forces in play is of no less weight than the more subtle motives whose diffusion is more capillary. In the analyses which follow I will try to show how numerous are the elements in play and how complex their relationships. The sacrifice of any of them in the name of greater simplicity of symbolic representation simply means that one is burning on the altar of theory the density and many-sidedness of the text: it is a sacrifice which in the field of literary criticism is hardly likely to be productive.

I may from the outset anticipate the elements of the study introduced here and say that the overall schema furnished by the functions (which, while they follow each other in terms of a logic of their own, also constitute the various moments of the action) will be filled out stage by stage with schematic and graphic representations. These will be employed to indicate relationships between the characters and also between polarities (oppositions) or complementaries which signify (express with signs) the concrete character of the world narrated, or else abstractions (idea forces) arrived at through the actions of the characters or the way in which (by imposition of the author) the facts are perceived by them. I shall try not to leave out of account signs for motives, concepts, and words, which constitute not so much leitmotivs as vectors of the narration.[3] They provide a countercheck on the plane of language for schemata located on the content plane. In the same order of ideas, though this undertaking is more exacting, I shall do what I can to grasp stylistic correlatives of narrative mechanisms, so as to have the author himself confirm, if possible, my tentative outline analysis of the whole body of the text.

1.1. I shall follow a schematic arrangement in descending order, deriving my first descriptive elements from Boccaccio himself, for he takes us very close to a modern *analyse du récit*. Here is the theme of the day as Boccaccio formulates it:

Si ragiona delle beffe, le quali, o per amore o per salvamento di loro, le donne hanno già fatte a' lor mariti, senza essersene avveduti o no.

[Discourse is had of the tricks which, either for love or for their deliverance from peril, ladies have heretofore played their husbands, and whether they were by the said husbands detected or not.]

Three elements in particular are brought to our attention: the trick (*beffa*), the distinction "o per amore o per salvamento," and the distinction "senza esserne avveduti o no."

1.2. The *beffa* is not merely a question of self-defense; it also represents the humiliation of the husband, outmatched by the wife's intelligence or cunning.[4] And Boccaccio is careful to distinguish sudden accesses of talent called forth by necessity—"da subito consiglio aiutata" ("with an inspiration as happy as sudden," III.27), "la donna, alla quale Amore aveva già aguzzato co' suoi consigli l'ingegno" ("the lady, her wits sharpened by love," IV.16)—from a superiority which we might call constitutional (hence the opposition between "con la sua sagacità": "by her address," VIII.50, said of the wife; and "sciocca-mente": "foolishly," VIII.4, said of the husband). But on the whole, while the wife's intelligence is more often demonstrated by the facts than proclaimed, the husband's lack of intelligence is specifically stressed ("il bescio santio": "the poor simpleton," III.29; "quella bestia": "the fool," IV.13; "sciocca oppinione": "foolish purpose," IV.17, etc.) and underlined comparatively by the wife herself at V.52–53: "Tu non se' savio . . . quanto tu se' più sciocco e più bestiale, cotanto ne diviene la gloria mia minore . . . tu se' cieco di quegli [gli occhi] della mente" ("No wise man art thou . . . the more foolish and insensate thou art, the less glory have I . . . thou art [blind] of the mind's eye"). And it is a fact that the *beffe* are here a form of reprisal, nearly always approved of by those who tell the tales and by the author himself, for attitudes which run counter to Boccaccio's human ideal: jealousy (IV, V, VIII), bigotry (I, III). It is symptomatic that where such justification is absent, the *beffa* is less elaborate (II), or else the negative urge (jealousy and bigotry) is replaced by a positive urge (love) on the wife's part (VI, VII, IX; and note that in this series the husband is always viewed with a certain respect, even sympathy in VI, while in IX Boccaccio narrates the *beffa* with explicit moral reservations). Here then is an initial opposition: between negative motivations (jealousy or bigotry on the husband's part) and positive motivations (the wife's being in love). What is more, such opposition has an ideological importance: the bigoted, jealous husbands are always to some degree rich; one of them even has aristocratic ambitions which, parvenu that he is, he has satisfied by marrying a woman of noble birth: "ingentilire per moglie" ("thinking to compass gentility by matrimony," VIII.4). The lovers who are contrasted with them are the expression of an ideal in which youth and courtliness, good looks, and erotic vivacity all play their part. The lover is always young (I.6, II.8, III.4, IV.6, V.11, VI.5, VIII.5, IX.6; in VII his youth can be deduced from personal details given); often handsome (I.6, V.11, IX.6) and/or "leggiadro" (courtly: II.8, III.4, IX.6) or attractive ("piacevole," V.11, VI.5). At times he has more precisely defined qualities: quick to laughter ("pronto al riso," I.28, as is clear from the way he makes a joke of the assignation which does not materialize), elegant and poetic (III.7), quick to do anything that he has a mind to ("destro a qualunque cosa avesse voluto fare," IX.6). In certain cases the young man is rewarded by the woman after long and patient love (VIII.5); indeed his love may begin from hearsay in the troubadour convention, as in VII.5.[5] Nearly always it is these human and personal qualities which make him preferable to a husband richer or more noble but jealous or bigoted or overbearing; on one occasion, indeed, his social inferiority is deliberately underlined (VI.5). It is no accident that Lodovico in tale VII, who "assai di be' costumi e di buone cose aveva apprese" ("acquired very fine manners and other accomplishments") at the court of France, no less, disguises himself as a humble serving man and wins the woman's favors by his sighs and by the good grace with which he lets himself be beaten at chess (13), or by declaring—again in the troubadour tradition—that he is content to be able to love though unrequited (20). Only in tale II does the lover seem better born than the husband, a necessity in a plot where the wife's betrayal is seen as a compensation for her poverty and for the monotony it entails. The opposition of youth and age is explicitly declared as the causal driving force only in tale IX.[6]

1.3. The distinction "per amore o per salvamento" ("either for love or for deliverance from peril") establishes another differentiation, based no longer on the motivation of the betrayal but on that of the *beffa*. It is a fact, as we shall soon see, that in certain cases the betrayal is consummated after (and thanks to) the *beffa* (V, VII, IX). Thus the *beffa* organized "per amore" is an indispensable preliminary to the betrayal. In other cases, the *beffa* serves to save a wife surprised by her husband: and "save" is to be understood in the fullest sense, for reputation may be involved, and even the continuation of the intrigue. The distinction establishes two clear-cut groups: tales of courtly inspiration (courtly, however, in an approximate sense) versus those in which love is understood in a naturalistic sense alone. We are dealing, in substance, with types X and Y of section 2.2 below.

1.4. The final distinction proposed by Boccaccio is between *beffe* effected with and without the husband's knowledge ("senza essersene avveduti o no"). Here it might be advisable to substitute a tripartition for the bipartite division proposed. For if in one group of tales the *beffa* succeeds in hiding the betrayal from the husband (I–III, V, VI) and in the other the husband resigns himself to closing his eyes to a betrayal he has brought to light beyond any possibility of doubt (IV, VIII), there still remain others in which a much more refined technique is put into effect: the betrayal is sketched out or effected in the husband's presence but in circumstances which persuade him that it does not exist (VII, IX). While I shall return (in sec. 4.2) to these particular tales from the point of view of the opposition true/false, for the moment I wish merely to observe the way the groupings of these distinctions relate to the others. In fact the second group of our tripartition (IV, VIII) belongs to the series in which the motive for the betrayal is jealousy: the pretense that he knows nothing about a dishonor of which he is all too aware is a kind of retaliation for the husband.[7] The third group (VII, IX) falls under the head "per amore" versus "per salvamento." Such intellectualized cruelty is possible only for one who, with malice aforethought, holds all the cards and chooses both the moment and the terrain. It is sufficient to note Madonna Beatrice (VII), when she tells her lover that from the ferocious *beffa* contrived for her husband "ne seguirà meraviglioso diletto e piacere" ("the sequel . . . will be wondrously gladsome and delightful," 39).

The intermediate type (IV, VIII) constitutes a kind of zero degree with respect to the other two, in which the truth is either hidden or manifested and is then proved to be false. As for the two extreme types, they too are characterized in terms of clear-cut oppositions. When the deception is effected "senza essersene avveduti," the author underlines in a manner that is clearly ironic and comic the solidarity of the couple husband-wife: i.e., the wife, in the very act of deceiving, emphasizes her ties to the husband, in order to limit or eliminate his suspicions. Thus the *beffa* described in tale I is characterized by explicit emphases of this type: "Io non avrei mai avuto ardire d'andare *sola* a provarla; ma *ora che tu ci se'*, io vo' che noi andiamo ad incantarla" ("I should never have had courage to try it alone; but *as thou art here*, I propose that we go exorcise it [the ghost] together," 24) or "se ne vennero *amenduni* pianamente all'uscio" ("they . . . stole to the door [*both together*]," 25), so that even in the formula contrived to exorcise the ghost it is entreated, "Non far male né a me *né a Gianni mio*" ("No scratche unto me *or my*

Gianni do," 27). And in tale II husband and wife echo each other with phrases[8] like "Fate sicuramente meco, che *io son suo marito*" ("Have no fear, you can deal with me; for *I am her husband*," 28) and "*Mio marito* il netterà tutto" ("*My husband* will scour it [the tun] clean," 30); in III the wife says to her husband, who has arrived unexpectedly, "Tu ci bisognavi per dir certe orazioni" ("To say certain of the prayers thou shouldst have been with us," 31); in tale V the wife demonstrates at length to her husband that he is himself the supposed lover (52–58); finally, in VI we come to an alliance of wife and husband in defense of the lover, presented as the innocent victim of unjustified violence.

The "illusionistic" type of tale, more complex and psychologically elaborate as well, provides us with another interesting expository technique, what we might term the public proclamation of the trio—their banns, as it were. Husband, wife, and lover are introduced together, so that the adultery is carried forward in the teeth of the absurd. In tale VII Anichino has no sooner come into the couple's bedroom than the wife takes him by the hand and on the other side takes her husband's hand (29). In tale IX the wife goes to the place where the *beffa* has been organized having "on the one hand" her husband, and "on the other" the man who is about to become her lover (58); and at the end, "il misero marito schernito con lei insieme e col suo amante nel palagio se ne tornarono" ("the poor duped husband went back with her and her lover to the palace," 80).[9]

2.1. Such is the formalization proposed by the author and the preliminary deductions, integrations, and adjustments we might make of it. If we now proceed to a new formalization centered on the phases of the tale, we find it impossible not to take account of that ternary symmetry which is probably a kind of narrative universal, as has been noted over and over again, from Aristotle ("A whole is that which has a beginning, a middle and an end. A beginning is that which does not itself follow anything by causal necessity, but after which something naturally is or comes to be. An end, on the contrary, is that which itself naturally follows some other thing, either by necessity or as a rule, but has nothing following it. A middle is that which follows something as some other thing follows it")[10] to Bremond, with his elementary sequence of narrative possibles: (1) virtuality, (2) actualization, (3) scope obtained; or (1) improvement to be obtained, (2) process of improvement, (3) improvement obtained; with the variant (1) obstacle to be eliminated, (2) process of elimination, (3) obstacle eliminated.[11]

2.2. If we apply and integrate Bremond's schemata, then our tales can be reduced to two basic types. A first type (X), more elaborate, from a narrative point of view, but more linear, can be indicated with the abbreviation

F(alling in love)–B(*effa*) B(etrayal)–B′(etrayal effected)

It coincides with the series virtuality–actualization–scope obtained. It only remains to add that the actualization is carried into effect by means of a betrayal staged in such a way that the husband is reassured; thus any obstacle to the betrayal's continuation is eliminated from the outset. This pattern, which is ternary since B and B are identical, is found in tales V, VII, and IX.

In the other tales (type Y), only after an unforeseen event does the line virtuality–scope obtained come to coincide with the line obstacle to be eliminated–obstacle eliminated: the betrayal, in other words, would proceed undisturbed were it not for the husband's discovery (D), or threatened discovery, which makes the $B(effa)$ unavoidable. The pattern then becomes (1) virtuality, (2) actualization (a, obstacle to be eliminated; b, obstacle eliminated), (3) scope obtained. It should also be remarked that the betrayal has already taken place in these tales during the first phase, which is differentiated from the final phase by a shift in the degree of safety and possibility of repetition. It is a case less of virtuality than of incipient, aleatory realization. The schema is therefore

$$B–D–B–B′$$

and it holds good for tales I–IV, VI, VIII. The quaternary pattern might be reduced to a ternary series if D and B were held to be two phases of the actualization. But as a matter of fact D and B and distinct and clearly differentiated, for the suspense involved is an evident requirement: the more serious and more immediate the danger, the greater the surprise and amusement the wife's ingenious expedients will cause. And it is, on the contrary, moment B′ which is left out (in tales II, III, and VI), with the consequence of rendering the series a ternary one, or reduced to a single sentence or to a few cursory sentences: "E poi dell'altre volte, ritrovandosi con la donna, molto di questa incantazione rise con essolei" ("And many a hearty laugh had he and the lady over the exorcism during their subsequent intercourse," I.30); "Anichino e la donna ebbero assai agio di quello per avventura che avuto non avrebbono, a far di quello che loro era diletto e piacere" ("This affair . . . to them was the occasion that, with far less let than might else have

been, they were able to have solace and joyance of one another,"
VII.46). As a matter of fact, although the successful outcome of B
renders it highly likely, B′ is not the main point of the tale, which reaches
its climax in the lively agitation of the *beffa* itself.

2.3. It is interesting to compare the two basic patterns, F–*B* B–B′
and B–D–*B*–B′. First and foremost, the presence of F provides "psychological" explanations for the betrayal and allows an excursion between
F and *B*′ greater than that which can exist between B and B′, two facts
which accord significantly with a courtly character (which is especially
marked in VII and IX but not absent from V, given an initial assonance with a series of topographical indications which constitute a setting to be found from Piramus and Thisbe in Ovid to Marie de France's
Deus amanz). In the other tales these preliminaries are replaced by a
simple, concise indication of the motives for adultery. Thus F and B
are two moments, one emotional, the other carnal, of a substantially uniform situation where the movement is from B to B′. In terms of logic
B′, optional in the pattern B–D–*B*–B′, is obligatory in the type F–*B*
B–B′: in the former the goal has already been reached, one way or another, from the first moment; in the latter there is a very real virtuality
(F) which requires as its conclusion that the goal be reached (B′). In
contrast, *B* and B are fused together in type *X*, and the *beffa* comes to
consist precisely in a betrayal which is so presented that it can be denied.
It should be noticed that the fusion *B*B, which distinguishes between a
betrayal staged and denied and a betrayal which is carried through
(B′), exactly reproduces the double relationship of the *beffa* in these
"illusionistic" tales, toward the fantastic and toward the real.

3.1. Once the phases or moments of the action have been defined, its
unfolding can be followed in detail when account is taken of the distribution within each phase of the elements of a number of fundamental oppositive couples. For the moment, I shall give attention to three of these:
door open/door closed, outside/inside, above/below. These oppositions
are factual in character, not abstract: they refer to the home of the married couple, with its door shut to defend the fidelity of the wife, proclaim
her sinful absence, hide the adultery taking place within, etc.; open to
allow the wife's stealthy exit, the lover's entry, etc. (so that the extreme
points of the opposition are determined by those of another, complementary opposition: outside/inside, with reference now to the wife, now to
the husband, now to the lover); with its windows from which the person
inside converses with the person outside; with its stairs linking the two
successive barriers, the door of the house and the bedroom door. They

are oppositions whose nature is a little like that of a stage set: the characters move from the house to the piazza to the neighboring houses, their voices echoing back and forth.

I have called them factual oppositions, but they become operative only when their elements, with their calculated alternation, take on a deliberately oppositive value. Thus no account should be taken, in terms of an analysis, of the scattered allusions to open and closed doors that are frequent in all these stories—II.11: the husband finds "l'uscio serrato dentro" ("the door locked") and exclaims, thanking God,"Vedi come ella tosto serrò l'uscio dentro, come io ci uscii, acciò che alcuna persona entrar non ci potesse che noia le desse" ("Mark what haste she made to shut the door when I was gone forth, that none else might enter to give her trouble"); III.24: "Il compar tornò e . . . fu all'uscio della camera, e picchiò e chiamò la donna" ("The father returned . . . and was at the bedroom door, and knocked, and called the lady by her name"); VI.8: "picchiò alla porta" ("knocked at the door"); VI.11: "andasse ad aprire" ("bade . . . go open"); VI.13: "serratisi dentro" ("locked them in"); VI.21: "Io mi portai in su l'uscio della camera, e volendo egli entrar dentro, il ritenni" ("I planted myself in the doorway, and kept him from entering"); VII.27: "lasciò l'uscio della camera aperto" ("leaving . . . the door of the chamber open"); VII.28: "l'uscio rinserrato dentro" ("closed the door behind him"); VII.37: "l'uscio di quella [camera] dentro serrò" ("and locked the door [of the room]"; VIII.7: "di dover far venire Ruberto . . . all'uscio della casa sua e d'andargli ad aprire" ("that he [Ruberto] should come to the front door . . . whereupon she would get her down, and open the door"); VIII.14: "Giunto all'uscio e non aprendolo soavemente" ("And being come to the door, he opened it by no means gingerly"); VIII.21: "la serrò di fuori" ("locking the door of the room behind him").

It should be made clear, however, that the objective character of these oppositions does not exclude but indeed implies an erotic metaphor, which tale II shows in a form that is explicit and even coarse. Here the coupling of wife and lover takes place while the husband is inside the barrel, and a point is made of the fact that the vent of the barrel is stopped by the wife herself:"A lei accostatosi, che tutta chiusa teneva la bocca del doglio . . . ad effetto recò il giovinil desiderio" ("Whereupon he made up to the lady, who completely blocked the vent of the tun . . . [and] sated his youthful appetite," 34).

3.2. Thus we come to those tales in which the moments of the action and these oppositive couples are most satisfactorily integrated. Here is a representation of tale IV, following the phases B–D–B:

wife outside/husband inside   wife outside/husband inside
 (below)   (above)   (below)   (above)
         door open   door closed

              wife inside/husband outside
              (above)   (below)
                     door closed

In this tale, it will be remembered, the husband is made drunk by the wife and thus neutralized; he subsequently pretends to be drunk so as to unmask the wife he has every reason to suspect; he goes out of the house to denounce the betrayal he has discovered, but the wife turns the tables in such a way that she appears innocent and can accuse her husband of having spent the night in the taverns. Within the basic moments of the tale, we have an alternation of outside/inside oppositive localizations: first the wife is outside and the husband inside (moments 1 and 2), then the husband is outside and the wife inside. As for the opposition open/closed, during the betrayal the door is open, a sign of sin; with the discovery of the betrayal, the closed door denounces and sets the seal on the adultery, setting up a barrier between the wife, a sinner, outside and the husband inside. In a third moment the door, still closed, denounces the (nonexistent) sin of the husband, which the wife will make public. It should be noted that the opposition above/below appears here too: almost always the person inside comes to the upper window to speak to the person outside, who is at street level. The person who is above *seems* innocent (whether he is or not), while the person below *seems* guilty.

Going on now to tale VIII, still analyzing the moments B, D, and *B*, we have

wife inside   husband inside   wife inside
 (above)   (above)   (above)
        lover outside   husband outside   lover outside
         (below)   (below)   (below)

1. wife inside (above)   husband inside (above)
2. wife inside (above)   husband outside (below)

As can be seen, the wife always remains inside the house and above (in the room or on the stairs); the lover—whose intervention is merely virtual—is always outside, and soon enough in flight. The husband, however, continues moving from outside inside, and from above below, in his furious desire to strike at both the lover and the wife. It is precisely this dynamism, born of blind rage, which makes the *beffa* possible: in fact, while the husband is outside to wreak violence on the lover, the wife inside prepares her escape from the violence which she knows is threatening (and puts the serving girl in the bedroom as her substitute). The *beffa* thus comprises two phases: first the husband is above and intends to beat his wife; then he is outside and below, searching out the relatives before whom he intends to accuse her. And it will be precisely "at the top of the stairs" ("in capo delle scale," 23), i.e., in a dominant position, that her brothers and mother as well as her poor husband will find her, to receive from her all the (obviously falsified) proofs of her innocence. Once again, the person who is above *seems* innocent, the one below, guilty.

In tale V, the three moments are F, *B*B, B′; here the situation takes on the following configurations successively:

<table>
<tr><td>wife inside
husband outside
door closed/aperture open</td><td>wife inside
husband outside
door closed/passage through roof</td></tr>
</table>

wife inside
husband outside
door open

This tale places its shifts of perspective close to each other and grades them gradually. We are dealing with a tale of a jealous husband; thus the wife's seclusion is strict and unrelenting (vectors: "guardia": "close watch," 8, 16; "Non osava farsi ad alcuna finestra": "She dared not so much as show herself at a window," 9; "a finestra far non si potea": "as she might not show herself at the window," 11; "rinchiusa": kept "so close," 18, etc.). She always stays *inside*. But the wife manages to find *inside*, precisely in the dwelling next door, what she is unable to search for *outside*: the "finestra" she cannot lean out of finds an etic[12] variant in the aperture ("pertugio" or "fessura") through which she attracts the attention of the young fellow lodger (11, 13, 14, 16). This etic variant is inserted between the phrases which link the emic shift from a closed door (for jealousy) to an open door (for the ending of jealousy and for betrayal now made easy). The closed door of the first moment already stands in secondary opposition to the "pertugio" and then (second moment) to the passage over the roof, thanks to which the betrayal is effected on the first occasion ("Truova modo che su per lo tetto tu venghi stanotte di qua": "Contrive to come in tonight by the roof," 40). Finally, the door itself will be opened in a third moment. The opposition outside/inside also goes through various stages, as it is referred to the husband and to the wife: in the first and third moments, the husband's absence is independent of his wife's will, though it offers her excellent opportunities; in the second moment, however, it is the wife who provokes the outside/inside opposition, persuading her husband to stay outside on guard, awaiting a priest-lover who does not exist, while the real lover comes inside through the roof and inside meets with the wife.

3.3. In tale VI the moments of the action (B–D–*B*) are grouped primarily in virtue of the inside/outside opposition, but the situations they present are considerably complicated by sudden reversals which derive from the presence of two lovers rather than one. The parallelism of the two lovers is stressed by Boccaccio, who gives them names with the same initial and with a diminutive suffix of endearment (Leonetto, Lambertuccio). Furthermore, with regard to the first the woman is the lover ("s'innamorò d'un giovane . . . assai piacevole e costumato, come che di gran nazione non fosse": she "became enamoured of a gallant . . . who, though of no high rank, was not a little debonair and courteous," 5); with regard to the second, she is the object of love, a love borne with because it is advantageous to her ("Di lei un cavalier . . . s'innamorò forte . . . essendo possente uomo": "A gentleman . . . grew mightily enamoured of her . . . who was a powerful signior," 6). In short, representing Leonetto as L_1, Lambertuccio L_2, and the husband as H, the love relationships can be represented as follows (arrows indicate the object of love):

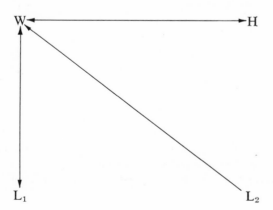

The phases of the story follow the deterioration of an ideal situation (W and L_1 inside, H and L_2 outside), in that first L_2 takes the place of L_1, at least physically (as the dynamic dotted line indicates: W and L_2 inside, L_1 hidden, H outside):

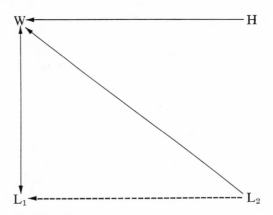

Then H replaces L_2, obliging the wife to contrive an ingenious stratagem (W and H inside, L_1 hidden, L_2 outside):

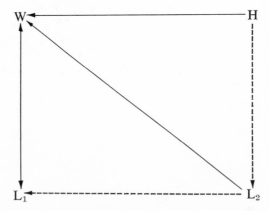

The stratagem consists in exploiting the hitherto potential rivalry of L_1 and L_2, shifting it from the erotic plane to the social-personal plane: the arrogance with which the powerful Lambertuccio forces himself on the woman (6) and the timid nature of the modest Leonetto (11, 25) give rise to a fabrication which will explain the presence of both in the house (16–17) and which, arousing the chivalrous generosity of the husband, creates a momentary alliance WH in defense of L_1, thus:

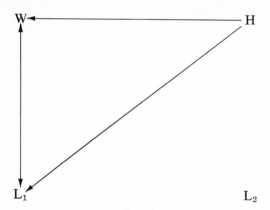

The fact that the hostile relations between Leonetto and Lambertuccio cancel each other out, bringing about the following figure,

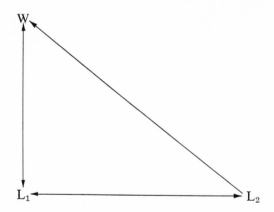

is of merely anecdotal interest, in that it shows the way a writer exploits the geometric potential of his pattern to the full.

4.1. At a final level of formalization, relationships can be shown empirically between the characters and certain basic situations or attitudes susceptible of conceptual synthesis. These relationships are grouped to form oppositive symmetries, either in their reference to different actants or when the same actant is seen by one or another component of the "triangle."

In tale I, the contraposition of H and L (lover) can be summed up in these two triangles, which present contrary elements in the same position:

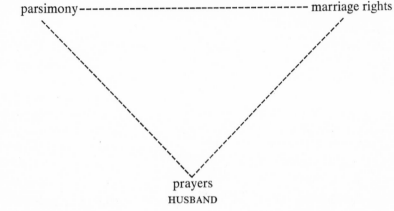

prayers
HUSBAND

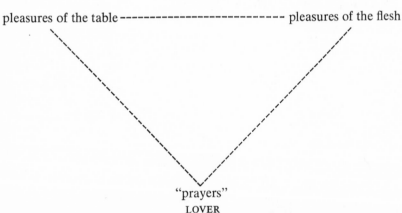

"prayers"
LOVER

The constitution of the triangle is suggested by Boccaccio himself, for he unites all the elements in play in a single sentence: "A grande agio e con molto piacere *cenò* e albergò con la donna; ed ella, *standogli in braccio,* la notte gl'insegnò da sei delle *laude* di suo marito" (he "did most comfortably, and to his no small satisfaction, *sup* and sleep with the lady, who *lying in his arms* taught him that night some six of her husbands *lauds*," 9). Here we find the pleasures of the table ("cenò") and of the flesh ("standogli in braccio") and the metaphorical and obscene use of terms related to prayer ("laude"). Taking this sentence as a starting point, it is possible to define completely the vectors of the oppositions indicated in the triangles. That between prayer in its literal sense and prayer in its metaphorical sense is fundamental: in fact, in the tale it is the husband's bigotry which provides the occasion and the incentive for the betrayal.

"Prayers" is to be taken in the literal sense when reference is to the husband (the friars "gli insegnarono di buone orazioni e davangli il paternostro in volgare," etc.: "would teach him good orisons, and give him the paternoster in the vernacular," 5). Prayers are also linked to the marriage bed, a place so far removed from voluptuousness as to be almost sacramental: "Io dissi dianzi il Te lucis ante e la 'ntemerata e tante altre buone orazioni quando al letto ci andammo" ("Before we got into bed I repeated the *Te lucis*, and the *Intemerata*, and divers other good orisons," 15); "Segnai il letto da ogni canto" ("I made the sign of the cross . . . at each corner of the bed," 20), etc. We have just seen, however, what "laude" are for the lovers. Indeed the point is reached of including obscene expressions in the "prayer" which the wife recites against the "ghost": "A coda ritta ci venisti, a coda ritta te n'andrai" ("Tail erect, thou cam'st, tail erect, take thy flight," 27). This usage is also playfully employed by the narrator, Emilia, who promises, in setting out to tell the tale, "Potrete una santa e buona orazione e molto a ciò valevole apparare" (her audience may learn "a holy, salutary and most efficacious orison," 3); and it is caught up again by Dioneo at X.10, 2.

The oppositive relationship between parsimony and the pleasures of the table appears at 12–13, where the "great capons," the "many fresh eggs," and the "good flagon of wine" prepared for Federigo contrast with the "little salted meat" ("poco di carne salata") boiled for Gianni, the husband, on his unexpected arrival. But most interesting of all is the correlation between pleasures of the table and pleasures of the flesh, because it takes us to the heart of the hedonism which for Boccaccio was a life-enhancing value. This correlation is underlined by a curious commutative exercise: the tale is provided with two optional endings. In the first, Federigo loses his night of love but makes up for it by dining "in all ease" ("a grande agio," 30) on the capons and the wine left him by his lover; in the second, he "was fain to take himself off, having neither slept nor supped" ("andatosene, senza albergo e senza cena era la notte rimaso," 32).

Passing to tale III, we can show with two triangles the different aspects in which the lover, Rinaldo, appears to the wife and to the husband:

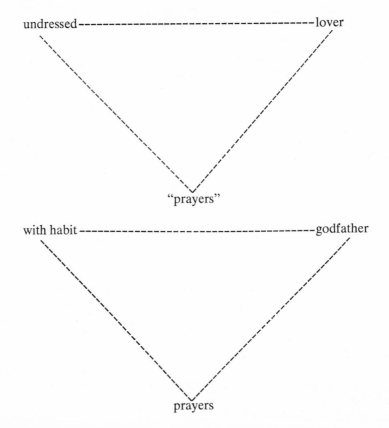

Rinaldo has agreed to become godfather for the couple with the precise aim of approaching more easily the wife with whom he is in love; after much dissipation, he has adopted monastic dress. The second figure shows Rinaldo's appearance with respect to the husband: he wears the habit (in this case the cowl does indeed make the monk); he is godfather and recites prayers in the house he visits none too honestly. The first figure shows him in his relations with the wife. The removal of his habit is repeatedly emphasized: "Qualora io avrò," he says at the moment he seduces her, "questa cappa fuor di dosso . . . io vi parrò uno uomo fatto come gli altri, e non frate" ("When I divest myself of this habit . . . you will see that I am a man furnished as other men, and no friar," 15). The relationship is that of lover, and here too prayers are used as an obscene metaphor. Here are the nodal points (vectors) in the text itself: godfather/lover, "Voi siete mio compare" ("You are my child's godfather"), says the wife, resisting his first advances (16); when she at last accepts them, she gives in "nonostante il comparatico" (notwithstanding "the godfather in the lover"). Indeed she gives herself to Rinaldo "sotto la coverta del comparatico" ("under cover of the friar's sponsorship," 22). Finally, the godfather relationship takes on the function of a cover-up during the *beffa* ("Frate Rinaldo nostro compare ci venne" ["In came Fra Rinaldo, our sponsor," 28]) symbolically as well (the godson rapidly caught up in his arms, 30). With habit/ undressed: "Era frate Rinaldo spogliato, cioè senza cappa e senza scapolare, in tonicella" ("Fra Rinaldo . . . was undressed, that is to say, had thrown off his habit and hood, and was in his tunic," 26); "Se io fossi pur vestito, qualche modo ci avrebbe" ("If I had but my habit and hood on me in any sort, 'twould be another matter" [justification], 26). After the wife has ably saved the situation, "erasi rivestito a bello agio e avevasi recato il fanciullo in braccio" ("he was in his canonicals, and quite at his ease, and had the boy in his arms," 35). We can see already how the habit and the sponsorship are linked together during the *beffa*: the friar, now dressed, takes his godson in his arms. The prayers also link up: he says he has waited for the husband's arrival to pronounce them (see sec. 1.4); but here, by a happy stroke, the shift from literal to figurative sense is rendered concrete by doubling Rinaldo and his brother friar.[13] It is the other friar who goes up "nel palco di sopra" (into the pigeon house) with the servant girl "ad insegnarle il paternostro" ("to teach her the paternoster," 23: figurative), while Rinaldo shuts himself up in the room with his lover; it is the other friar who is credited with the recitation of thaumaturgical prayers (31: literal). Hence the dialogue, whose comic nature derives from the biplanar structure of literal and metaphoric: "Frate Rinaldo, quelle quattro orazioni che m'imponeste, io l'ho dette tutte" ("Fra Rinaldo, those four prayers that you bade me say, I have said them all," 39); "Fratel mio, tu hai buona lena, e hai fatto bene. Io per me, quando mio compar venne, non n'aveva dette che due" ("Then well done, my brother . . . well-breathed thou must be. For my part, I had said but two," 40).

A different kind of relationship can be pointed out in tales VII and IX. These two have distinctive pertinent traits: (1) the story begins before the wife has betrayed the husband (see sec. 2.3), and (2) the future lover is in the service of the husband, so that in accepting the love of the wife he fails in his duty to his master. Both tales thus recount a passage from Fi(delity) to B(etrayal) on the part of the wife and the (future) lover:

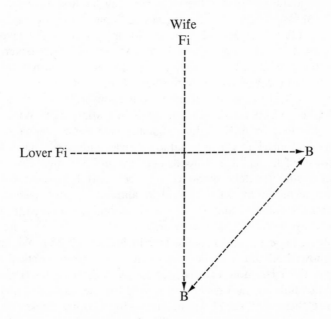

The characterizing element also common to both tales is that the passage Fi - - - - - - → B is effected after the husband has been made to catch a glimpse or even to see it clearly; but this is done in such a way that it can be denied and rendered incredible. On the other hand, the tales are differentiated in the sense that in VII it is only the future lover who is shown to be unfaithful, and this in order that he will then appear more faithful still, while in IX wife and future lover together initiate the betrayal they will subsequently have means of denying. In short, for the husband in VII the situation appears to be

Wife
Fi

Lover   (Fi------------------► B) -------------------►Fi

while for the husband in IX it appears thus:

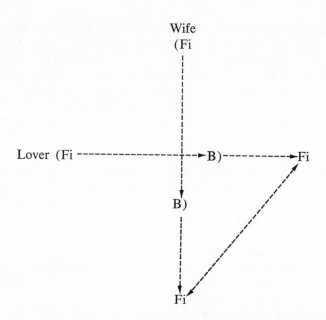

4.2. In these last two tales the wife manages to turn the truth upside
down in her husband's eyes either by an able alignment of suspicions,
indications, and proofs in her favor or by having outright recourse to a
supposedly magic spell (IX). The perspective is determined by the opposition t(rue)/f(alse) already mentioned (sec. 1.4).[14] From this point
of view too the tales of Day VII lend themselves to progressively abstract operations in relation to the specific situations set forth. In general, it might be affirmed that the usual love triangle is hidden from the
vision of the husband which is false, while it is put into effect from the
wife's viewpoint, which is the true one:

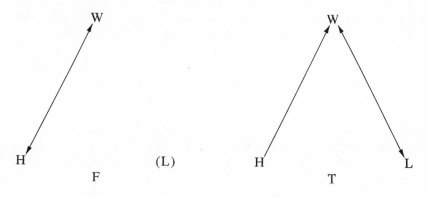

"Viewpoint" immediately clarifies the difference between the oppositions studied up to this moment, all of which pertain to the factual
level (inside/outside; open/closed, etc.) or the attitudes of the actors
in their reciprocal relationships—which are thus in a certain sense fields
of force (fidelity/betrayal)—and this particular opposition, whereby
the same facts are transformed when they are perceived by one or by
another of the main actors or even by secondary characters. It is an
opposition which thus functions as a commutator, changing the lighting
and what it illumines in terms of which person is watching the stage.

Tales VII and IX make use of this commutator with consummate
skill. The husband, in fact, is introduced into the field of this opposition, but in such a way that what he sees (t) seems impossible (f), with
the consequences that he judges to be f what actually takes place in
reality (t).[15] In other words, going back to the figures, the husband is
brought to refer to pole f the passage (Fi - - - - $\rightarrow$ B) and consequently
to situate at pole t a passage - - - - - - - - $\rightarrow$ Fi based on nothing more
than the first polarization. However, since (Fi - - - - - $\rightarrow$ B) belongs to
t, - - - - - $\rightarrow$ Fi belongs to f.

Boccaccio emphasizes the introduction of the husband within the t/f
polarity in several ways. He frequently uses verbs related to visual and
cognitive experience: "acciò che questa cosa non mi bisognasse *con*
troppe *pruove mostrare* e per farlati *toccare e vedere*" ("that I might
not need other evidence than that of thine own senses to prove his guilt to
thee," VII.34); "la fedeltà del tuo famiglio *cognoscere*" ("*prove* the
loyalty of thy retainer," VII.35); "Io il convengo *vedere*" ("Meet . . .
it is . . . that I should go *see*," VII.36); "Per certo tu di' il *vero*" ("Indeed . . . thou sayest *sooth*," VII.45); "Ben vo' *vedere* se questo pero
è incantato" ("I am minded *to see* if this pear-tree be enchanted,"
IX.69); "Nicostrato, al qual *vero* parea ciò che dicea l'uno e l'altro"
("Nicostrato . . . deeming that what they both averred must be *true*,"
IX.76). In structural terms, the author employs rapid alternations (tale
IX) between the opposition of "vedere" ("see," 61, 64, 65, 66, 67, 68,
69) and "sognare," "farneticare," "smemorare," "trasvedere" ("dream,"
"rave," "forget," "mistake," 60, 61, 62, 63, 66, 67, 73). But the most
explicit appearance of this device in stylistic terms is found in those sentences in which truth and falsehood, affirmation and negation, experience and opinion follow and cancel each other out: "Io mi *credeva* che
fosse ciò che tu *di'* . . . ma me ha egli *sgannata*" ("I *thought* that he was
all thou *sayest* . . . but he has *undeceived* me," VII.33); "Pirro, *vera-
mente* io *credo* che tu *sogni*" ("Pyrrhus . . . I *verily believe* thou *dream-
est*," IX.62); "Potrebbe egli esser *vero* che gli *paresse ver* ciò ch'e'*dice*"

("Can it be that it *really seems* to him to be as he *says*," IX.64); "Io *veggio* e *so* che voi *falsamente* avete *veduto*" ("I now *see* and *know* that thou hast also *seen* a *false* show," VII.71); "Egli vi fosse *paruto* che io facessi quello che io so *certissimamente* che io non *pensai*, non che io facessi mai" ("[You thought] that you *saw* me doing that which *most assuredly*, so far from doing, I never so much as *thought of*," VII.73).

Tale V has already been examined in the succession of its phases and in relation to the oppositions open/closed, outside/inside (sec. 3.2). The second opposition is basic when we are dealing with a jealous husband who keeps his wife shut away in the house. It is onto this opposition that the wife projects another for her own ends, that of t/f. While as we have seen, she manages to find *inside* what her husband fears she will obtain *outside*, she finds *outside* (at church) the means of meeting *inside* (the house) with her lover, inducing her husband to stay *outside* on guard. But her false confession to her husband has one overriding aim: it confuses him with the t/f polarity in such a way as to cure his jealousy and at the same time to ensure that the course of adultery at least will run smooth. In a manner not far removed from that of tales VII and IX, though on a purely enunciative plane, the wife confesses her betrayal, but in such terms that she will subsequently be able to deny its existence. First, that is, she declares what is false; then she substitutes as truth a second falsehood, thus:

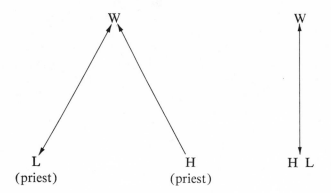

On the left we have the usual triangle (see sec. 1.4), which the wife is disposed to act out. But by revealing it to her husband disguised as a priest and at the same time describing her lover as a priest, she is preparing to "discover" the truth—i.e., the second fiction—affirming the identify of H and L in their common title: "Io ti dissi che io amava un prete: e non eri tu, il quale io a gran torto amo, fatto prete?" ("I told thee that I loved a priest; and wast not thou, whom I love, though ill enough dost thou deserve it, turned priest?" V.55).

Here, then, the *beffa* is based on a kind of mirror image (H is doubled in H + L), of which once again there are clear stylistic signs. The husband's jealousy is due to the fact that "*come* egli molto l'*amava* e molto bella la teneva . . . *così* estimava che ogn'uom l'*amasse* e che ella a tutti paresse bella e ancora che ella s'ingegnasse *così* di piacere *altrui come a lui*" ("*loving* her greatly, and esteeming her exceeding fair . . . he *must needs* suppose that every man *loved* her, and esteemed her fair, and that she, moreover, was as zealous *to stand well with every other man as with himself*," 7). The wife exclaims, "Credi tu, marito mio, che io sia *cieca degli occhi* della testa, *come* tu se' *cieco di quegli* della mente?" ("Deemest thou, my husband, that I am as *blind of the bodily eye as* thou art *of the mind's eye?*" 53). And at the end, she says of her husband, "*Quando* la gelosia gli bisognava del tutto se la spogliò, *così come, quando* bisogno non gli era, se l'aveva vestita" ("And thus having cause for jealousy, he discarded it, as he had erstwhile been jealous without cause," 59).

In tales IV and VIII there is also a play of illusion based on the t/f interchange, but in the sense that the husband, though he well knows t (i.e., the reality of the betrayal), is obliged to consider it f by the situation and even more particularly by the bystanders (relations or neighbors), ably transformed by his wife into her accomplices and defenders. In short, the wife involves her potential defenders in her action of falsification (t - - - - → f) and with their support forces her husband to accept it. He is quite aware of the truth, even though in IV there is a moment in which he allows himself to be convinced by his wife's shrewd argumentation to the point of going to help her out of the well into which he thinks she has fallen, and in VIII he is so shaken by the intrigues that he wavers in his opinion: "Rimase come uno smemorato, seco stesso non sappiendo se quello che fatto avea era stato vero o s'egli aveva sognato" ("[He stood there] like one dazed, not witting whether his late doings were actual fact or but a dream," 50). It should be noted that the falsification effected by the wife is bidirectional: she denies her own fault, which is real, and replaces it with one of her husband's, fictitious this time, thereby effecting a reversal of the situation well summed up at 26 by Ghita: "Egli dice appunto che io ho fatto ciò che io credo che egli abbia fatto egli" (the husband "tells you that I have done just what, I doubt not, he has done himself").[16] Thus in IV Tofano is accused of spending his nights in the taverns (24);[17] in IX

Arriguccio is accused of the same thing, with the additional charge that he patronizes prostitutes ("cattive femmine," 42). There is no fitter punishment for jealousy than the knowledge that one is betrayed and that it is impossible to react (see sec. 1.4). As for the mediation of the bystanders, it integrates and improves the punishment. It is a particular which once again takes us to the heart of Boccaccio's beliefs: the jealous husband who looks for witnesses to his dishonor aggravates a possessive (not elective or free) conception of marriage with a sort of legal attestation to its failure, not taking into account the dictates of either discretion or common sense.[18] Recourse to the wife's relatives (threatened in IV.12 and actual in VIII.24–25) involves the whole clan in the betrayal, and placed by the wife in perspective f, they not unnaturally take her part and threaten vengeance. There are evident social overtones in VIII, where the husband who wanted to "compass gentility by matrimony" has his humble origins and the mésalliance flung in his face by his wife's aristocratic mother (45–48); the absence of these overtones in IV explains why the neighbors, with greater dramatic simplicity, exercise the function reserved for the relatives in IX; in this case, the relatives arrive only later.[19]

The ideological guidelines are perfectly obvious. Here in IV are the threats of the husband: "Tu non ci tornerai infino a tanto che io di questa cosa, in presenza de' parenti tuoi e de' vicini, te n'avrò fatto quello onore che ti si conviene" ("Rest assured that thou shalt never recross this threshold, until I have done thee such honour as is meet for thee in the presence of thy kinsfolk and neighbours," 12), and Boccaccio's explicit comments: "Quella bestia era pur disposto a volere che tutti gli aretini sapessero la loro vergogna, laddove niun la sapeva" ("For the fool was determined that all Arezzo should know their shame, whereof as yet none wist aught," 13) and "Tofano bestia, d'altra parte, diceva come il fatto era stato, e minacciava forte" ("Tofano, on his part, told [the neighbors], dolt that he was, just what had happened, and was mightily menacing," 25). We may also note the way the husband's return to his senses ("rinsavimento") is announced—to his wife he "diè licenza che ogni suo piacer facesse, ma sì saviamente, che egli non se ne avvedesse" (promised "to give her leave to amuse herself to her heart's content, provided she used such discretion that he should not be ware of it," 30). And in VIII we meet with threats that are all but identical, even in the way they are formulated: "Io andrò per li tuoi fratelli, e dirò loro le tue buone opere; e appresso che essi vengan per te e faccianne quello che essi credono che loro onor sia e meninte; ché per certo in questa casa non starai tu mai più" ("I go to find thy brothers, and shall do them to wit of thy good works; and then they may come here, and deal with thee as they may deem their honour demands, and take thee hence, for be sure thou shalt no more abide in this house," 21), and the measured wisdom of what the wife says to her husband in the presence of her relatives: "Perché fai tu tener me rea femina con tua gran vergogna, dove io non sono?" ("Why givest thou me, to thy own great shame, the reputation of a lewd woman, when such I am not?" 34).

The t/f opposition is achieved more simply in the four other tales. In these the wife limits herself on her husband's arrival to justifying the presence of the lover, presenting him in another, more likely guise: as buyer of the barrel (II), as godfather come to cure his godson (III), as one who has taken refuge in the house to escape his persecutor (VI), and here the persecutor is in reality the second lover. Or else her work of falsification has as its object not persons but words; this is the case in I, where a warning of danger to the lover is disguised as a charm against the ghost.[20]

5. Here our analyses come to an end. In keeping with my initial program, I have repeatedly gone back over the same tales each time they lent themselves to one or another possibility of formalization. The reader will find it easy to arrange in columns under the number of each tale the schemata or the interpretations which fit it. As soon as he does this, the mechanisms brought to light will once more be rendered operative; the basic functions of the tale, reducible in this case to only two types of conformation (X and Y), will find their motivations in a constellation made up of the three principal actors, according to their character and social standing. The passage from one function to another (seen as a phase in the tale) will prove to be determined by the impact of correlative systems peculiar to the competing characters, and it may be characterized by movements within the factual oppositions. The apogee of the comic parabola will coincide with varied and skillful use of commutations. Finally, the vectors and their stylistic correlations will open the way to a linking of the field of abstraction and the field of the verbally concrete, suggesting the mirror-image relationships between expression and substance planes.

Bringing together the various types of analysis may prove useful in another manner. For if there are times when the analyses dovetail perfectly, at others they serve to throw into relief sutures between themes of heterogeneous origin, such indeed that they do not necessarily bring about reciprocal involvement. This is the case, for example, in tale V (see secs. 3.2 and 4.2) and in tale IX (see n. 15 above). In these instances it is the writer's ability—and this should be emphasized—which intervenes more or less decisively to motivate what otherwise might seem gratuitous. Thus in tale V the lying confession serves (as we have seen) to allay the husband's suspicions and at the same time to neutralize him and make the first assignation possible; in tale IX the opening section sets the husband on a path which eliminates the distinction between falsehood and truth.[21] This combination of themes is here confirmed by the sources; but analyses of the kind sketched out on other occasions might well favor the detection of sources which the author or his models have contaminated.

In conclusion, it is perhaps worthwhile stressing yet again the way in which these abstractive operations, far from obscuring the author's narrative individuality, enable us to define it more rigorously, even with respect to sources which it seems have been fairly faithfully followed (see nn. 3, 6, 8, 9, 17, 19 above). But until now I have deferred reference to tale VI. The schemata outlined in section 3.3 find their significance in an inverse relationship between L_1 and L_2 in terms of their social standing and favor in love. Passages from phase to phase of the tale are directly arranged by the wife so as to effect an artfully contrived repetition of attitudes typical of the two characters: disarmed fright (in a lover called Leonetto, "little lion"!) and sheer arrogance. Now in the sources of the tale[22] L_1 is the squire/servant of L_2, who is the only true lover admitted on a permanent basis. Sent as a messenger by L_2, L_1 receives the favors of the wife simply on her abandoned impulse. The opposition between love chosen and love imposed is thus absent, as is the functionalization of L_2's arrogance at the moment of the *beffa*; for in the sources it is no more than an instrument. The mechanism is analogous, but its component parts are quite different. Schematization here shows the way Boccaccio has renewed the theme.

This manner of reducing to unity analyses initially divided out might be viewed as an experimental verification of the "system of the systems," as the formalists envisage it. In fact, in this way systems of the most varied nature, which have been isolated for purposes of demonstration, are brought together again and inserted one into another: systems which in their totality come to constitute a further system, the literary work itself. What I think must be rejected is the conception of a perfect, pre-established harmony between first-degree systems, the conception of an absolute homogeneity which the critic, trembling with joy, brings to light with a triumphant Q.E.D. Such harmony may be absent; consideration of its absence has been for us, as it generally is, both useful and instructive. On other occasions harmony is expressly avoided, and it is from the contrast between systems or from their collision that the artist will derive his effects. This is not Boccaccio's case, or at least it is not the case with the tales we have considered; but the insights suggested by the method we have just put to the test may well prove rich in future developments.

Five

Comical Structure in the Tale of Alatiel

1. If one were to set out to show that the history of literary criticism has been both an exciting and a discouraging chase within a twisting labyrinth, from the many examples available he might select studies devoted to the tale of Alatiel (*Decameron*, II.7).[1] A start might be made with the protagonist. For Hauvette she is "the pitiable image of female frailty represented by a soul straightforward and pure; one who is concerned for her reputation, yearning after serene felicity and happy married trust, but who gives herself up, weeping the while, to her conquerers, because in reality it is love she loves." For Bosco, on the other hand, she is a creature of farce: "Whether crying or immediately consoled, whether she proposes to be honest or falls short of her proposals, delights in love play or concocts stories to trick and mock her credulous old father; in the kindest interpretation, she is a figure of farce." For Getto Alatiel, "in her enforced lack of conversation, her periods of alternate weeping and consolation, both on a totally physiological level, lives as a happy toy in the hands of both Fortune and the various men who take turns in representing Fortune's place." Baratto says, "The character, a symbol of human weakness, is also, thanks to her natural sensuality, a symbol of resistance to events." Or again, for other critics "the figure of this woman has heroic traits: morally superior to a cruel fortune, impregnable in her inmost spirit" (Petronio); "She has a character so tempered that it resists with requisite courage each and every brush with fortune: prepared for the worst but ready also to enjoy the best" (Muscetta). Almansi places us on an entirely different plane. "Alatiel is not a 'beautiful woman'; she is a superhuman character, a character of myth or, at the very least, one who shows her kinship with myth . . . ; her inability to communicate . . . is a sign which shows Alatiel's isolation due to her superhuman character."

As for the plan of the tale, there is no more agreement here. According to Bosco, "all these men who, as soon as they see Alatiel, fall in love with her mechanically and with clockwork regularity and instantly plot treason and murder in order to possess her—these are not men at all, they are mass-produced puppets, all alike, all of straw, however much (and it is not much) the events of which they are protagonists vary one from another. Attention cannot remain alert with the tone Boccaccio assumes here; he is a clerk of the court who impassively drones the long list of a prisoner's crimes." In like manner, Grabher sees the tale of Alatiel as one of those "in which Fortune plays the main role" and where in general "there is more imaginative effort than fantasy, more mechanical combination of cases— all too uniform at times—than artistic transformation of reality." Indeed "a variety of leads which here . . . seem to be hinted at are overwhelmed by the mechanical succession and repetition of merely casual elements." Again, according to Petronio, "the greater part of all the adventures through which Alatiel passes follow each other flatly, with mechanical and shallow regularity." Getto's judgment is pitched in quite a different key; for him we are dealing with "the text that is closest to Ariosto, given its open, volatile feeling, and the vast space of the Mediterranean in which it takes place, given the gaily carefree adventurous rhythm which drives it onward, an adventure entrusted to the caprice of chance rather than the calculation of human initiative." As for Baratto, "facts and characters are given less weight than their coordination to form the thread of a life, their crowding together into the paratactic rhythm of the tale. . . . It is the rhythm of repetition, the rapid succession of relationships, which attracts the narrator."

But what is the sense (or the moral) of the tale? According to Hauvette, it "translates with rare force the tyrannic domination of love over human life; it is the tragedy of that beauty which, because it is too much desired, becomes the plaything of the most savage passions." In like manner, for Petronio, "running from end to end of the tale is a serious, downright tragic motif, which Boccaccio makes clear as early as the proem ("quanto sventuratamente fosse bella") and insists upon later: "la sua sventurata bellezza." Almansi, however, in line with his interpretation of the protagonist, states that "the deaths with which the disastrous erotic career of Alatiel is strewn are not merely dramatic deaths, to be pitied; they are sacred deaths, deaths for the faith." For Muscetta ours is "a tale of a blithely paradoxical education"; on the other hand, according to Getto, "in this tale it will be easy to divine a yearning for the capricious variation of Fortune and for continual adaptation to it on the woman's part (and this is an invariable motif of the unique and unmistakable theme, the savoir vivre which was so dear to Boccaccio's imagination)." For Baratto the meaning of the tale is to be found in "the irresistible impulse of the forces of nature which bring wisdom, which constitute a source of smiling optimism versus the pessimism aroused by the pressure of the accidents of chance."

As for overall judgments, they range from "masterpiece," a label unhesitatingly applied by Flora and Muscetta, to Bosco's sharp criticism: "The desire and preoccupation with overdoing things is so intense that in this tale there is scarcely any feeling of joy for the tale's sake, that feeling which makes other adventures so delightful. The tone is, we have said, impassive, dull, flat, though from time to time there does emerge some sign of life, as in the scene of starkest horror in which the madman drags away the body of Ciuriaci or in the other, mischievous scene of Alatiel and the merchant whom the little bed invites to 'stuzzicarsi' [tease each other]. These scenes live, but their very coexistence in the same tale demonstrates its fundamental falsity, its lack of a vital imaginative center."

I shall end this rapid survey with the overall judgments of Sapegno and Flora, which most nearly coincide, as we shall see, with those suggested by my own analysis. Sapegno: "Even the tale of Alatiel . . . , which has been judged monotonous, insipid, hovering between high drama and farce, is alive, at least if one does not split hairs over the character of the heroine but gives himself up wholeheartedly to the varied movement of the tale—the generation, ever the same yet ever different, of furious passions around an impassive idol of beauty. Nor should a tragic situation be looked for (of the kind we should have if Alatiel were represented as an almost fatal creature endowed with a terrible gift, who arouses wherever she goes furious passions, violent struggle, and death) or poorly farcical movement. Rather, we have here Boccaccio's superior irony, the form taken by his humane but always realistic pity." Flora: "The tale of Alatiel deals with the love of adventure itself, with the unfolding of events in their ingenious fatality, rather than with any particular human feeling. For Boccaccio did not set out to make of Alatiel a woman who bears, in her face and her heart, an awareness of the kind of beauty which incites men to conquest through horrendous crimes; nor has he given his men any inner wavering between the poles of good and evil; his intention was to narrate the visible and obvious particulars of an adventure, because the very character of that adventure inspired him by its mere movement."

In the pages that follow an attempt will be made to arrive at an interpretation which puts to use the advantages afforded by a total reading of the narrative discourse, as opposed to selection on each occasion of details held to be symptomatic or the acceptance (which can never be sufficiently cautious) of the author's own programmatic statements.

2. The main technique which operates in the tale can be brought to light simply by analyzing the heading:

> Il soldano di Babilonia ne manda una sua figliuola a marito al re del Garbo, la quale per diversi accidenti in spazio di quattro anni *alle mani di nove uomini* perviene in diversi luoghi: ultimamente, restituita al padre *per pulcella*, ne va al re del Garbo, come prima faceva, per moglie.

> [The soldan of Babylon sends one of his daughters overseas, designing to marry her to the king of Algarve. By divers adventures she comes in the space of four years *into the hands of nine men* in divers places. At last she is restored to her father, whom she quits again *in the guise of a virgin*, and, as was at first intended, is married to the king of Algarve.]

If the words I have italicized are eliminated, one is left with a schema typical of the Alexandrian romance:[2]

> Promise of marriage–delaying misadventures–accomplishment of marriage

The narration of delaying misadventures usually involves keeping faith both morally and physically, to the point of heroism for a future husband. Boccaccio's most striking innovation with respect to the scheme he adopts is the fact that Alatiel not only defends her chastity half-heartedly at best; she actually gives herself up quite cheerfully to the many men who lay hands on her. Despite all this, however, it is as a virgin ("pulcella") that she achieves her long delayed marriage.[3]

Two consequences of this method of treating the plot stand out at once. (1) The series of misadventures traces not the continuous line of faith maintained but a broken line of progressive unions which are the inevitable conclusion of the misadventures themselves. (2) The final return to the father and the betrothal encanopy and with spirited sleight of hand draw the curtains around a marriage which, according to the rules, should set the seal on the constancy and fidelity of the male or female protagonist.

Both of these consequences place the tale decisively in the realm of the comic. Its comic character lies in the contrast between the tragic events and the erotic outcome; between a long parenthesis of utter dissipation, however extenuating the circumstances, and the final apotheosis, crowned with marriage; and between noncooperation in and effective enjoyment of pleasure. These are to my mind the only coordinates within which interpretation of the tale can be attempted.

3. Given this inversion of the Alexandrian romance, loss of virginity in Alatiel's case could hardly remain one misadventure among many. The inversion involves accommodation so that each of her mishaps is provided with an erotic outcome: each new embrace enriches the comic dimension of her final restitution as virgin; and it is all the more enjoyable as the device is shown to be explicitly repetitive[4] with respect to the dramatic or directly tragic onset of each new sequence. A characteristic quality of this mechanism of repetition is thus the substantial affinity of its sequences; but it also gives rise to a particular exploitation of numerical effects, e.g., "essa che con otto uomini forse diecemilia volte giaciuta era" ("she, who had lain with eight men in all, perhaps, ten thousand times," 121). The mechanism thus puts this simple pattern into effect:

A takes possession of Alatiel
A becomes her lover
[A dies at the hands of B]
B takes possession of Alatiel
B becomes her lover
[B dies at the hands of C]
And so on for C, D, etc.

The only changes in the pattern concern the function which is bracketed here. B in fact does not reach the point of killing A when Alatiel passes from the Genoese sailor to the prince of Morea (45) and from the duke of Athens to Constanzio (73); A dies without the intervention of B in the cases of Osbech replaced by Antioco (79–80) and Antioco replaced by the Cyprian merchant (83–86).

In an iterative mechanism of this kind the actual number is irrelevant; it is only important that it be high. It is curious to note in this regard a divergence between the *rubrica*, which speaks of nine men, and paragraph 121, which cites eight. This situation arises from the episode which follows the killing of Marato (40–41): after a bloody encounter with his brother and erstwhile accomplice, the sailor is too seriously wounded to take advantage of the woman he has won (42–44). The *rubrica* is thus quite accurate when it says "pervenire alle mani" ("come . . . into the hands of") and includes the sailor, and paragraph 121 is no less so when in its turn it refers to "lying with" ("giacere con") and by so doing excludes him. Finally, compare paragraph 7, where the author speaks of "fare nuove nozze da ["about"] nove volte" ("being wedded nine several times").

Within the system of the expectations aroused by a romance of the Alexandrian pattern, our curiosity is made to focus on the way in which the protagonist (male or female) will manage to escape intact from each new misadventure. In the schema as Boccaccio has renovated it, however, expectation is soon oriented—one grasps the repetitive nature of the pattern soon enough—toward the invariably erotic conclusion of every episode: curiosity about the outcome gives way to more relaxed attention to events themselves, while these are worked out in breadth and with a wealth of detail. Thus Boccaccio has functionalized narrations, frequently tragic enough in themselves, in the service of the comic character of the whole. For the dramatic adventures often overlap with Alatiel's own personal history (and soon enough she reveals herself as unsinkable), and this (with the relaxing of tensions implied thereby) renders even more comic their ultimate conclusion "sotto le lenzuola" ("between the sheets," 80).

As for the contradiction between these reiterated couplings and the earlier matrimonial engagement, it is kept alive and even amplified by virtue of the fact that the adventures themselves often stray over into the matrimonial field: "diliberò . . . di volerla per moglie" (decided "he would take her to wife," 21); "non a guisa d'amica, ma di sua propria moglie la trattava" ("treating her not as his mistress but as his wife," 46); "sua moglie la fece, e celebrò le nozze, e con lei si giacque più mesi lieto" ("made her his wife out of hand with all due form and ceremony. And so for several months he enjoyed her," 77); "disse che era sua moglie" ("gave her out as his wife," 88). Or, more ironically, this effect is achieved by means of expressions like "fare nuove nozze da nove volte" (7), "fecero parentado" ("they were indeed man and wife," 89; used only here; cf., distantly, Branca: "faccendola parente di messer Domenedio," VIII.II.38).

4. Boccaccio so orders it that corresponding to this iterative scheme of the action is a sort of passive sensuality on the woman's part. Once initiated into the pleasures of love, she submits perforce to a whole variety of "changes of ownership"; and she then adapts willingly enough to the pleasures which each new situation at any rate offers. In her passage from naiveté to false naiveté, Alatiel continues to be the victim of her own fate (and no less of her beauty). The reader's amusement lies in observing how misadventures so varied are nonetheless so deliciously spiced.

But the storyteller's most happy stroke is making Alatiel practically mute, given her captors' different languages, "sì come a colei alla quale parecchi anni a guisa quasi di sorda e di mutola era convenuta vivere, per lo non aver persona inteso, né essa essere stata intesa da persona" ("which counted for much with one who for some years had been, as it were, compelled to live the life of a deaf mute, finding none whom she could understand or by whom she might be understood," 80). It may seem contradictory that she should then speak, in fluent and well-contrived phrases, from the moment she meets Antigono. Yet this too squares with a rigorous design, which can be synthesized as follows:

(incommunicability + individuality lost) : carnal contact = (communicability + individuality maintained) : chastity

Her "mutism" means that for Alatiel, once the secrets of sex have been revealed, intercourse becomes the only form of language. Tossed from one man to another, she cannot express herself; in particular, she cannot evoke pity or compassion—one should note the insistence on the theme of loneliness: "strignendola necessità di consiglio, per ciò che quivi tutta sola si vedeva" ("being in sore need of counsel, all alone as she was," 16); "sì come a colei che quivi sola senza aiuto o consiglio d'alcun si vedea" ("to find herself thus alone with none to afford her either succour or counsel," 43). Hence the almost Pavlovian reflex which leads her to find in lovemaking the comfort she cannot otherwise obtain: "La donna amaramente e della sua prima sciagura e di questa vicenda *si dolfe* molto; ma Marato, col santo Cresci in man che Iddio ci diè, *la cominciò* per sì fatta maniera *a consolare*" ("This new misadventure, following so hard upon the former, caused the lady no small *chagrin*; but Marato, with the aid of the good Saint Crescent-in-hand that God has given us, *found means* to afford her such *consolation*," 37); "Più giorni la bella donna *pianse la sua disavventura*, ma pur poi da Constanzio *riconfortata*, come l'altre volte fatto s'avea, s'incominciò a prendere piacere di ciò che la fortuna avanti l'apparecchiava" ("So, after some days of repose, the lady ceased *to bewail her harsh destiny* and, suffering Constantine *to console her* as his predecessors had done, began once more to enjoy the good gifts which Fortune sent her," 75).

   In addition to denying her the possibility of communication, this "mutism" deprives Alatiel of her individuality, rendering total a prudential proposal of secrecy she had formulated at the outset of her adventures: "Alle sue femine, che più che tre rimase non le ne erano, comandò che ad alcuna persona mai manifestassero chi fossero, salvo se in parte si trovassero dove aiuto manifesto alla lor libertà conoscessero"

("Wherefore she bade the three women, who were all that were left to her, on no account to let any know who they were, unless they were so circumstanced that they might safely count on assistance in effecting their escape," 24). Pericone thinks that "costei dovere esser gran gentil donna" ("she must be some great lady," 20); as for the prince of Morea, "vedendola oltre alla bellezza ornata di costumi reali, non potendo altramenti saper chi ella si fosse, nobile donna dovere essere l'estimò" ("the royal bearing, which enhanced the lady's charms, did not escape the prince, who, being unable to discover her true rank, set her down as at any rate of noble lineage," 46). And the mystery of her nobility comes to contribute in no small measure to the fascination she exerts (cf. 22, 46).

But these two positional elements, "mutism" and loss of individuality, combine in the "reification"[5] of Alatiel, a silent beauty descended, as it were, from another world. Boccaccio opportunely insists on this "reification": "Convennersi di fare l'acquisto di questo amor comune, quasi amore così questo dovesse patire, come la mercatantia o i guadagni fanno" ("[They] resolved to make conquest of the lady on joint account: as if love admitted of being held in partnership like merchandise or money," 39); "lei sì come maravigliosa *cosa* guardava" ("looked on her as on *something* marvelous," 50); "appena seco poteva credere lei essere *cosa* mortale" ("was scarce able to believe that she was of mortal *mold*," 50); "sì bella *cosa* avendo al suo piacere" ("to have so fair a *creature* to solace him," 51); "mai sì bella *cosa* non aver veduta" ("he had never seen so beautiful a *creature*," 65); "per avere una così bella *cosa*" ("to have so beautiful a *thing*," 67). In order to confirm a relationship between "mutism" and reification, we may consider the following phrase from the novella of Gentile de' Garisendi: "Messere, bella *cosa* è questa vostra, ma ella ne par mutola" (X.IV.34),[6] while the relationship between (feigned) mutism and erotic activity at once brings to mind the tale of Masetto di Lamporecchio (III.I), with its full accompaniment of sources and analogues.

It should now be clear why there is so marked a division between Alatiel "dumb" and Alatiel speaking: her "return to speech" is a return to her own individuality which, apart from anything else, turns the incognito just abandoned into a smoke screen hiding a past of amorous exploits, involuntary though they were. Antigono renders this explicit: "Madonna, poi che occulto è stato ne' vostri infortuni chi voi siete, senza fallo più cara che mai vi renderò al vostro padre, e appresso per moglie al re del Garbo" ("Madam, as throughout this train of misfortunes you have happily escaped recognition, I undertake to restore you to your father in such sort that you shall be dearer to him than ever before, and be afterwards married to the king of Algarve," 101). It is no accident that although the last two lovers (Antioco and the merchant) know Alatiel's language, Boccaccio still does not allow his heroine a single word (whereas Antioco makes a fine speech at 83–85).

The same twofold division serves further to explain the differing attitude of the author toward his protagonist. From the beginning of her imprisonment with Pericone (8–25) and the moment of her meeting Antioco (90–120)[7] Alatiel is a noble personage, dressed in a style befitting her status in terms of rhetorical convention: her decisions are independent, her gestures dignified, her discourses learned. It is during the long parenthesis of her adventures that Boccaccio allows himself to treat of her in the middle style, often with mischievous double entendre: "Non avendo mai davanti saputo con che corno gli uomini cozzano" ("She knew not till then with what horn men butt," 39); "col santo Cresci in man che Iddio ci diè" ("with the aid of Saint Crescent-in-hand that God has given us," 37); "Quasi da iguale appetito tirati, cominciatisi a stuzzicare insieme . . . insieme fecero parentado" ("And by a common impulse they began to wanton together, insomuch that . . . they were indeed man and wife," 89). Thus we find resolved on a structural and stylistic level an aspect which critics have often felt was a form of psychological incongruity.

5. At this point we may move more easily to the second terms of the "proportion" arrived at in the preceding paragraph, i.e., to the opposition between carnal contact and chastity. The nucleus of the tale is the sizable enclave found within a marriage saga based on the schema discussed at the beginning of this chapter:

> promise of marriage–retarding misadventures–achievement of marriage

This schema may be considered from within the following system of probabilities:

$$\text{chastity} \begin{cases} \text{chastity maintained} \longrightarrow \text{marriage} \\ \\ \text{carnal contact} \end{cases}$$

where, naturally enough, carnal contact not only stands in contradiction to an ideal protagonist but should also rule out ipso facto any possibility of a happy ending (marriage). When the two schemata are integrated, we have

$$\left\{ \begin{array}{l} \text{1. chastity} \\ \text{2. promised marriage} \end{array} \right. \quad \left\{ \begin{array}{l} \text{3. chastity maintained} \\ \text{4. retarding misadventures} \\ \text{5. carnal contact} \end{array} \right\} \quad \text{6. marriage}$$

where the succession 1–2, 3–4, 6 is the norm within the conventions of the romance, while the succession 1–2, 4–5, 6 is clearly unacceptable (6, which implies 3, excludes its contrary, 5). The schema Alatiel makes her own is 1–2, 3–4, whose two culminating moments are represented by her "orazion picciola" to her companions in misfortune, which is still sincere: "Sommamente confortandole a conservare la loro castità, affermando sé aver seco proposto che mai di lei se non il suo marito goderebbe" ("She also exhorted them most earnestly to preserve their chastity, averring that she was firmly resolved that none but her husband should enjoy her," 24); and also, in the form of verbal disguise,[8] by the sublimated account of her adventures proffered to her father and confirmed by Antigono with regard to just this question, chastity: "quanto quegli gentili uomini e donne, colli quali venne dicessero della onesta vita la quale con le religiose donne aveva tenuta e della sua virtù e de' suoi laudevoli costumi" ("all that the gentlemen and ladies who accompanied her said of the virtuous and gracious and noble life which she had led with the devout ladies," 117); "Voi vi potete vantare d'avere la più bella figliuola e la più onesta e la più valorosa che altro signore che oggi corona porti" ("You may make it your boast that among all the daughters of all your peers that wear the crown none can be matched with yours for virtue and true worth," 118). This is the way in which Alatiel is able to arrive at 6, the third phase.

The opposition of chastity maintained and carnal contact is thus neutralized by Alatiel herself in a misleading discourse which culminates in her allusion to the devotion which, during so many years' absence in a foreign land, she had shown to "san Cresci in Valcava, a cui le femine di quel paese voglion molto bene" ("Saint Crescent-in-Hollow, who is held in great honor by the women of that country," 109). This neutralization is decisive for any overall interpretation of the tale: Alatiel takes on herself, in a stylistically elevated context, Boccaccio's burlesque double entendre and by the very fact of so doing confirms the slightly malicious point of view from which he had observed her vicissitudes.

The tale thus stands revealed as one of the many in the *Decameron* which are based on a species of fraud (*inganno*), a wider category than *beffa* in that while it includes unfair defense of one's own interest, it excludes spite toward the betrothed. In this kind of tale amusement arises from the use made of the true/false commutator.[9] In other words, while one group of characters (the Soldan and the king of Garbo) believe that Alatiel's history actuates the schema 1–2, 3–4 and as a consequence find it perfectly natural that it should end with phase 6, the reader looks over the shoulders of the protagonist, Antigono, and the writer and knows very well that the real schema is 1–2, 4–5. He then finds it hilarious that despite everything, the history should end in phase 6. In short, the whole point is the setting up between 5 and 6 of a relationship of inclusion rather than exclusion.

This contrivance is put into effect (typically, for Boccaccio) through the art of words. The cunning to which Alatiel is unable to have recourse in defense of her chastity directs her words instead to just this demonstration—that she has spent four years in a life of inviolate sanctity. Her words—and those of her accomplice Antigono—impose a more dignified, acceptable reality which replaces and thus nullifies the real one. This illusionistic use of language, common enough to Boccaccio the narrator, indeed peculiar to him in this role, is a functional element within the system of the tale. In fact we might compare the "proportion" discussed in paragraph 4 with the schema we have arrived at in the present paragraph. If it is true that

(incommunicability + individuality lost) : carnal contact = (communicability + individuality maintained) : chastity

as in the schema earlier displayed, then points 1–2 and 6 belong to the second member of the proportion; the binomial 4–5, which really belongs to the first member of the proportion, is shifted to the second (and is transformed to 3–4) by permutation of the first elements: incommunicability → communicability, individuality lost → individuality maintained. The recovery of speech and social status have their repercussions retroactively on the series of retarding misadventures, replacing the parallel element with its opposite (carnal contact → chastity maintained).

6. A "tragic" reading of the tale finds only weak support in the prologue. The prologue is serious, even solemn (in appearance), but it should appear suspect for this very reason: prologues that are *engagé*, at times even on the theological plane (we might recall I.I.), are often used by Boccaccio as a means of smuggling in themes that are in some measure daring, while on the artistic plane he also exploits the comic element arising from the fall from an initially elevated tone to the uninhibited level of the tale that follows.

More significant, in our case, is the cut-and-dried summing up:

Ed essa che con otto uomini forse diecemila volte giaciuta era,
allato a lui si coricò per pulcella, e fecegliele credere che così fosse;
e reina con lui lietamente poi più tempo visse. E perciò si disse:
"Bocca basciata non perde ventura, anzi rinnuova come fa la luna."

[So she, who had lain with eight men in all, perhaps, ten thousand
times, was bedded with him as a virgin and made him believe that
a virgin she was, and lived long and happily with him as his queen:
wherefore 'twas said—"Mouth, for kisses, was never the worse:
like as the moon reneweth her course," 121–22.]

Here we should note the kind of moral conveyed by the proverb and
the fact that what is underlined is the hoodwinking of the king of Garbo
and the right royal satisfaction of our involuntary heroine of sex. Furthermore, and even more particularly, there is a particular emphasis laid
on the erotic element, and this is done once more by the use of numbers. The impossibility of the figure (intercourse 10,000 times!) merely
confirms the qualifying function, in terms of narrative logic, of intercourse itself.

No less symptomatic are the reactions of the female auditors:

Sospirato fu molto dalle donne per li vari casi della bella donna:
ma chi sa che cagione moveva que' sospiri? forse v'eran di quelle
che non meno per vaghezza di così spesse nozze che per pietà di
colei sospiravano.

[The ladies heaved many sighs over the various fortunes of the fair
lady: but what prompted those sighs who shall say? with some,
perchance, 'twas as much envy as pity of one to whose lot fell so
many nights of delight, 2]

In this example the contrasted nouns ("vaghezza," "pietà") and the
means of effecting the contrast ("non meno . . . che") represent well the
relative weights of the erotic element (with the self-satisfied participation of the audience) and the pathetic element (where participation
cannot go beyond compassion).

But is the prologue really as solemn as it sounds? It is not, I think,
altogether free from a certain archness. The statement that

se dirittamente oprar volessimo, a quello prendere e possedere ci
dovremmo disporre che Colui ci donasse, il quale sol ciò che ci fa
bisogno conosce e puolci dare

[if we would act rightly, we ought to school ourselves to take and be
content with that which He gives us, who alone knows and can
afford us that of which we have need, 6]

recalls, and not on the formal plane alone, the metaphor of "Santo
Cresci in man che Iddio ci diè" (37). It was given us, then, by "Colui
. . . il quale sol ciò che ci fa bisogno conosce"; and it does seem rather
counterproductive, when the intention is to preach against the beauty of
women, to tell us "quanto sventuratamente fosse bella una saracina, alla
quale in forse quattro anni avvenne per la sua bellezza di fare nuove
nozze da nove volte" ("the coil of misadventures in which her beauty
involved a fair Saracen, who in the course of, perhaps, four years
was wedded nine several times," 7), where the only illustration of
"sventuratamente" is "fare nuove nozze da nove volte."

7. The interpretation of a work of art may be considered all the more
valid the more it allows constituent elements to be disengaged. The
present structural description, as is proper to this method, is based on
an overall analysis of the work's narrative articulations and their functions. If this is admitted, it will follow that while some part of earlier
interpretations must be rejected as no longer adequate (e.g., those which
do not understand the rhythmic and comic value of the repetition device), others can be salvaged on condition that they are integrated into
a different interpretative structure.

For example, appeals to the way fortune and nature (and thus sex
as well) influence the events the tale narrates undoubtedly call upon
constituent elements of Boccaccio's ideology. It is inevitable that such
elements should be present in II.VII as well, except that, if our interpretation is correct, it is not on these that the story hinges. On other
points the interpretations of earlier critics can be held to, on condition
that they are integrated into the pattern that has now come to light. I
allude, for example, to the tragic aspects (Getto goes so far as to write
that the killing of the prince of Morea constitutes a "splendid scene
which would not be out of place in any Elizabethan or, it may be, even
in Shakespeare himself").[10] Tragic details are unquestionably present,
but the function they fulfill is precisely localized. The victims of the
tragedy are characters who come onstage one after another only to be
carried off almost at once (as corpses), hardly giving the reader time or
motive to identify with them. In other words, they are stand-ins, soon
forgotten. The one and only protagonist is Alatiel herself; for her, every
drama ends in another bout of intercourse, with its related switch of
husband or lover. The erotic-burlesque conclusion which unfailingly

crowns each of the sequences will hardly permit one to apply the term "tragedy" whatever poetic one subscribes to; it seems, rather, to lend support to Sapegno's reference to "superior irony."

Of even more far-reaching and indisputable value is the weight of the "sea voyage" theme, not only because it explicitly squares with the scheme of Alexandrian romance. Almansi writes that "the sea/wind group in the tale of Alatiel, and in this tale alone, forms a symbolic node or, rather, a symbolic tangle, necessarily inextricable, not susceptible of paraphrase, caught up in the net of its own suggestive allusiveness." I would not, however, go on to maintain the parallelism "of sea passions and human passions, unleashed elements and unrestrained instincts, flight and orgasms." The tale's only tempest precedes the series of couplings and deaths that form the plot; there is no parallelism, then, but symbolic anticipation, if that[11] (or better, in a less ambitious hermeneutics, a narrative expedient which gives good results).

I believe that Boccaccio's insistence on voyages and flight by sea is the result of a definite artistic calculation: it offsets the temporal concentration of events in terms of spatial dispersion. This technique is concomitant with others whose aim is to keep Alatiel in a precarious but continuing equilibrium between ingenuousness and calculation, reluctance and surrender. Each change of setting—geographical, social, or topographical—constitutes a break with what has gone before, distancing and all but obliterating it. So true is this that the final homecoming will reduce to zero voyages, misadventures, and erotic experiences. It is as if the four years had never been, as if the sea had closed over them as over a wake some thousands of leagues in length.

Six

A Conceptual Analysis of the First Eclogue of Garcilaso

1.1. A text like Garcilaso's *First Eclogue* challenges the critic by its very perfection.[1] This perfection is so clearly built up out of preexisting cultural elements (the bucolic genre, from its Latin models down to its recent embodiment in Renaissance achievement, Petrarchan language in its Spanish acceptation, not without Mannerist anticipations) that it constitutes an invitation to comparative analysis, to a learned search for sources and deviations from them. Such research, though undoubtedly of value (and which sixteenth-century scholars had themselves already initiated),[2] all too readily lead at the moment of critical evaluation to disparate and heterogeneous results—to local appreciation unrelated to overall pattern. It would, however, be no less misleading to give no weight at all to Garcilaso's literary background, interpreting his work in terms of formulae alien to his cultural conceptions.

The geometry of the *First Eclogue* is clear and deliberate. Equally clear is the fact that the two laments which all but fill it are placed beside each other to form a diptych, which allows the realization of a whole series of finely calculated affinities and differences. The materials Garcilaso employs in the eclogue as a whole, commonplaces for the most part, appear often in the laments of the two shepherds, but here their functions are different and at times opposed. The sixteenth-century poet, working with a rigorously defined linguistic and stylistic repertoire, was thus able to express himself in an original way either by uttering a commonplace in a new voice or by subtly bringing one into line with the function it was destined to assume at a particular point of the text.

In the analysis which follows, I have sought to bring to light in the groups of stanzas attributed to each of the shepherds (who elaborate traditional themes—the abandoned lover, the lover whose lady is dead—in an accumulation of forms and *topoi* no less canonical, through rhetorical questions, *adynata*, apostrophes, *ubi sunt*, contrapositions, personifications) the conceptual line along which Garcilaso moves with unrivaled technical skill. It is a line which develops among semic oppositions of general validity, though I have accepted the arrangement sanctioned by the Petrarchan ideological system because it is this alone which justifies the value they assume in Garcilaso.

Such an attempt to show, by means of lexemes, the semes and the semic system which underlie Garcilaso's discourse in the *First Eclogue* could obviously enough be extended to include other works of either Garcilaso or his contemporaries. This, however, has not been my aim here. The thesis which this chapter will set out to develop and demonstrate is that the structure of this eclogue is sustained by a combination of opposed directional tensions: the diurnal cycle of the sun is its symbol in the narrative section; its metaphor in the lyrical section. Around this metaphor, which the two mourning shepherds use antinomically, the opposing pairs of concepts which dominate the text have been arranged. The directional tensions, in short, polarize the semic field of the text and by so doing bring about its definition.

1.2. Garcilaso's *First Eclogue* is made up of thirty stanzas, all with the scheme A11 B11 C11 B11 A11 C11 c7 d7 E11 E11 F11 e7 F11.[3] The arrangement of the stanzas creates a rigorous geometrical pattern:[4]

Dedication	stanzas 1–3	(lines 1–42)
Narration	stanza 4	(lines 43–56)
Salicio's lament	stanzas 5–16	(lines 57–224)
Narration	stanza 17	(lines 225–38)
Nemoroso's lament	stanzas 18–29	(lines 239–407)
Narration	stanza 30	(lines 408–21)

Thus we have three stanzas of dedication, three of narration, and two lyrical sections of twelve stanzas, i.e., multiples of three.[5]

1.3. The dedication is coordinated with the content of the eclogue through a variety of procedures. First it opens with the "argument" (1–6), thus introducing the two shepherds at the outset and in terms that will be recurrent in the narration: "cantar" ("to sing," 4), "canto" ("song," 49); "dulce lamentar . . . sus quexas" ("sweet lamentation . . . their complaints," 1, 3), "se quexava tan dulce[mente]" ("complained as sweetly," 53), "Las fieras . . . dexan el sossegado . . . sueño por escuchar mi llanto triste" ("The wild beasts . . . wake from their peaceful sleep to listen to my plaints," 203–6). It ends with the invitation "Escucha tú el cantar de mis pastores" ("Listen to the singing of my shepherds," 42). Next, it has internal connections with the "argument": "atentas" ("heedful," 5), "atento" ("attending," 10). And third, there are verbal and thematic anticipations of the laments: the theme of the chase (17–20) which reappears in Nemoroso's lament (380, 389–91), the image of the "yedra" (ivy, 38) which returns in Salicio's lament (135–36).

1.4. Connections between the narrative sections and the laments are closer still. (*a*) The *locus amoenus*, with the "agua clara" which crosses the "fresco y verde prado" ("fresh green meadow") in the "verdura" (grass, 46–48), is described not only by the poet but also by Salicio: "Ves aquí un prado lleno de verdura, . . . ves aquí un agua clara" ("Here you see a meadow full of grass, . . . here you see a clear stream," 216–18); also "en esta agua que corre clara y pura" ("in this clear and pure running stream," 178); and it is called upon as a witness by Nemoroso: "corrientes aguas puras . . . verde prado de fresca sombra lleno" ("flowing, pure, and crystalline waters, . . . green meadow full of cool shadow," 239–44). (*b*) The stream which crosses the meadow leads to the metaphor of the stream of tears, alluded to by Salicio in the last line of each stanza in his lament: "Salid sin duelo, lágrimas, corriendo" ("Fall, tears, abundantly and flow," 70, 84, 98, 112, etc.), directly treated in the intermediate narrative stanza (17): "soltó de llanto una profunda vena" ("broke a deep vein of tears," 227), and taken up again by Nemoroso: "Yo hago con mis ojos / crecer, lloviendo, el fruto miserable" ("With the water from my eyes I nourish this miserable crop," 308–9). (*c*) Finally, it is to the murmuring of the stream that Salicio seeks to adapt the rhythm of his song: "El con canto acordado / al rumor que sonava / del agua que passava, / se quexava . . . " ("With his voice tuned to the sound of the moving water, he complained . . . ," 49–52).

Other connective elements include "el monte," the "altíssimo monte" of the narrative stanzas (46, 228, 417), and the "ganado" (flocks) or "ovejas" (sheep) mentioned in the dedication (4) and the conclusion (420), but naturally also frequently in the laments.

1.5. The first and last of the three narrative stanzas mark as equal the duration of the laments and the passage of the sun from dawn to sunset. Compare stanza 4,

Saliendo de las ondas encendido,
rayava de los montes el altura
el sol . . .

[Rising on fire from the waves, the sun was streaking
the mountain tops, 43–45],

with stanza 30,

Nunca pusieran fin al triste lloro

. . . .

si mirando las nuves coloradas,
al tramontar del sol bordadas[6] d'oro,
no vieran que era ya passado el día.

[The shepherds would never have put an end to their
sad weeping . . . if they had not seen red clouds
edged with gold, as the sun sank behind the mountains,
and realized that day was done, 408–13.]

Such a procedure has precedents in the bucolic genre but is here utilized metaphorically.[7] For the moment, it is sufficient to note that the diurnal cycle of the sun is a correlative of poetic time, while the murmuring of the stream (1.3) is a correlative of poetic rhythm.

2.1. The laments of the shepherds, of equal length and with an equal number of stanzas, are nevertheless differentiated from a formal point of view. In Salicio's lament all the stanzas, with the exception of the last, end with the same verse ("Salid sin duelo lágrimas, corriendo") which functions as a refrain; consequently, the rhyme of the third from last verse is a fixed one: -iendo (see the scheme outlined in sec. 1.2). In Nemoroso's lament, however, the last verse constantly changes.

Both shepherds bewail separation from their beloved, separations whose causes are quite different. Galatea has left Salicio to join another shepherd; Elisa is dead. It follows that the desire for death expressed by both shepherds is differently motivated: Salicio wants to leave a world in which Galatea is no longer his, while Nemoroso desires to be reunited with Elisa in eternity.

An examination of the words "muerte" and "morir" in the lament of Salicio is symptomatic. They always refer to Salicio himself and are cast, through a variety of grammatical procedures, in a proximate future. Used in their normal sense, they are often in contraposition with "vida": "Estoy muriendo, y aun la vida temo" ("I am dying, and yet I fear to live," 60); "y tú, desta mi vida ya olvidada, / sin mostrar un pequeño sentimiento / de que por ti Salicio triste muera" ("and you, who have now forgotten this life of mine and show not the smallest regret that sad Salicio is dying for you," 85–87). Further, "causar la muerte d'un estrecho amigo" ("drives her close friend to his death," 94), "yo estoy muriendo" ("I am dying," 96), and "mi morir" ("my death," 202). The shepherd's imminent death depends on the loss of positive value of "vida" and "bivir" once they are deprived of the only value they had for him—Galatea's love: "aun la *vida temo*; / Témola con razón, pues tú me dexas, / Que *no ay sin ti el bivir para qué sea*" ("and yet I fear to live, and rightly fear it, since you abandon me, and without you there is no reason why life should be," 60–62). Thus the singer finds himself between two poles, life and death, and he tends toward the latter. Life, devoid of Galatea's love, has lost its attraction. Thus[8]

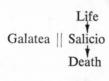

In Nemoroso's lament, "muerte," when not hypostasis and antagonist (340, 344), is twice referred to the beloved (293, 393). Its contraposition to "vida" involves the different fate of the two lovers. "Vida" is, in fact, always that of Nemoroso, and attributes of sorrow accompany it: "los agudos filos de la *muerte* [of Elisa] . . . los cansados años de mi *vida*" ("the sharp shears of *death* . . . the weary years of my own *life*," 262–64), "a la pessada *vida* y enojosa" ("a heavy and tiresome *life*," 293). The life-death opposition is thus also an opposition between two states: Elisa has moved across to the second pole, whereas Nemoroso is still unwillingly at the first.

For Nemoroso life is now a burden, an effort. In contrast to Salicio's situation, what gave life its value has not itself failed but has been forced over into the field of death. So true is this that it is still possible to apply to Elisa the epithet "vida mía" (282). A conceptual system emerges which finds expression in stanza 23 in the equivalences of darkness, night = death; light, day = life; sun = Elisa. Elisa's passing from life to death inverts the terms of the two equivalences: light, day = death (thanks to the sun-Elisa); life (without the sun-Elisa) = darkness, night:

> tal es la tenebrosa
> *noche* de tu partir en que é quedado
> de sombra y de temor atormentado,
> hasta que *muerte* 'l tiempo determine
>   que a ver el desseado
> *sol* de tu clara vista m'encamine.

[Even so is the dark night of your departure, in which I am left troubled by shadow and fear until *death* shall fix the time when I shall set out to see the welcome *sun* of your clear gaze, 318–23.]

This is the only time that "muerte" is referred to Nemoroso, since, without any overtones of sadness, through verbal transformations it becomes an apotheosis in the last stanza of the lament. Nemoroso's desire to move to the pole of death can be synthesized thus:

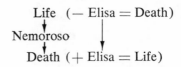

2.2. Therefore death is for Salicio a natural outcome of his suffering, while for Nemoroso it is touched with hope. Salicio's situation is expressed in "derritiendo / M'estoy en llanto eterno" ("I am dissolving in eternal weeping," 194–95), or even more clearly in the following lines, where he imagines he is dissolved in tears:

> No ay coraçón que baste,
> aunque fuesse de piedra,
> viendo mi amada yedra
> de mí arrancada, en otro muro asida,
> y mi parra en otro olmo entretexida,
> que no *s'esté con llanto deshaziendo*
> *hasta acabar la vida.*

[No heart, not even a heart of stone, would be so strong as not *to dissolve itself in tears until its life ebbed away*, on seeing my beloved ivy wrenched from me and clinging to another wall, and my vine entangled with another elm, 132–39.]

It is quite evident that all the refrains "Salid sin duelo, lágrimas, corriendo" converge on these central lines (which close stanza 6): each tear is a fragment of life which departs. Death is a passive outcome, a form of wasting away.

Nemoroso's state, however, still allows for descriptions and variations, contemplating consolatory fetishisms (stanza 26), assuming an appearance of weariness, though with the prospect of an early restorative abandonment. Compare "En esta triste valle, donde agora / me entristezco y me *canso* en el reposo / Estuve ya contento y *descansado*" ("In this same valley where now I find sadness and *weariness*, I was then contented and *happy in my repose*," 253–55), "El importuno / Dolor me dexa *descansar* un rato" ("My wearisome grief *gives me a little rest*," 364–65), and "pessada vida" ("heavy life," 293) with "otros valles floridos y sombríos / donde *descanse* y siempre pueda verte / Ante los ojos míos, / Sin miedo y sobresalto de perderte" ("other flowered and shady valleys, where I may *rest* and always be able to see you before my eyes, without the fear and dread of losing you," 404–7).

3. Essential to an understanding of the two laments is, then, the fact that Salicio's turning toward death is a turn in a direction opposite to that of Galatea's movement toward her new lover, whereas Nemoroso's drift toward death is a move in the same direction as Elisa's enforced departure. And it is precisely to this play of opposing directions that the diurnal cycle of the sun has been adapted. Salicio does not feel in harmony with that phase of the sun's increase, sunrise, the symbol of replenished life and joy which are extraneous to him; Nemoroso's feelings accompany the sun's declining phase, a symbol of the death which will take him to his Elisa. This emerges quite strikingly if we compare stanza 6 (Salicio) with stanza 23 (Nemoroso):

El *sol* tiende los rayos de su *lumbre*
por montes y por valles, despertando
las aves y animales y la gente:
quál por el ayre claro va bolando,
quál por el verde valle o alta cumbre
paciendo va segura y libremente,
   quál con el *sol* presente
   va de nuevo al oficio
   y al usado exercicio
do su natura o menester l'inclina:
siempre 'stá en llanto esta ánima mezquina,
quando la *sombra* el mundo va cubriendo,
   o la luz se avezina.
Salid sin duelo, lágrimas, *corriendo*.

[The *sun* darts the rays of his *fire* over mountains and valleys, rousing birds, beasts, and men; those go flying through the clear air, those through the green valley or over the lofty heights, safely and freely pasturing; and men, now that the *sun* is here, go once more to their work and to the customary employment to which their nature or their need inclines them. But this miserable creature is in tears when *shadows* come to cover the world or when the light draws near. Fall, tears, abundantly and *flow*, 71–84.]

Como al partir del *sol* la *sombra* crece,
y en cayendo su rayo, se levanta
la negra escuridad que 'l mundo cubre,

de do viene el temor que nos espanta
y la medrosa forma en que s'offrece
aquella que la noche nos encubre
    hasta que 'l *sol* descubre
    su luz pura y hermosa:
    tal es la tenebrosa
noche de tu partir en que é quedado
de *sombra* y de temor atormentado,
hasta que muerte 'l tiempo determine
    que a ver el desseado
sol de tu clara vista m'*encamine.*

[As when the *sun* departs the *shadows* grow and, as its rays sink,
the black darkness rises to cover the world, whence comes the fear
that strikes us and the fearful shape assumed by what the night hides
from us, until the *sun* reveals its pure and lovely light: even so
is the dark night of your departure, in which I am left troubled
by *shadow* and fear until death shall fix the time when *I shall set
out* to see the welcome sun of your clear gaze, 310–23.]

It should be noted that "sol" is in a parallel position in the first and
seventh lines of both stanzas, although in 23 there is another "sol" in
the final line, a symbol of the beloved herself. The sun in the literal
sense has, in stanza 6, a progressive movement which exercises its influence on living creatures ("tiende," 71 → "va," 74, 76, 78); the static
state of sorrow contrasts with it ("siempre 'stá en llanto," 81), where
the only movement is the hopeless one of tears ("Salid . . . corriendo,"
84). In stanza 23 it is the other way around—the sun's movement is a
moving away ("partir," 310) and a corresponding advance of shadow
and darkness ("la sombra crece," 310; "se levanta / la negra escuridad," 311–12). The transition to the symbolic use of "sol" is marked
by the new "partir" (319), referring to the woman but accompanied
by the same "sombra" and "temor" (320) which the sun's departure
caused (310, 313). The singer is shown in movement toward the
beloved-sun ("m'encamine," 323), a movement subtended by a temporal drive ("hasta que muerte 'l tiempo determine," 321). This deliberate contrast between the two stanzas is underlined by the homogeneity of the expression even at a lexical level ("rayos," 71, "rayo,"
311; "sombra," 82, 310; "luz," 83, 317), by a common reference to
the sun's cycle (82–83; 315–17), and by the fact that the two verbs of
movement are located in final position: "corriendo" (84), "m'encamine" (323).

All this can be synthesized in the two figures which follow. (In the second figure the equations Life = Night and Death = Day are motivated by what we have set forth in sec. 2.1, and by the identification Elisa = Sun):

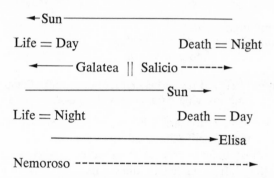

4.1. Within this simple schema nearly all the details of the execution will be found coherent. We might particularly note in Salicio's lament the prevalence of allocutive expressions. From the outset, the woman's name is pronounced and set between a pair of similes which give the measure of her cruelty:

¡O más dura que mármol a mis quexas
y al encendido fuego en que me quemo
más elada que nieve, Galatea!

[O harder than marble to my plaints, and colder than snow to the flaming fire in which I burn, O Galatea! 57–59.]

Then she is named no more, for the very good reason that she is apostrophized more directly with insistent personal pronouns and adjectives: "tú," 61, 85, 147, 207, 209; "ti," 62, 65, 87, 99, 100, 102, 167, 174, 187, 188, 220, "te," 67, 172, 183, 184, 185; "tu," 108, 127, 130; "tus," 128, 132. Only once is another person—God—apostrophized, and even then it is as witness to Galatea's inhuman behavior (91–95).

Connected with this insistent invocation of the beloved are innumerable expressions pertaining to displacement—movement away from Salicio: "tú me dexas" ("you abandon me," 61), "dexas llevar . . . al viento / El amor" ("do you permit the wind to bear away . . . the love," 88–89), "quitándolo de mi" ("taking it from me," 159); movement toward the new lover: "bolviste" ("have you turned," 128), "pusiste" ("have you given," 130), "dando a quien diste" ("since you gave . . . to whom you did," 158). A series which is rendered more effectively metaphoric as a result of the degree of violence conferred on the images is the following:

> viendo mi amada yedra
> de mí *arrancada*, en otro muro asida,
> y mi parra en otro olmo *entretexida*

[on seeing my beloved ivy *wrenched* from me and clinging to another wall, and my vine *entangled* with another elm, 135–37.]

Two types of consideration are inherent in this displacement. The first has to do with the objective impossibility of justification. This is built around a contrast between the starting point (Salicio) and the goal (the rival), the shift in Galatea's affections. For this concept, use is made of the traditional bucolic argument which lists the merits (175–78) and the wealth (183–96) of the abandoned beloved. Even more incisive is the contrast that results from the repetition of "trocar" in the following lines (which are the development of the earlier line, "¿Por quién tan sin respeto me trocaste?": "Whom have you so inconsiderately put in my place?" 129):

> y cierto no *trocara* mi figura
> con esse que de mí s'está reyendo;
>   ¡*trocara* mi ventura!

[And I certainly would not *change* features with the man who is now laughing at me, but I would *change* my luck with him! 179–81.]

The second type of consideration involves the break in synchronization between the movement (of abandonment) of the beloved and the stability of Salicio's love:

> ¿D'un alma te desdeñas ser señora
> donde siempre *moraste*, no pudiendo
>   della salir un ora?

[Do you despise yourself for being the mistress of a soul in which you have always *dwelt*, unable to leave it for an hour? 67–69];

> ¡Ay, quán diferente era
> y quán d'otra manera
> lo que en tu falso pecho se escondía!

[How different and how contrary was the feeling hidden in your false breast! 106–8.]

This stability in love is now stability in grief for Salicio, who is still characterized by expressions of durative aspect: "Estoy muriendo" ("I am dying," 60), "Siempre 'stá en llanto esta ánima mezquina" ("But this miserable creature is in tears," 81), "Yo estoy muriendo" ("I am dying," 96), "Yva siguiendo" ("I went on," 124), "que no s'esté con llanto deshaziendo" ("so . . . as not to dissolve itself in tears," 138), "derritiendo / M'estoy en llanto eterno" ("if I am dissolving in eternal weeping," 194–95).

His very tears seem to allude to a flight from himself. Note in the refrain the use of the verb "salir" ("leave"), which verbal repetition and conceptual cross-reference throw into particular relief:

¿D'un alma te desdeñas ser señora
donde siempre moraste, no pudiendo
   della *salir* un ora?
Salid, sin duelo, lágrimas, corriendo

[Do you despire yourself for being the mistress of a soul in which you have always dwelt, unable to *leave* it for an hour? *Fall*, tears, abundantly and flow, 67–70];

que 'l más seguro tema con recelo
perder lo que estuviere posseyendo.
   Salid fuera sin duelo,
salid sin duelo, lágrimas, corriendo

[Why the most secure should fear and suspect the *loss* of what he once possessed. *Fall* abundantly, *fall,* tears, abundantly and flow, 151–54]

as well as the concomitance of presentiments and refrain in the series of images which link together the ideas of flowing and of flight:

. . . por nuevo camino *el agua s'iva*;
. . . .
el curso *enagenado* yva siguiendo
   del agua *fugitiva*.
Salid sin duelo, lagrimas, corriendo.

[The water was flowing . . . down a new channel . . . I went on along the course of the evasive water, with distracted mind. Fall, tears, abundantly and flow, 122–26.]

Note that "enagenado" will be picked up again in the stanza which follows, where it is attributed to the beloved (147).

As a result, the eversion which the last stanza effects is of extreme subtlety. Movement, symbolic prerogative of his tears, though in Galatea's case real (and in the opposite direction), is now predicated of Salicio himself; resigned to the fact that he has been abandoned, it is now he who leaves the places his beloved holds dear. Galatea's movement of displacement, now taken for granted in its affective aspect, no longer needs support in local terms. The woman may take possession of the landscape she loves, and it is Salicio who, with a final renunciation, leaves it. I would underscore the way "dexar" is insisted upon, being applied alternately to the beloved and to the shepherd, and also the play that is made at a semantic and phonic level, with "hallar" and "alexar," "quitar" and "quedar":

> Mas ya que a socorrer aquí no vienes,
> no *dexes* el lugar que tanto amaste,
> que bien podrás venir de mí segura.
> Yo *dexaré* el lugar do me *dexaste*
>
> . . . .
>
> quiçá aquí *hallarás*, pues yo m'*alexo*,
> al que todo mi bien *quitar* me puede,
>   que pues el bien le *dexo*,
> no es mucho que 'l lugar también le *quede*.

[But since you do not come here to rescue me, do not *forsake* the place that you so loved, for you will surely be able to come without fear of me. I will *forsake* the place where you *forsook* me. . . . Perhaps, since I am going away, you will *meet* him here who may *rob* me of all my treasure; for since I *leave* him my treasure, it matters little if he *has* the place too, 211–14.]

Thus a movement traced out from the very first stanza comes full circle here: "más dura que marmol a mis quexas" ("harder than marble to my plaints," 57), "tú me dexas" ("you abandon me," 61), "de ti con lágrimas me quexo" ("I complain of you with my tears," 220), "Yo dexaré el lugar do me dexaste" ("I will forsake the place where you forsook me," 214).

4.2. In Salicio's lament the two lovers are ideally face to face, even though the woman is absent and the only voice heard is that of the shepherd himself. In Nemoroso's lament there are other actors. It is as if both shepherds needed to find someone who could be held "responsible" for bearing the weight of their recriminations, whereas in Salicio's case it is the woman who is actually responsible, Nemoroso has to attribute his unhappiness to extraneous "persons," since both he and his beloved are, in their different ways, victims of hostile forces. Hence his apostrophes to Death and, since Elisa has died in childbed, to Lucina (Diana), who was deaf to her invocations.

Because of this transference of responsibility, Elisa is apostrophized only in the final stanza (an exact inversion with respect to Galatea), where she is called upon to intercede to hasten the shepherd's death. Elsewhere her name appears in nonallocutive form ("A Elissa vi a mi lado": "I found Elisa by my side," 258) or as a means of loving evocation, calling up as present one who is present no longer (282, 353). This repetition is as effective as Salicio's insistence on "tú," "te," etc., toward Galatea.

Death, often called by name, is personified accusingly in lines 344–47. But Lucina is much more decisively anthropomorphized. To her the whole of stanza 28 is directed, in which, with attributes lyric poetry as a rule reserved for *belles dames san merci* ("cruda, / inexorable diosa": "cruel, inexorable goddess," 367–77; "¡Y tú, ingrata, riendo / dexas morir mi bien . . . !": "And do you laugh, ungrateful one, and let my treasure die . . . ," 392–93), she is accused of culpable and even erotic amusements ("¿Yvate tanto en un pastor dormido?": "Were you so taken up with a shepherd?" 38). This discovery of a female antagonist introduces into Nemoroso's lament the antagonistic relationship proper to Salicio and Galatea. In the first lament Salicio can seek the aid or the testimony of the gods against a beloved who is now his enemy; in the second, Nemoroso and his beloved are together arrayed against the divinity who has brought about their separation.

The fact that different persons are apostrophized, and particularly that no blame can be attached to Elisa, brings about an even distribution of second person pronouns and adjectives between the two hostile divinities ("ti," 345 to Death; "tu," 387, 389; "tú," 379, 392 to Lucina; "tus," 391) and Elisa ("tu," 319, 323; "tus," 352; "-te," 370; "te," 397; "-tigo," 401), an incomparably smaller number than in Galatea's case.

The abandonment effected unintentionally by Elisa is referred to in terms which are different from those used for Galatea: "partida," 266, "partir," 319; the expressions used for Death ("llevó," 342) and for Lucina ("dexas morir," 393) are much stronger. In reality, "dexar" is used once, but with a plural object which, by extending the sorrow felt by Nemoroso for the abandonment to include his surroundings and the things he loves ("Después que nos dexaste": "since you have left us," 296), creates a tone of listless melancholy.

It is not just that he has been left alone; the singer suffers because he has not been called on to undertake the same journey as Elisa. An inseparable connection, between the woman's eyes and the lover's soul, has been interrupted:

¿Dó están agora aquellos claros ojos
que *llevavan* tras sí, como colgada,
mi alma, doquier que ellos se *bolvián*?[9]

[Where now are those bright eyes that *drew* my soul after them, as if it were their prisoner, wherever they *turned*? 267–69.]

It is the goddess Death who has arrogated to herself the use of "llevar," object of the woman herself (342). And now there is another inseparable connection, that between sorrow and "sentido":

no me podrán *quitar* el dolorido
  sentir si ya del todo
primero no me *quitan* el *sentido*.

[No one can *rid* me of my *grievous* feelings unless they *relieve* me first of all *feelings*, 349–51.]

Thus the apparent inviolability of Nemoroso's life is deplored, for it impedes the journey he so much longs for. Its continuance is likened to the darkness, to the cramped space of a prison:

. . . Mi vida,
  que 's más que 'l hierro fuerte,
pues no la á quebrantado tu partida

[My life must be harder than iron, seeing that your departure has not snapped it, 264–66];

solo, desamparado,
ciego, sin lumbre, en cárcel tenebrosa

[alone, forsaken, blind, and lightless in a dark cell, 294–95],

which is like that of the tomb which encloses Elisa's body:

Aquesto todo agora ya s'encierra
. . . .
en la friá, desierta y dura tierra

[All these . . . are now buried in the cold, barren, hard earth, 279–81].

4.3. The difference in the separations is further reflected in the different attitudes of the two shepherds toward nature.[10] This aspect too is highlighted in parallel stanzas—the fourth of each lament: Salicio, 18; Nemoroso, 21:

> Por ti el silencio de la selva umbrosa
> por ti la esquividad y apartamiento
> del solitario monte m'agradava;
> por ti la verde yerva, el fresco viento,
> el blanco lirio y colorada rosa
> y dulce primavera deseava.
>   ¡Ay, quánto m'engañava!
>   ¡Ay, quán diferente era
>   y quan d'otra manera
> lo que en tu falso pecho se escondía!

[On your account the silence of the shady forest, on your account the indifference and remoteness of the solitary mountain pleased me; for you I desired the green grass, the fresh wind, the white lily and red rose, and the sweet spring. Oh, how I was deceived! How different and how contrary was the feeling hidden in your false breast! 99–108.]

> Quien me dixera, Elissa, vida mía,
> quando en aqueste valle al fresco viento
> andávamos cogiendo tiernas flores,
> que avía de ver, con largo apartamiento,
> venir el triste y solitario día
> que diesse amargo fin a mis amores?
>   El cielo en mis dolores
>   cargó la mano tanto
>   que a sempiterno llanto
> y a triste soledad m'a condenado.

[Who could have told me, Elisa, my dear life, when we were walking in this valley in the cool breeze, gathering the delicate flowers, that it would see the sad and solitary day come, with its wide separation, to put a bitter end to my love? The heavens have dealt me grief with so heavy a hand that they have condemned me to perpetual tears and sad solitude, 282–91.]

Note on one hand the natural elements in common ("fresco viento," 102, 283; "lirio . . . rosa," 103; and "tiernas flores," 284) and on the other the different definitions of responsibility: the beloved's infidelity (106–8), the cruelty of fate (288–91). But the most striking element is the way images of solitude are employed. In Salicio's words, the solitude of an earlier day is in part prefiguration, in part symbol of an institutional fact, for his contact with nature was effected through Galatea's mediation or the thought of her (observe the triple anaphora "por ti"). In Nemoroso's lament, however, the past is described as a common participation, by himself and Elisa, in the life of nature (marked by the plural "andávamos," 284); in contrast, solitude characterizes the present. These different perspectives are given relief by the attribution, respectively, to past and present of "apartamiento" and "solitario" in the laments of Salicio (100, 101) and Nemoroso (285, 286).

We might say that in terms of the three poles of the man-woman-nature relationship, Galatea, by leaving Salicio, has broken off mediation between him and nature. On the other hand, Elisa, taken at once from Nemoroso and from the world, has linked Nemoroso and nature together in a sort of common bereavement. This explains the alienation Salicio feels toward nature (see sec. 3 for the sun's cycle) and his final decision to abandon the place where he had been happy (see stanza 16, where Galatea's love for the place, though not Salicio's is spoken of). In stanza 15 it is nature which seems to approach Salicio, sympathetic to his sorrow. But the movement serves merely to throw into contrasted relief Galatea's lack of feeling, and there is no reciprocation on Salicio's part toward nature's participation. In contrast, Nemoroso feels his sorrow as something cosmic, believing that not he alone but the whole of the landscape he loves so well has been left desolate upon Elisa's death. The pathos of "nos dexaste" has already been noted; we should add that Nemoroso lingers among the plants and animals either searching for signs of their participation or else endlessly verifying in them the loss of his beloved. Hence the frequency of the deictics: "aquí," 242, 257, 352; "donde," 249, 251, 253; "este," 253; "aqueste," 283; "estor," 306; "allí," 358. The functionality of this use is confirmed both by explicit formulations (the opening invocation addressed to the streams, the trees, the meadow, the birds, the ivy, all witnesses to past happiness and present despair) and by the fact that "esta" and "aqueste" are contrasted with "aquel" referred to the beloved ("aquellos . . . ojos": "those . . . eyes," 267; "aquella boz": "that voice," 372) and especially to the hour of her death ("aquella noche," 367; "aquel duro trance de Lucina": "that harsh ordeal of Lucina," 371; "aquel passo": "that predicament," 378). Furthermore, when so many local determinations are present, adverbs of place are emphasized in interrogative phrases, a precise echo of the *ubi sunt* formula (267–77):

¿Dó están agora aquellos claros ojos . . . ?
¿Dó está la blanca mano . . . ?
Los cabellos . . .
¿adónde 'stán, adónde el blanco pecho?
¿Dó la columna . . . ?

[Where now are those bright eyes . . . ?
That hair . . . where is that white hand . . . ?
Where is that soft breast?
Where is the column . . . ?]

Of necessity the question is not left open but answered in all its cruelty: "en la fría, desierta y dura tierra" (281).

Nemoroso does not look at nature with detachment, with Salicio's sense of not belonging. Indeed for him it is syntonized to the point of deteriorating physically after Elisa's death. Stanza 5 describes the interruption of vital energies, the sterility of the earth, the choking embrace of the weeds. Nemoroso's weeping, which now waters only thistles and thorns, underlines this connection between personal and cosmic grief. Thus Nemoroso's lament finds itself in harmony with the shadows of the sunset, and he can give himself up to this movement of all things toward the night (see sec. 3). If he wishes to leave the "lugar," which participated first in his joy, now in his sorrow, he does so only for the mirage of another place, beyond this earth, where happiness can begin anew (stanza 29).

5.1. Galatea's betrayal is seen by Salicio as a break in the natural order.[11] It is expressed in philosophical terms, with reference to the conjunction ("juntar") of naturally extraneous elements ("discordia," "differente"):[12]

¿Que no s'esperará d' aquí adelante,
por difícil que sea y por incierto,
o que discordia no será juntada?

[What can we not expect henceforth, what difficult and doubtful event may not come to pass? Or what discord will not be reconciled? 141–43.]

Materia diste al mundo de 'sperança
d'alcançar lo impossible y no pensado
y de hazer juntar lo differente.

[You gave the world cause to hope that it might attain the impossible and unthought of and that it might join contraries, 155–57.]

By virtue of such formulation, the *impossibilia topos* is made more far-reaching. In "La cordera paciente / con el lobo hambriento / hará su ajuntamiento, / y con las simples aves sin rüydo / harán las bravas sierpes ya su nido" ("Now the patient ewe will join with the hungry wolf, and bold serpents will now noiselessly make their nests with the simple birds," 161–66), Garcilaso, with his habitual coherence, uses "ajuntamiento" ("coupling"), which ties in with earlier uses of "juntar."

The breach in the natural order entails the collapse of all belief in the stability of things: "enxemplo a todos quantos cubre 'l cielo, / que 'l más seguro tema con recelo / perder lo que estuviere posseyendo" ("example to all who live beneath the heavens, why the most secure should fear and suspect the loss of what he once possessed," 150–52), which serves as the perfect framework for the contrapositions which are so frequent in the lament: "más dura que mármol a mis quexas / y al encendido fuego en que me quemo / más elada que nieve" ("harder than marble to my plaints and colder than snow to the flaming fire in which I burn," 57–59); "Estoy muriendo, y aun la vida temo" ("I am dying, and yet I fear to live," 60). It finds its affective correspondence in stanza 15, where a symmetrical break in the natural order brings in, as sharers in Salicio's grief, objects and beings unendowed with human feelings, in contrast to Galatea's indifference: "Con mi llorar las piedras enternecen / su natural dureza y la quebrantan; / los árboles parece que s'inclinan" ("With my weeping the stones are moved from their natural hardness and break it; the trees seem to bend down," 197–99).

The past with its happiness is thus seen as deception. Typical are such exclamations as in stanza 8 (105–7) which open with a memory of calm wanderings once bright with overwhelming love. And typical are the forebodings (109–11), the warning dreams (116–25), which project present unhappiness onto the past.

Thus, as Salicio recounts the course of his love, it becomes a progressive awareness of negativity. Galatea's faithlessness, which her womanly beauty and passion hide, turns into an outright betrayal which admits no appeal. The stanzas of the lament trace out the parabola, from the incredulous questionings of stanza 5 through the dejection of stanza 6 and the appeal to God in stanza 7. Stanzas 8 and 9, with their memories of the full flood of a love touched by premonition, serve by contrast to accentuate stanza 10, which dwells cruelly on Galatea's union with her new lover. This stanza constitutes the climax of Salicio's cry of grief; it is the sixth of the lament whose first half it concludes. The four stanzas that follow are of a more rationally argumentative cast. They set the betrayal either within the framework of the laws of nature it violates or within a scale of values which points up its unreasonableness. Stanzas 13 and 14 bring the lament to a close on a note of final defeat: "Y cierto no trocara mi figura / con esse que de mí s'está reyendo; / ¡trocara mi ventura!" ("And I certainly would not change features with the man who is now laughing at me; but I would change my luck with him!" 179–81); "¡Mas qué vale el tener, si derritiendo / m'estoy en llanto eterno!" ("But what is the good of ownership if I am dissolving in eternal weeping!" 194–95). Nature confirms this defeat (stanza 15), for while it participates in Salicio's grief, it takes it upon itself to show a pity of which the woman has become incapable (207–9).

We may safely say, then, that the order of Salicio's arguments reproduces the phases of his beloved's abandonment of him. The final stanza (16) quite unexpectedly shows Salicio's movement in the opposite direction; its motives are argued in detail:

> Mas ya que a socorrer aquí no vienes,
> no *dexes* el *lugar* que tanto amaste,
> que bien podrás venir de mi segura.
> Yo *dexaré* el *lugar* do me *dexaste*
> . . . .
> quiçá aquí hallarás, pues yo m'alexo,
> al que todo mi *bien* quitar me puede,
>   que pues el *bien* le *dexo*,
> no es mucho que 'l *lugar* también le quede.

[But since you do not come here to rescue me, do not *forsake* the place that you so loved, for you will surely be able to come without fear of me. I will *forsake* the place where you *forsook* me. . . . Perhaps, since I am going away, you will meet him here who may rob me of all my *treasure*; for since I *leave* him my *treasure*, it little matters if he has the *place* too, 211–24.]

We are close to a schematization: invitation to the beloved, who has left him, not to leave the place she still loves (as the shepherd does not); renunciation in favor of the rival who has taken away his treasure and his "lugar," its accidental accompaniment. Salicio now abandons the "lugar" to the woman who loves it, since he is no longer included in her affection.

Salicio's grieved wanderings lead to (and at once leave) a well-defined locality which, caught in all its colors and delights, ill matches the shepherd's exacerbated spirit. It is in this section of the lament, and here alone, that deictic forms abound with insistent anaphora, whereas Nemoroso's lament is permeated with them (see sec. 5.1):

> *Ves aquí* un prado lleno de verdura,
>   *ves aquí* un'espessura
>   *ves aquí* un agua clara,
>   en otro tiempo chara

> [*Here you see* a meadow full of grass, *here you see* a thicket,
> *here you see* a clear stream which was once dear to you, 216–19].

Salicio's despair is made more complete the more it is brought into relation to reality. It is no accident that his words of renunciation in the final stanza replace, for the first and last time, the tearful refrain which closes the other stanzas.[13]

5.2. Whereas Salicio's sorrowful journey sets out from the beloved to end with the "lugar," Nemoroso's sets out from the "lugar" and ends with the beloved (a further movement, however, will take him toward a different "lugar" wherein there will be no more grief). The "lugar-bien" connection is thus rigorously maintained. If the "bien" has failed the singer, then this is the work of fate ("¡O bien caduco, vano y pressuroso!": "O perishable, vain, and swift-footed prosperity," 256), and he can search without bitterness in the "lugar" for traces of his lost happiness. Thus Nemoroso's lament is in opposition to Salicio's not merely because the "lugar" is found at its beginning—where indeed it is invoked and personified—but because the past, rather than seen as pregnant with anticipated sorrow, is juxtaposed with the present whose exact contrary it is:

> en este triste valle, donde agora
> me entristezco y me canso en el reposo,
> estuve ya contento y descansado.

> [And in this same valley where now I find sadness and weariness,
> I was then contented and happy in my repose, 253–55.]

It is the result of an inversion not merely cruel but quite unlooked for:

> ¿Quién me dixiera, Elissa, vida mía,
> quando en aqueste valle al fresco viento
> andávamos cogiendo tiernas flores,
> que avía de ver, con largo apartamiento,
> venir el triste y solitario día
> que diesse amargo fin a mis amores?

[Who could have told me, Elisa, my dear life, when we were walking
in this valley in the cool breeze, gathering the delicate flowers,
that it would see the sad and solitary day come, with its wide
separation, to put a bitter end to my love? 282–87.]

The past is thus for Nemoroso an object of prolonged melancholic
meditation, and from it he culls moments of uncomplicated happiness
("Acuérdome, durmiendo aquí algún ora, / Que, despertando, a Elissa
vi a mi lado": "I remember how once when I slept here I found Elisa
by my side when I awoke," 257–58; and again, lines 283–84, just
quoted); on each occasion it is the "lugar" which sets his imagination
afire (besides dominating stanzas 18–19, it reappears in 21).

Nemoroso's lament too falls neatly into two equal groups of six stanzas
(18–23, 24–29); each group begins with two coupled stanzas (18–19,
24–25), for the discourse overflows the limits of the first and only ends
in the second. The sixth stanza (23) announces an expectation of
death = life, which will then appear in the twelfth (29) as impatience to
set out on the journey to the other world. In both parts of the lament
the beloved is described as a physical presence preserved intact by
memory: these stanzas are placed at the center of each group; i.e., they
are the third (20) and the ninth (26). In the first there is a *descriptio*,
inserted into the heart-rending formula of the *ubi sunt* ("¿Dó están agora
aquellos claros ojos . . . ? Dó está la blanca mano . . . ? Los cabellos
. . . el blanco pecho," etc.); in the second there is a pathetic lingering
over the only relic snatched from dissolution, the lock of hair Nemoroso
bathes with comforting tears.

But overall one has a sense of approach: uncertain memories of lost
happiness give place (27) to precise, actualizing evocation ("verte
presente agora me parece": "I seem to see you before me," 370) of the
last moments of his beloved's life, a bridge between happiness and unhappiness. In the same way, the descriptive stanza (20), which ends on
the hopeless realization that "aquesto todo agora ya s'encierra, / por des-
ventura mía, / en la fría, desierta y dura tierra" ("all these, alas, for
me are now buried in the cold, barren, hard earth," 279–81), is coun-
terbalanced by the preservation of the lock of hair, still live to the caress
of loving hands (26). Nemoroso seems to approach his beloved progressively as he moves through the chronology of his memories; but he is
also preparing himself for the inverse parabola: the past, which once
united him with Elisa, will recur as the present in another region, that
of death. He does not move away, as does Salicio, from the "lugar";
what he awaits is a happy transference with Elisa into its otherworldly
copy, where separation is no longer possible, or even fear: "sin miedo

y sobresalto de perderte" ("without the fear and dread of losing you,"
407), which recalls by contrast Salicio's "que 'l más seguro tema con
recelo / perder lo que estuviere posseyendo" ("why the most secure
should fear and suspect the loss of what he once possessed," 151–52).

5.3. Salicio, deserted by his beloved for a rival, ends by handing over
the entire "lugar" as well, thereby adding renunciation to renunciation
(one enforced, the other voluntary). Elisa, carried off by death, has at
one and the same time abandoned Nemoroso and the "lugar," both of
whom mourn her. The displacement which Nemoroso awaits will carry
him off to his beloved in the heaven of Venus. For this reason, with a
curve as precise as that of Salicio's, Nemoroso's lament, after opening
with an invocation to a fraternal landscape, closes with the longing for
other landscapes, a longing for displacement which is predicated by himself with vehement anaphora: "Busquemos *otro* llano, / busquemos
otros montes y *otros* ríos, / *otros* valles floridos y sombríos" ("We may
seek *another* plain, we may seek *other* mountains and *other* rivers, *other*
flowered and shady valleys," 402–4).

If we schematize the relationships between "lugar," the two shepherds, and their loves, the result is the following:

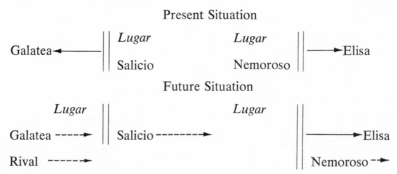

In short, the "lugar" is a fixed pointer behind which occur (and in relation to which are measured) the movements of displacement of the
characters (and of the sun). Until the last stanza of the eclogue, both
shepherds are actually in the "lugar." The abandonment they are victims
of has involved the "lugar" as well, and Salicio quite explicitly states
this (212), as does Nemoroso (296). Elisa's displacement has taken an
opposite direction from that of Galatea (see scheme in sec. 3): Elisa has
gone toward the sunset = death; Galatea follows the cycle of the grow-
ing sun (= life), from which in his despair Salicio is cut off.

The final stanza of each lament closes with a decision to abandon
the "lugar." It is clear that Nemoroso wants to reach Elisa in the other

world, and so, as he looks at the sunset, he is following the traces of her final journey. And Salicio? In his case is it just a question of rendering the renunciation more complete? Is it, as is usually thought, no more than a last desperate homage to Galatea? It seems to me that his journey is in the same direction as Nemoroso's, and that just as Nemoroso desires to remove the distance that keeps him from Elisa, so Salicio leaves the "lugar" to Galatea and in so doing maintains the same distance from her that she herself has interposed by leaving him. The distance—and this is repeated over and over again—is that of death (4). Salicio's continual talk of approaching death can hardly be merely verbal, and it is certainly not an expedient to move to pity one whom he knows will no longer listen to him. The statement that he will abandon the "lugar" is a contained, desperately calm way of bidding farewell to life.

What the ideological structure leads us to discern finds its confirmation in the source. In Virgil's *Eighth Eclogue*, Damon ends with this cry:

Omnia vel medium fiant mare. Vivite, silvae;
Praeceps aerii specula de montis in undas
Deferar; extremum hoc munus morientis habeto.

[Let all become mid-ocean. Farewell, woods; headlong from some
towering mountain crag I will plunge into the waves; take this
as the last gift of a dying man, 58–60.]

And the same thing is said, once due weight has been given to the subtlety of allusion, in the close of Garcilaso's eclogue:

la sombra se veýa
venir corriendo apriessa
ya por la falda espessa
del altíssimo monte, y recordando
ambos como de sueño, y acabando
el fugitivo sol, de luz escaso
   su ganado llevando,
se fueron recogiendo passo a passo.

[The shadows could be seen now hurrying apace down the thick
slope of the highest mountain; and, both awaking as if from sleep
when the fleeting sun went down, they drove their flocks off in
the thin light and returned step by step homeward, 414–21.]

This similar movement of both shepherds toward the setting sun, while the lengthening shadows rise to cover them, is the image of their journey toward the kingdom of death.

Seven

Rectilinear and Spiral Constructions in *Don Quixote*

1. Unhurriedly but irresistibly, the lanky knight-errant Don Quixote rides down century after century, his rotund, proverb-spouting squire at his back. It is an image which dozens of painters, engravers, and theatrical producers have striven to capture, while philosophers, critics, and writers of all kinds have extolled the two symbols, one of blind faith in an ideal which no outrage or refutation can tarnish, the other of common sense and reality, solid if unlovely.

It is all too clear that the text of the novel itself is in contrast less with the elements of this stylization than with its one-sidedness; what are needed are definitions at once more detailed and less rigid. We even find, in defense of a free-floating figuration which has broken away from its matrix, the adoption of an expedient: Cervantes is presented as a guileless writer who is no match for his own character. In this way the immortal pair, knight and squire, are taken out of the incompetent hands of the writer and acquire, thanks to their enthusiastic interpreters, the right to an autonomous existence (Unamuno).

Critics have long since abandoned positions of this kind, at least at the level of consciousness. But the fact that Don Quixote and Sancho have been transformed into symbols, at whatever cost in simplification and distortion, does at least serve to place Cervantes among that tiny group of writers whose characters are immortal: from Shakespeare's Hamlet to Flaubert's Madame Bovary (other cases are more often those of adoption rather than paternity: from Oedipus through Tristan and Yseult down to Faust). Usage—as the dictionaries attest—pays no mean respect, classing "Don Quixote" as a common noun in various languages. The *O.E.D.* itself registers "quixotic," "quixotical," "quixotism," "quixoticism," "quixotry," and the verb "to quixotize" (in Spanish, along with "quijote," "quijotería," "quijotescamente," "quijotesco," and "quijotismo," we also find "sanchopancesco").

We must thus adopt for our reading a standpoint which will not detach the character from the novel (or, worse still, set him at loggerheads with it) but will allow us to take account of interpretations for which Cervantes's text itself furnishes some excuse. It will be even better if character and novel are found to be so complex as to require a multiplicity of careful approaches, even if these will necessarily leave unexplained that part of a work of art which constitutes its reserves of vitality.

Two preliminary assertions concern the nature of Cervantes's relation to his work and the forms to which it gives rise. On one hand there exists an extreme critical awareness, so marked that it makes *Don Quixote* a forerunner of the essay-novel; on the other, a method of composition which unfolds along the time axis with virtually no going back (in terms of reelaboration) over what is already written; this goes hand in hand with the absence of any overall plan and a readiness to disregard whatever partial plans there are. From these two assertions emerges the outline of a critical approach which, rather than fixing in advance the themes and structures of the book, will adjust its own development and reassessment to progressive elaboration, in a kind of feedback.

As far as the actual drafting of the novel is concerned, it is of considerable importance that its two parts are separated by an interval of ten years. In the first, after bringing Don Quixote home and entrusting him to his niece and the governess, Cervantes hints at a further "expedition" on the part of his hero, but the epitaphs and funeral verses for Don Quixote, Sancho, and Dulcinea convey an impression of closing the account. Furthermore, although he does allude to a continuation, with his Ariosto-like finale he does not seem to exclude the possibility that others will take it upon themselves to provide one: "Forse altri canterà con miglior plettro" ("perhaps others will sing with better plectrum").[1]

Ten years later, however, we find Cervantes putting the finishing touches to a second part of his novel, even larger than the first. In 1614 a certain Avellaneda had anticipated him and taken up the invitation of the first part to write a second—in competition and in disaccord with Cervantes. The second part of the authentic *Don Quixote* thus becomes not merely complement but defense and apology.

There is as well ample internal evidence in both parts to show that the drafting of the novel coincided with its structuring. We might note, for example, the different lengths of the first two "expeditions": chapters 2–5 and 7–52. Furthermore, in the first Don Quixote is not yet flanked by his deuteragonist and double, Sancho. Finally, he gives the impression of oscillating between two cultural stereotypes: romances of chivalry (which will subsequently dominate uncontested) and popular verse romances, which he adapts to fit his own adventures and with whose protagonists he identifies (a clue, as we shall see, to the stimulus given by a little-known *Entremés de los romances*). Some of the invariants of *Don Quixote* thus appear for the first time only in the second "expedition."

In the second part of the novel there is an equally evident turning point in the narrative. Its occasion is a polemical attitude to Avellaneda's *Don Quixote*: not only is this text made the object of a number of disparaging allusions; it further stimulates Cervantes to characterize his "true" Don Quixote by explicit contrast. This has tangible consequences for the plot as well: for Don Quixote, following a program laid down at 1.25 and confirmed at 2.4, 57, was to have attended a tournament at Saragossa; he changes his itinerary, however, when he learns that Saragossa has already been visited by Avellaneda's Don Quixote (2.59).

Avellaneda's imitation is referred to, and insistently (dedication and introduction, obviously enough, having been written last), only from chapter 59 on. This points unequivocally to a one-way technique of composition within which in all likelihood the disagreeable event has been registered in the form of an immediate reaction on the part of the writer. There was a further motive, too, for not going back over what had already been written—the need to publish the authentic second part as quickly as possible and thus block the diffusion of its competitor. The final chapters, as has frequently been pointed out, betray a sketchy, somewhat hectic mode of composition.

Once we have separated, as far as possible, the reactions of his characters from his own, in the relaxed atmosphere of the literary dialogue Cervantes informs us of his personal choices and the theoretical judgments elaborated for their support. The two longest episodes of this type of literary criticism (episodes because they are skillfully fitted in with Don Quixote's own adventures) are the inventory of the hero's library, drawn up by the parish priest and the barber in a (not wholly) facetious literary *auto da fé* (1.6), and the discussion between canon and parish priest while they carry home, shut up in a cage, the knight who is convinced that he is enchanted (1.47–48).

But the entire novel is shot through with literary discussion and judgment. Innkeepers and goatherds, fledgling scholars, maidens and near-maidens, all reveal their pleasing vices as readers and express, each in his own way, preferences and reactions; head and shoulders above them all is Don Quixote, who—apart from those moments in which he identifies directly with the heroes of his favorite books—expresses himself as a refined man of letters with regard to artistic problems and techniques and at times writes verse himself. In other words, *Don Quixote* can be made to yield (as Canavaggio and Riley in particular have shown) a wealth of theoretical assertions and explicit judgments.

This, however, is not enough to give us the measure of Cervantes's critical finesse. The passages just referred to show a writer well informed about sixteenth-century poetic theorizing, whose central problems (of Aristotelian origin) he maintains. But there can be few works, at least taken as a whole, further removed from the poetics they subscribe to. What needs investigation, then, is the degree to which Cervantes was conscious of a phase difference between his literary theory and his literary practice, to the advantage of the latter, with its extraordinarily modern approach.

This consciousness will emerge, rather than from explicit avowals, from a glance at the complex system of mediations which have been placed between the author and his work. The person who signs the dedications of both parts and who declares himself the author in their respective prologues (already inclined to present himself as "coauthor") appears as the compiler of contradictory traditions (1.1, 2), only to become in 1.8 the "second author" of a tale which the anonymous "first author" seems to have put together from still earlier writings. From 1.9 on there is fictitious recourse to the Arabic manuscript of a Cide Hamete Benengeli, a device which seems to have served its turn by the end of the first part (1.52), where there is some talk of adventures to come based on oral tradition, and where a conclusion is made with the epitaphs and encomiums found in yet another manuscript, that of the Academics of Argamasilla. Finally, in the second part Cide Hamete reemerges without explanation as the sole source of the text.

The expedient of a fictitious source, now called upon to bear (false) witness of veracity, now jokingly made to shoulder responsibility for affirmations of the incredible, has a long tradition in romances of chivalry (one remembers Turpino in the *Orlando furioso*), and elsewhere. But Cervantes has divined in the device a means not only of constructing a dividing interspace between himself and his tale but also of adapting this space to the scale of his motivations.

Long before the invention of Cide Hamete's manuscripts, when Don Quixote is still alone and without a history, he says to himself, "¡Oh, tú, sabio encantador, quienquiera que seas, a quien ha de tocar el ser coronista desta peregrina historia! Ruégote que no te olvides de mi buen Rocinante," etc. ("And thou, O sage magician, whoever thou art, to whom it shall fall to be the chronicler of this wondrous history, forget not, I entreat thee, my good Rocinante," etc., 1.2). Cide Hamete is thus evoked by the character even before he has come into action as "first author." We thus have a writer (Cervantes) who invents a character (Don Quixote) who invents an author (Cide Hamete) to serve as source of the author's (Cervantes's) work. And on several occasions (1.11, 21) it seems that Don Quixote's actions are or may well be influenced by initiatives of the author Cide Hamete.

This Borges-like construction allows Cervantes playfully to lay responsibility for what is recounted at the door of an infidel (who as such is not trustworthy—how many oaths in the name of Allah are we implicitly invited not to believe) and magician (who as such is custodian of information to which no mere mortal could aspire). Cide Hamete thus has at his disposal an immense range from credibility to unreliability, while the "second author," Cervantes, can pose at one moment as not directly responsible for what he relates and at another as a critic who calls in question or qualifies the affirmations of his source. This doubling of the writer shadows forth the crisis (= "separation," "choice," "judgment") between Renaissance and baroque. In the first person, Cervantes is spokesman for Renaissance poetics; disguised as Cide Hamete, he creates characters and events which are baroque in their feeling for violent contrast, in their calculated disharmony, in their sense of the transience of the real.

2. *Don Quixote* speaks not only of Don Quixote and Sancho. Both characters dominate the reader's attention and memory; but if we were to leave out of account the many chapters in which they do not appear, we would falsify the framework of the novel and (even more damagingly) its meaning. Taking stock of *Don Quixote's* structure is indispensable in order to understand what relations are established from part to part and the exigencies they are intended to meet.

In broad outline, *Don Quixote* is a brochette-structured novel, to use Shklovsky's term, frequently broken up by inserted narrative episodes which are at times extraneous to the plot, at times grafted onto it. They are insertions which constitute vertical sections, as it were, within the serial horizontal character of the adventures of knight and squire. The way in which these episodes are inserted varies: we move from the technique of the "discovered manuscript" (the case of the *Curioso impertinente,* 1.33–35) to that of the tale recounted by the insert's protagonist (the *Historia del cautivo*, 1.39–41), or in a succession of separate episodes by the protagonists (Cardenio, 1.24, 27, and Dorotea, 1.28) or by a narrator (the history of Marcela, 1.12–13).

The different manner of actuating these insertions is naturally enough the result of deliberate *variatio*, but it is no less related to the possibility that their characters may take part in the main plot. Such participation may be merely fortuitous (they call forth the madness or, it may be, the wisdom of Don Quixote, enriching and exemplifying these qualities in greater depth), or it may be substantial (as with Dorotea, who accepts readily enough the role of Micomicona); it may even be nonexistent (the *Curioso impertinente*). This is a structural problem to which Cervantes must have devoted much thought, as appears from what is said at 2:44:

> Dicen que en el propio original desta historia se lee que llegando Cide Hamete a escribir este capítulo, no le tradujo su intérprete como él le había escrito, que fué un modo de queja que tuvo el moro de sí mismo por haber tomado entre manos una historia tan seca y tan limitada como esta de don Quijote, por parecerle que siempre había de hablar dél y de Sancho, sin osar estenderse a otras digresiones y episodios más graves y más entretenidos; y decía que el ir siempre atenido el entendimiento, la mano y la pluma a escribir de un solo sujeto y hablar por las bocas de pocas personas era un trabajo incomportable, cuyo fruto no redundaba en el de su autor, y que por huir deste inconveniente había usado en la primera parte del artificio de algunas novelas, como fueron la del *Curioso impertinente* y la del *Capitan cautivo*, que están como separadas de la historia, puesto que las demás que allí se cuentan son casos sucedidos al mismo don Quijote, que no podían dejar de escribirse. También pensó, como él dice, que muchos, llevados de la atención que piden las hazañas de don Quijote, no la darían a las novelas, y pasarían por ellas, o con priesa, o con enfado, sin advertir la gala y artificio que en sí contienen, el cual se mostrara bien al descubierto cuando por sí solas, sin arrimarse a las locuras de don Quijote ni a las sandeces de Sancho, salieran a luz; y así, en esta segunda parte no quiso ingerir novelas sueltas ni pegadizas, sino algunos episodios que lo pareciesen, nacidos de los mesmos sucesos que la verdad ofrece, y aun éstos, limitadamente y con solas las palabras que bastan a declararlos; y pues se contiene y cierra en los estrechos límites de la narración, teniendo habilidad, suficiencia y entendimiento para tratar del universo todo, pide no se desprecie su trabajo, y se le den alabanzas no por lo que escribe, sino por lo que ha dejado de escribir.

[It is stated, they say, in the true original of this history, that
when Cid Hamet came to write this chapter, his interpreter did not
translate it as he wrote it—that is, as a kind of complaint the Moor
made against himself for having taken in hand a story so dry and
of so little variety as this of Don Quixote, for he found himself forced
to speak perpetually of him and Sancho, without venturing to
indulge in digressions and episodes more serious and more interesting.
He said, too, that to go on, mind, hand, and pen always restricted
to writing upon one single subject, and speaking through the mouths
of a few characters, was intolerable drudgery, the result of which
was never equal to the author's labor, and that to avoid this he had
in the First Part availed himself of the device of novels, like *The
Ill-advised Curiosity* and *The Captive Captain*, which stand, as it
were, apart from the story; the others that are given there being
incidents which occurred to Don Quixote himself and could not be
omitted. He also thought, he says, that many, engrossed by the
interest attaching to the exploits of Don Quixote, would take none
in the novels, and pass them over hastily or impatiently without
noticing the elegance and art of their composition, which would be
very manifest were they published by themselves and not as mere
adjuncts to the crazes of Don Quixote or the simplicities of Sancho.
Therefore in this Second Part he thought it best not to insert novels,
either separate or interwoven, but only episodes, something like
them, arising out of the circumstances the facts present; and even
these sparingly, and with no more words than suffice to make them
plain; and as he confines and restricts himself to the narrow limits
of the narrative, though he has ability, capacity, and brains enough
to deal with the whole universe, he requests that his labors may not
be despised, and that credit be given him, not for what he writes,
but for what he has refrained from writing.]

It is a fact that in the second part the episodes are shorter and all
closely linked to the main plot—thus the *Bodas de Camacho* (2.20–
21), the narration of Doña Rodríguez (2.48), the histories of Claudia
Jerónima (2.9) and Ana Félix (2.65), and the innocent escapade of
Don Diego's daughter (2.49). On the other hand, the second part reveals the first lengthy separation of Don Quixote and Sancho, during
the whole episode of Sancho as governor (2.45–53).

There has been some talk of possible relations between *Don
Quixote* and picaresque novels. The answer, highly uncertain if borrowings at the content level are sought, must be affirmative when attention is given to structure. *Don Quixote* resembles a picaresque novel in
the virtually infinite, open-ended, serial nature of its episodes (brochette

construction); in the way in which it is presented as an itinerary through contemporary society, particularly at the level of the lower classes (and we have the tavern, the servant girl of easy virtue, convicts, swineherds, and so on); in the constant "search for employment," which in the case of Don Quixote is transformed into a "quest for heroic undertakings." It was along the lines of the relatively slight idea of the initial "expedition" that Cervantes was able to develop the tale horizontally and to take up its narration after ten years, this time ensuring its undoubted conclusion with the death of the protagonist, so that no one would be led to take it up yet again with a third, fourth, or *n*th part.

On the other hand, the technique of inserting episodes derives from poems of chivalry (and I might mention once again the *Orlando furioso*, for it is from Ariosto that the tale of the *Curioso impertinente* in fact derives). Such episodes are more likely to be fully integrated into the narrative the less predominant in them is the role of the protagonist. In extreme instances we have a technique of interweaving (*entrelacement*), which builds a whole mosaic out of a plurality of events which have the same functional quotient.

With *Don Quixote* we are at the opposite extreme. The history of knight and squire maintains its linearity, which the inserted episodes may stop short but not sidetrack. The episodes may be hung along the thread of the tale, but they are not twisted into it. Only rarely do the episode characters cross Don Quixote's path a second time, and even more rarely are the consequences appreciable when they do. Parity of alternation—a dovetailing technique—appears only on the very few occasions when Don Quixote and Sancho are separated (1.26–29, 2.44–53), and it creates problems for both.

If the inserted tales are not functional to the plot of the novel, they are functional on the thematic level. There is no need to go into sixteenth-century disquisitions on literary genres to remark at once that all these inserts have one element in common, love, and that they belong almost exclusively to the pastoral or sentimental genre (the exception is the prisoner's history, which is an adventure story). A first approximation, which will immediately prove useful, might be the following observation: all these love stories fill the vacuum at the level of feeling created by Don Quixote's totally fantastic cerebral cult of Dulcinea.

Don Quixote's conception of love, in fact, goes far beyond what has been called the courtly love paradox, where invocations are made on the understanding that they will go unsatisfied and indeed are the more exalted and inspired as the loved one is more distant, unattainable, or even of doubtful existence (which is precisely the case with Dulcinea del Toboso). Don Quixote, unlike the greater part of the novel's characters, excludes with almost monastic rigor any concession to courtliness whatsoever. The same extremism appears in his conception of adventure: it must be disinterested and inspired by love of glory alone.

Thus Cervantes felt the need to lead Don Quixote on his one-sided spiritual itinerary through the midst of characters and events which represent fairly extensive areas of narrative invention, at least as it was codified in his time. Don Quixote's gaze is steadfastly fixed on the goals he dreams of, while those of the characters in the episodes no less persistently move over persons and things; Don Quixote's feeling is as immovable in its self-sufficiency as the feelings of the others are inclined to bursts of passion, gratitude, revenge; the needle of Don Quixote's compass points to his unattainable north while that of the others swings wildly under the influence of impulse, situation, and more or less fortuitous events.

It would be easy enough to show how the pastoral genre (and its sentimental variant) corresponded to the literary ideals of the Renaissance with the unremitting conventionality of its situations and developments and its fiction of masking the usually well-to-do young as shepherds inclined to declamation and poetic improvisation. It offered a happy utopia of rural life, simplicity of feeling, poetry lived or at least livable. It was the most organic proposal for realization of the courtly conceptions which had been elaborated by the troubadours, Petrarch, and his sixteenth-century followers.

The Arcadian fiction gave concrete form to that taste for decorum, for nobility of taste and of verbal expression, quintessentially expressed by the theorists in accordance with the aspirations of the more refined circles. The subtle distinction between truth and verisimilitude which assigned the second only to narrative literature offered a solidly based justification for the pastoral genre. How far Cervantes himself shared this particular conception is evident from the fact that he was the author of a *Galatea*, oriented toward Neoplatonizing allegory though it is, and never entirely abandoned the idea of composing a second part for it.

We might say then that the narrative inserts express the exigencies of reality, however difficult this may seem for the modern reader to accept, far removed as he is from the literary conventions of the sixteenth century and predisposed to react negatively when faced with artificiality of framework and plot—able at most to enjoy no more than elegance of style and the striking particular.

It is enough to observe that if the novel unfolds on two different planes, one of quixotic unreality and the other of reality itself (indeed implying a gentleman's agreement between writer and reader about veracity), then the characters of the episodes rightly belong to the plane of reality as established by the author: so true is this that Dorotea participates in the harmless conspiracy which is to lead the hero back into the fold.

The inserts are placed in the novel to represent still a further reality, that of social depth. Don Quixote, poor *hidalgo* and false knight, and the peasant Sancho are flanked in the inserts by representatives of the nobility, landowners, administrators, clerics. It should be noted that, were the episodes left aside, in the first part of *Don Quixote* the knight would meet for the most part only persons whose social standing and education are inferior to his own. For this reason too, the inserts are less vital in the second part, where personages of considerable social status—the duke and then Don Antonio Moreno—monopolize the Knight of the Rueful Countenance at length and intervene decisively in events concerning him. In this second part aristocratic society does not need to go to Don Quixote; Don Quixote comes to them and accepts their hospitality and, unfortunately, their terms too.

3. But the reality of these insertions has yet an additional function. *Don Quixote* is a sort of gallery of the literary genres of its epoch: the romance of chivalry, however parodistic an approach, which consists in part in recourse to patterns typical of the picaresque novel; and the pastoral genre, the adventure story, the *novella*, and the literary dialogue. Nor should the love lyric be forgotten, for it is a common element in both the insertions and Don Quixote's own adventures (while examples of the folk genre of the *romances* are found in these last alone).

The whole history of the romance/novel genre may be seen as a series of attempts to mix various types of novel: first the Arthurian with the Charlemagne cycle, then the romance of chivalry and the Byzantine novel with the sentimental novel and the Arcadian romance. In the case of *Don Quixote* this mixture is less a solution than a suspension which leaves its components unaltered; Cervantes has ably arranged the sequences belonging to different genres without allowing either contamination or reconciliation of their characteristic traits. It is the nature of Don Quixote himself which calls for the combination instead of fusion of literary genres.

Don Quixote's position with respect to reality centrifuges the noblest and the most vulgar elements that coexist within it. The protagonist chases after chimerae, after impracticable ideals, and releases from every situation or environment, almost as an equal and opposite reaction, its prosaic aspects, its triviality. Don Quixote's idealism might be looked at as an uncommonly effective stimulation toward realism. The stage of each of his undertakings is the distance between the two extremes; the hero's defeat lies in an awareness, constantly removed, of how very short in his case that distance is.

Recourse to other literary genres aims meanwhile at neutralizing the noble/vulgar opposition, in the sense that it creates a literary climate within which tonal excursions are more contained; reality is stylized along a register of moderate elevation, where the feelings under which it is entirely subsumed constitute a fixed system whose predisposition avoids disorganization and banality. Feelings, good or evil, float ever higher above the unadorned and rugged earth; and they can drift readily enough from negative to positive.

This in all likelihood is the calculation Cervantes made, in full accordance with Renaissance poetics. But Cervantes is a bifrontal author: had he trusted only to the dictates of his speculations as critic, he would have written the *Galatea* and the *Persiles,* certainly not *Don Quixote.* What characterizes Cervantes's method of working is a dialectic between brilliant insights and careful calculation, between free invention and critical control. Calculation and control belong to the realm of the already acquired, of the codified, of the Renaissance in decline; intuitions and inventions can already head directly toward the impending baroque.

For this reason the mad knight provides the writer with more powerful, indeed overwhelming stimuli than the characters in the insertions can supply: Don Quixote moves in a space from which madness withdraws precision of confines and rigor of control. It is a space within which the comic and the grotesque run riot (extraneous as they are to Renaissance conceptions of harmony, which admitted at most a smile of ironic superiority), where figures lose their natural contours, and in which there erupts a new feeling for landscape.

Intuitions, I suggested; but they are intuitions which Cervantes has organized and institutionalized. It is significant that in the second part, while the reduction of the insertions ensures a preponderant role for Don Quixote, the deformation of reality is no longer put down exclusively to the knight's madness but is also the result of the often cruel fantasy of those he deals with. It is as if the deformation of reality, from the outset the fruit of a sick mind, has at this stage become a repeatable and definable act.

Thus it is that in the course of composition Cervantes has discovered a new measure of things; he has registered it, but without making it his own. If we prefer, we may say that he has sent his hero to scout out the new territory and has put the results of his experience to use, but without participating in it. The spiral pattern we found in relations among the writer, his character, the "first author" (Cide Hamete), and the work reappears here in relations among reality, likelihood, dream, and invention of new reality. We thus have two clearly related spiral forms which allow multiplication of perspectives and hidden surveillance. Only by safeguarding his own wisdom (as writer as well) was Cervantes able to recount Don Quixote's madness; only by holding fast to a Renaissance poetic could he render effective his baroque visions, leading them where he would.

4. But the moment has come to discuss Don Qixote's madness. As to its genesis, Cervantes leaves us in no doubt: after so many years spent reading romances of chivalry, "del poco dormir y del mucho leer se le secó el celebro, de manera, que vino a perder el juicio. Llenósele la fantasía de todo aquello que leía en los libros, así de encantamentos como de pendencias, batallas, desafíos, heridas, requiebros, amores, tormentas y disparates imposibles; y asentósele de tal modo en la imaginación que era verdad toda aquella máquina de aquellas sonadas soñadas invenciones que leía, que para él no había historia más cierta en el mundo" ("what with little sleep and much reading his brains got so dry that he lost his wits. His fancy grew full of what he used to read about in his books, enchantments, quarrels, battles, challenges, wounds, wooings, loves, agonies, and all sorts of impossible nonsense; and it so possessed his mind that the whole fabric of invention and fancy he read of was true, that to him no history in the world had more reality in it," 1.1).

In condemning his protagonist to madness, Cervantes thus actuates a definite polemical program, for which he will give detailed justification in the two critically oriented episodes I have referred to (the examination of the library and the conversation between canon and curate). His target was a controversy which was particularly relevant in the years 1605–15, given the enduring popularity of the chivalric romance, a consumer product despite its links with medieval ideals and conventions (by now anachronistic), and given also the frequently expressed condemnations in the name of good taste and even of religion itself.

The motives of Cervantes's own disapproval of romances of chivalry can be reduced, not without simplification, to two: the disregard of their authors for the Aristotelian norm of verisimilitude and the far-fetched character of their style. In other words, they offend against reality of events and discourses (against likelihood, harmony, and decorum). Erasmus, whom subtle ties link to Cervantes, expressed concepts similar to these. But Cervantes's attitude is hedged in with careful qualification: many examples of chivalric literature are found to be blameless and are even commended after a mock trial. These are works which have taken on a particular historical value and which conform, positively or negatively (by virtue of the slightness of the infractions), to the paradigms of Cervantes's own predilections.

And since the condemnation of chivalric literature is not all-embracing, Don Quixote's infatuation is neither isolated nor exceptional. The whole romance is one long procession of enthusiasts of the genre, from the bibliophile host, only less credulous than Don Quixote himself (1.32); to Ginés de Pasamonte, the puppet master (2.26); to the ecclesiastical critics, the curate and the canon, who show that they are absolute experts in the field. Don Quixote's fault, then, is not that he reads books of chivalry but that he believes them. Even more, he believes that the adventures they tell of are still possible.

In his madness, Don Quixote has models (the heroes of the romances) and behavior patterns (their achievements). As far as the models are concerned, he oscillates between identification and emulation, always keeping his attention fixed on the noblest, most generous, most perfect and most enamored of knights—Lancelot and Amadis of Gaul; the patterns they provide serve for the decisions he must make in relation to situations, but they serve even more to *create* situations.

It has been said that *Don Quixote*, in parodying romances of chivalry, ends up being a romance of chivalry itself. This is not a contradiction but a logical consequence of the undertaking: Don Quixote holds in his mind all the principal stereotypes of chivalric action; it is enough for reality to provide a single trait (or its appearance) for him to announce the presence of the whole stereotype and behave accordingly. Instead of an "imitation of Christ," an a priori pattern for so many lives of the saints, Don Quixote seeks to put into effect an "imitation of the perfect knight." It is here that we find the deepest motivation of the brochette structure. In the life of a knight-errant an event is conditioned by the personality of the hero and by his developments in relation to his surroundings, while in the life of Don Quixote there is a well-defined intention—to exhaust, as in an "imitation of Christ," the entire range of possibilities for a knight-errant's adventures, where these are considered as given from the outset. Their order thus becomes purely arbitrary.

It is no less an encounter between a personality and a series of situations than a list of "possibilities" from which one progressively crosses off those which have chanced to reveal an appearance of realization.

Each "possibility" is an episode which has as its point of reference not those which precede or come after it but, rather, the romances assimilated and unified by Don Quixote. Don Quixote really has made a formalization of chivalric "possibilities"; he gives one example when he tells Sancho (1.21) a series of episodes which are typical of a knight's life. These take on color as they go along, they connect, proliferate, and come very near to being something that has actually taken place. The possibility of changing the order of the episodes about is pointed out by Cervantes himself, with his usual acumen (1.2).

Here we come to the heart of the matter, the basis of Cervantes's contention. What he stigmatizes is less the passion for books of chivalry than the confusion of literature with life. Romances of chivalry, insofar as they are romances of action, have a considerable potential for mystifying their readers; but his madness would have been no different had Don Quixote taken too seriously, for example, pastoral romances. This is no mere hypothesis: Don Quixote declares over and over that he is or has been tempted by the idea of becoming a shepherd in love rather than a knight-errant. Hence the book's universal appeal, an appeal no outdated controversy would have permitted.

Don Quixote is soaked in literature. He knows whole romances of chivalry by heart; he has even tried his hand at writing them, and he continues to compose love poetry; he lives to relive the adventures of a knight-errant and sees himself as a potential character of romance. While waiting for a historian to make him immortal, he is his own historian:

> ¿Quién duda, sino que en los venideros tiempos, cuando salga a luz la veradera historia de mis famosos hechos, que el sabio que los escribiere no ponga, cuando llegue a contar esta mi primera salida tan de mañana, desta manera?: "Apenas había el rubicundo Apolo tendido por la faz de la ancha y espaciosa tierra las doradas hebras de sus hermosos cabellos, y apenas los pequeños y pintados pajarillos con sus arpadas lenguas habían saludado con dulce y meliflua armonía la venida de la rosada Aurora . . . cuando el famoso caballero Don Quijote del la Mancha, dejando las ociosas plumas, subió sobre su famoso caballo Rocinante, y comenzó a caminar por el antiguó y conocido campo de Montiel."

> [Who knows but that in time to come, when the veracious history of my famous deeds is made known, the sage who writes it, when he has to set forth my first sally in the early morning, will do it after this fashion? "Scarce had the rubicund Apollo spread o'er the face of the broad spacious earth the golden threads of his bright hair,

scarce had the little birds of painted plumage attuned their notes to
hail with dulcet and mellifluous harmony the coming of the rosy
Dawn . . . when the renowned knight Don Quixote of La Mancha,
quitting the lazy down, mounted his celebrated steed Rocinante
and began to traverse the ancient and famous Campo de Montiel,"
1.2.]

Not only is literature taken for life; it even takes precedence over life.
Don Quixote has hardly left home when he exclaims, "Dichosa edad y
siglo dichoso aquel adonde saldrán a luz las famosas hazañas mías,
dignas de entallarse en bronces, esculpirse en mármoles y pintarse en
tablas, para memoria en lo futuro" ("Happy the age, happy the time . . .
in which shall be made known my deeds of fame, worthy to be moulded
in brass, carved in marble, limned in pictures, for a memorial forever,"
ibid.). This is not overweening self-confidence: Don Quixote's whole
history will be a comparison of the novel to be written and that actually
written by the facts, for the latter is failure.

Confusing literature with life means in fact confusing the ideal with
its material explication, the motive with the gesture, the scope with its
celebration. And Don Quixote, who proclaims the defense of the weak
and the persecuted, the struggle for justice, the religious soldiering of
chivalry, merely aggravates the sufferings of those he defends, violates
the laws of civil society, and risks the rigors of the Inquisition. Impa-
tient to run through the chapters of his "imitation," he does not reflect
on its legitimacy or on the consequences of his actions in the precise context in which they unfold.

Hence Cervantes's ambivalent attitude toward his hero. He can hardly
not share Don Quixote's heroic and generous dream; but he considers it
a form of madness (i.e., alienation from reality) that one should look to
literary models for the means of actuation that time, place, and opportunity ought rather to suggest. The things Don Quixote believes in are
in no sense ridiculous; indeed they are distinctly noble. However, what
he lacks is a capacity for measuring them against reality so as to win
them back from sterile canonization, rendering them feasible and vital.

The original idea grew in Cervantes's mind together with an awareness that the split personality of Don Quixote (sane in all that does not
involve chivalry) allowed him to move through yet another of his beloved spiral discourses: this time a literary discourse on the limits of
literature. This is conducted in such a way that it ends up celebrating—
through the work itself—the unending expansion of the limits themselves. Because if *Don Quixote*, with its insertions, embraces the idea of
literature as escape into verisimilitude (linking up with a more elabo-

rated strand of Cervantes's narrative, from *Galatea* to *Persiles*), it also consecrates with its central action the idea of literature as escape into the unreal and, for this very reason, as conquest of new narrative realities (thereby bringing to fruition intuitions and "discoveries" of the *novelas ejemplares*).

It would seem that the type of madness with which Don Quixote is stricken was fairly frequent: Don Francisco of Portugal, Melchor Cano, Alonso de Fuentes, El Pinciano, and Don Luis de Zapata tell anecdotes of persons who were overcredulous about romances of chivalry, who were at times deluded into imitating their heroes. The immediate forerunner (echoed directly at certain points) seems to have been the *Entremés de los romances*, in which a poor peasant, Bartolo, by dint of reading romances gets it into his head that he is a knight, and abandoning his newly wedded wife, he sets out on adventures of his own imagining, ending up each time in humiliating and ridiculous circumstances. He applies to himself particular passages of the romances and identifies with the protagonists in exactly the same way as Don Quixote, who takes over expressions and attitudes of Lancelot and Amadis (but he too, particularly at the beginning of his adventures, has recourse to episodes from the romances).

It would be simple-minded to look to psychiatry (although it has been done) for a definition of the hidalgo's mental illness. What matters are the manifestations which the writer attributes to the madness in question. Since these vary as the story proceeds, any attempt at clinical definition would find itself coinciding with a diagram of the inventive processes themselves and the different phases of the book's structuring.

A fundamental fact, repeated as a leitmotiv by all those who come into contact with Don Quixote or who speak of him, is the "specialization" of his madness: informed, wise, judicious, shrewd, little short of a master is Don Quixote, as long as there is no question of chivalry. It is chivalric romances which have exalted him to the point of inspiring in him the program of reviving knight-errantry. Hence the desultory progression: Don Quixote in his right mind, who rushes headlong into insanity under the stimulus of any kind of allusion to the themes or characters of chivalry, Don Quixote who turns back to the high road of good sense the moment his interest deviates from those areas which constitute a danger to his reason. This segmentation reflects over shorter stretches that of the episodes in their linear succession.

On the other hand, it may be asked (and legitimately, as long as the answer remains in the terrain of literature) whether Cervantes wished to attribute to his hero a pathological madness, uncontrollable at least during its attacks, or (as Madariaga and Maldonado de Guevara propose) a more subtly nuanced and ambiguous form. Critical opinion is almost at one in resisting the second hypothesis, encouraged as it is by the indomitable persistence of a symbolic image of Don Quixote, venerable for his blind faith in the ideal or ridiculous in having forced this ideal to measure up to a (however triumphantly) shabby reality.

I believe, however, that Don Quixote's madness is to a considerable extent flawed and unstable; that his faith is primarily a strong will to believe. Many indications of this forced nature of his madness show through right from the beginning; we might take as their synthesis "Yo pienso, y es así verdad" ("I think, and it is the truth") which precedes an almost programmatic statement on Don Quixote's part (1.8). The veracity of the assertion rests on the subjective nature of the conviction, hence it is transformed into a consequence. And what does Don Quixote say to the merchants of Toledo who ask for proof of Dulcinea's superhuman beauty? Something that in all probability corresponds to the solution he has found for his own inner doubts: "Si os la mostrara ¿qué hiciérades vosotros en confesar una verdad tan notoria? La importancia está en que sin verla lo habéis de creer, confesar, afirmar, jurar y defender" ("If I were to show her to you, . . . what merit would you have in confessing a truth so manifest? The essential point is that without seeing her you must believe, confess, affirm, swear, and defend it," 1.4).

It is clear that the will to believe is held in check by the objective obstacle, by reality. The greatest victory Don Quixote wins is thus the somnambulist duel with the wine skins, torn to shreds by the sword blows the knight believes he has administered to an evil giant (1.35). This is a special case; as a rule, Don Quixote has to beat a retreat and adopt far-fetched justifications, suggested for the most part by Sancho, tacitly recognizing thereby the limited range of his will to believe. But he also invents a specific logical technique for inverting the illusion/ reality relation: the hypothesis of the enchanter. It is not the knight who has confused (or wished to confuse) windmills and giants; it is the envious enchanter who has made giants appear as windmills (1.8). It is not the knight's imagination that enlarges and ennobles reality; it is the enchanter who shrinks and mortifies it. Not even this unexceptionable account keeping can be considered the working of a benighted mind; it is rather, perhaps, a delirium that is in the last resort desperate.

And perhaps Cervantes has tried to put us on the right track with the episode of the Sierra Morena (1.23–25). Cardenio moves almost as a mirror image or an anticipation of Don Quixote. He too suffers from a madness which alternates with long periods of sanity; he too participates passionately in vicissitudes derived from chivalric romances: he lives among rocks in a savage condition, as will the knight at a certain point, in imitation of Orlando and Amadis of Gaul. But Cardenio's madness is really blinding, bestial; that of Don Quixote is madness of the second degree, lucid, reasoning—a product of predetermined decision rather than unaccountable mood. Sancho's common sense declares, "Todo esto es fingido y cosa contrahecha y de burlas" ("The whole thing is feigned and counterfeit and in joke"). A sophistical will to believe leads Don Quixote to reply, "Todas estas cosas que hago no son de burlas sino muy de veras" ("All these things I am doing are not in joke but very much in earnest,"and "de veras" means "believing in them," not "driven by ungovernable fury").

In the second part we are faced with admitted mystification if we are prepared to take in this sense a remark which escapes the knight after the adventure of Clavileño: to Sancho, who describes with unbridled imagination the seven kids (the Pleiades) which he has seen in his astral ride, Don Quixote whispers, "Sancho, pues vos queréis que se os crea lo que habéis visto en el cielo, yo quiero que vos me creáis a mí lo que vi en la cueva de Montesinos. Y no os digo más" ("Sancho, as you would have us believe what you saw in heaven, I require you to believe me as to what I saw in the cave of Montesinos; I say no more," 2.41).

But it is a mystification suffered to the end, for it corresponds to a pathetic search for external confirmation of a declining faith that is withering away. There is no presumption but, rather, a shiver of uncertainty in the question Don Quixote puts to the enchanted head: "Dime tú, el que respondes: ¿Fué verdad, o fué sueño lo que yo cuento que me pasó en la cueva de Montesinos?" ("Tell me, thou that answerest, was that which I describe as having happened to me in the cave of Montesinos the truth or a dream?" 2.62). In fact he is calmed after a reply that is anything but clear-cut: "A lo de la cueva hay mucho que decir: de todo tiene" ("As to the question of the cave, . . . there is much to be said; there is something of both in it"). In addition, Cervantes has Cide Hamete say quite brutally of the Montesinos adventure, "Se tiene por cierto que al tiempo de su fin y muerte dicen[2] que se retrató della y dijo que él la había inventado, por parecerle que convenía y cuadraba bien con las aventuras que había leído en sus historias" ("Though certain it is they say that at the time of his death he retracted and said he had invented it, thinking it matched and tallied with the adventures he had read of in his histories," 2.24). In any event the episode of Montesinos brings us to the second part of the romance, and this calls for a separate discussion. The change Don Quixote has undergone when he reappears after ten years is quite marked, for he rides the wave of the first part's success. In the first part of the book, adventures arise as a rule out of a meeting between an occasion-stimulus and the imagination of the hero who, on the basis of a single trait, believes he divines an entire, nonexistent Gestalt he then enters into. The schematization of situations typical of romances of chivalry turns Don Quixote into an inventor of situations; the setback is predetermined by the absolute incompatibility of the real and the literary situation. In the first part, Don Quixote at least passes from exaltation to a meditated engagement to remedy the consequences. His pride may be more or less fierce, but he never feels (or confesses to feeling) that it has been wounded; his language, reflecting all his variations of mood, is in admirable alternation noble or subdued, studied or inspired, didactic or captious.

The first part of *Don Quixote* is the story of how the hero does *not* become the hero of a romance of chivalry; but it is also the story of the birth of a hero of romance: Cervantes's romance. The context of the second part is radically altered by this element: all the characters, including the protagonist himself, know of the existence of the first part of the book. Don Quixote's new vicissitudes, presented as authentic, are influenced by a literary knowledge of earlier authentic events. We thus have the impact on life of two types of book: books of chivalry (false), dominating the intelligence and actions of Don Quixote, and the romance of Cervantes (truthful, historical) which has popularized the image of the knight—meanwhile changing both the environment in which he moves and the knight himself.

The first part of the romance, in short, has provided an objective recognition of that form of self-development which the succession of adventures had brought about. Now Don Quixote is sure of himself; he is what he has made himself and is, thanks to the book's circulation, a character. No longer do we find improvisation and caprices of fancy: Don Quixote speaks and acts in a way that enriches and perfects the traits of a character, and he does so with dignified awareness. His language too has now become more sure of itself; it is more even and moves through a whole range of tones, elevated if somewhat restricted. His is a self-control which not even madness can escape. And as the madness which is portrayed in this book is a transfiguring madness, Don Quixote no longer seems capable of transforming reality as he earlier did: taverns are no longer castles, herds of bulls or swine are no longer enemy armies, and the strokes of the lash which are to free Dulcinea from enchantment are paid for in hard cash.

The decline in Don Quixote's inventiveness is compensated for by the machinations of others. If the success of the romance means that everyone immediately recognizes the Knight of the Rueful Countenance and restrains their reactions to his oddities, there does seem to be insinuated in the minds of those who have to do with him the idea of putting his madness to use, as an amusement. The social elevation of the hero—in the second part he moves amidst noble and luxurious surroundings—has as its counterpart his involuntary participation in a nonstop party game, where he plays the flattered and petted laughing stock. It is no longer Don Quixote's imagination which creates different realities but that of his interlocutors which stages them for him. In the first part Don Quixote gulls himself; in the second he is gulled. The parabola from transfiguring madness to organized heterogeneous madness thus traces a narrative arc made up of the novel's first and second parts.

If this approach is tenable, the mythical personage (the knight of the ideal) and the comic character (the poor hidalgo concocting impracticable heroisms) must give place to a more tragic figure. For he is no less tragic in terms of the unfolding of his history. Not only is his will to believe repeatedly deluded and frustrated; at a certain point it even begins to wilt and dry up. And since Don Quixote's moral stature increases in proportion to the decrease of his will, the resonance is all the greater as the setback comes closer to being admitted.

In the first part imagination and a full joy in the mission to be carried out prevail over the eternally negative outcome of Don Quixote's undertakings. He rises again each time he is knocked down and proceeds unbowed toward ever new destinies. A lively dialectic is established between imagination and reality, even for the hero, for in however tangled a fashion, he is aware of it. But in the second part, we have a meeting between a complicated imagination, presumptuously scenographic (that of the hosts), and the last glimmerings of the knight's own imagination, predetermined and in substance mortified by the first.

Don Quixote's (third and last) setting forth is already surrounded with the shadows of illusion: the adulation and encouragement of Sansón Carrasco form an intricate net to ensnare the Knight of the Rueful Countenance. In addition, the pay which Sancho asks for and which Don Quixote wearily concedes, together with the frequent need to recognize the contractual function of money, constitute a surrender to practical considerations which earlier had been boldly ignored. But the tone of the second part is indicated cruelly from the very first adventure, the search for Dulcinea. On one hand there is Don Quixote, who recognizes at last, "En todos los días de mi vida no he visto a la sin par Dulcinea, ni jamás atravesé los umbrales de su palacio" ("I have never once in my life seen the peerless Dulcinea or crossed the threshold of her palace," 2.9); on the other, Sancho, who tries his hand at stage managing the knight's imagination, presenting him with a false Dulcinea and false handmaidens; Don Quixote cannot see in them anything other than what he does in fact see: rude peasant girls, and far from attractive at that.

The final "expedition" thus begins with the recognition of a check, which still rankles in the words pronounced shortly after: "Aunque en mi alma tienen su propio asiento las tristezas, las desgracias y las desventuras, no por eso se ha ahuyentado della la compasión que tengo de las ajenas desdichas" ("Though sorrows, misfortunes, and calamities have made my heart their abode, the compassion I feel for the misfortunes of others has not been thereby banished from it," 2.12). It ends with the most bitter humiliation, defeat in a duel, and Don Quixote's acceptance that he is "el más desdichado caballero de la tierra" ("the most unfortunate knight on earth"), with a request for death, now honor has been lost (2.64). The herd of swine that tramples Don Quixote and Sancho seems a materialization of this shame: "Esta afrenta es pena de mi pecado, y justo castigo del cielo es que a un caballero andante vencido le coman adivas, y le piquen avispas, y le hollen puercos" ("This insult is the penalty of my sin; and it is the righteous chastisement of heaven that jackals should devour a vanquished knight, and wasps sting him and pigs trample him under foot," 2.68). Only a few chapters earlier, knocked down by a herd of bulls, Don Quixote had come out with an expression worthy of a mystic: "Yo nací para vivir muriendo" ("I was born, Sancho, to live dying," 2.59).

But it is the adventure with the lions which most clearly displays Don Quixote's new tragic dimension. To the truly "inaudito animo" of the knight, who coolly faces a wild and famished beast without illusions or delusions, the lion reacts merely by stretching and yawning and finally, showing Don Quixote his rump, turns and lies down at the back of his cage(2.17). Don Quixote and the trembling onlookers talk of moral victory; but his failure to fight the lion symbolizes the impossibility of a dynamic contact, the closing of the world to the solicitations of the unfortunate knight. For it is not just success which is denied him but the process itself which would lead him to it.

5. Don Quixote and Sancho are closely linked in a complementary relationship. Sancho's common sense serves for some as a contrast to

Don Quixote's madness, while for others Don Quixote's madness is re-produced in Sancho on a more humble level (knight and squire would thus be tonal variants of a single prototype). Case by case, either of these interpretations is acceptable. What is important is precisely the fact that they can be interchanged—a confirmation on a combinatory level of the alternative nature of the two characters.

In general, if Don Quixote moves along a line of madness-wisdom, Sancho moves along a parallel line of credulity–common sense. Even limiting ourselves to these extreme polarizations, we thus have a four-fold possibility of combination, and these will be considerably multi-plied when all the intermediary stages are taken into account. What re-mains constant in Sancho, however, is a tendency to concretize things: as a rule his outbursts of imagination regard the concrete advantages of governing the island Don Quixote has promised him, and his common sense does not lose sight of egoism, fraud, or venality.

But any definition of Sancho, even more than in the case of Don Quixote, must take into account the way his personality develops throughout the book. There is, first and foremost, a sort of imitation on the part of the squire—Sancho's "quixotizing." Not only does he assimi-late the language and the codes of chivalry in his own way, to the point of being able to put together after a certain period delightful pastiches of noble style and elucidate to his own advantage the laws of chivalry (Don Quixote's title, "The Knight of the Rueful Countenance," derives from him, 1.19); he also takes to himself Don Quixote's own interpretative mechanisms.

It is enough to read together chapters 1.31 and 2.10 to find an iden-tical counterpoint between ennobling stylization and comic realism, ex-cept that Don Quixote and Sancho have exchanged tonality. Don Quixote says to Sancho, who has come back from an embassy to Dulcinea: "A buen seguro que la hallaste ensartando perlas, o bordando alguna empresa con oro de cañutillo, para este su cautivo caballero" ("Surely thou didst find her stringing pearls, or embroidering some de-vice in gold thread for this her enslaved knight"). And Sancho: "No la hallé sino ahechando dos hanegas de trigo en un corral de su casa" ("I did not, . . . but I found her winnowing two bushels of wheat in the yard of her house"). Or again: "Cuando llegaste junto á ella, ¿no sentiste un olor sabeo, una fragancia aromática y un no sé qué de bueno, que yo no acierto a dalle nombre? Digo, ¿un tuho o tufo como si estuvieras en la tienda de algún curioso guantero?" ("When thou camest close to her didst thou not perceive a Sabaean odor, an aromatic fragrance, a, I know not what, delicious, that I cannot find a name for; I mean a redolence, an exhalation, as if thou wert in the shop of some dainty glover?"). And Sancho: "Lo que sé decir es que sentí un olorcillo algo hombruno; y debía de ser que ella, con el mucho ejercicio, estaba sudada y algo correosa" ("All I can say is . . . that I did perceive a little odor, something goaty; it must have been that she was all in a sweat with hard work," 1.31).

And here, in contrast, is an exchange during and after the meeting with the three peasant girls whom Sancho has passed off as Dulcinea and her attendants. Sancho: "Sus doncellas y ella todas son una ascua de oro, todas mazorcas de perlas, todas son diamantes, todas rubíes, todas telas de brocado de más de diez altos" ("Her damsels and she are all one glow of gold, all bunches of pearls, all diamonds, all rubies, all cloth of brocade of more than ten borders"). Don Quixote: "No se contentaron estos traidores de haber vuelto y transformado a mi Dulcinea, sino que la transformaron y volvieron en una figura tan baja y tan fea como la de aquella aldeana, y juntamente le quitaron lo que es tan suyo de las principales señoras, que es el buen olor, por andar siempre entre ámbares y entre flores. Porque te hago saber, Sancho, que cuando llegué a subir a Dulcinea sobre su hacanea (según tú dices, que a mí me pareció borrica), me dió un olor de ajos crudos, que me encalabrinó y atosigó el alma" ("These traitors were not content with changing and transforming my Dulcinea, but they transformed and changed her into a shape as mean and ill-favored as that of the village girl yonder; and at the same time they robbed her of that which is such a peculiar property of ladies of distinction, that is to say, the sweet fragrance that comes of being always among perfumes and flowers. For I must tell thee, Sancho, that when I approached to put Dulcinea upon my hackney [as thou sayest it was, though to me it appeared a she-ass], she gave me a whiff of raw garlic that made my head reel, and poisoned my very heart," 2.10).

In other words, the squire becomes the principal agent in the knight's hoodwinking. But Sancho's deceptions are quite different in character from those contrived in cold blood by the duke and Antonio Moreno. Sancho deceives when he is in a tight corner, to avoid trouble which he considers unjust or excessive; his deceptions are an exception to his fidelity. Behind his reservations, his limitations, even his observations, there remains fixed an ingenuous adherence to Don Quixote's projects and thus to his world. To Sansón Carrasco, who talks to him about the first part of the book, Sancho says with irritation, "Atienda ese señor moro, o lo que es, a mirar lo que hace: que yo y mi señor le daremos tanto ripio a la mano in materia de aventuras y de sucesos diferentes, que pueda componer no sólo segunda parte, sino ciento" ("Let Master Moor [Cide Hamete], or whatever he is, pay attention to what he is doing, and I and my master will give him as much grouting ready to his hand in the way of adventures and accidents of all sorts, as would make up not only one second part but a hundred"). And he even adds, "Lo que yo sé decir es que si mi señor tomase mi consejo, ya habíamos de estar en esas campañas deshaciendo agravios y enderezando tuertos, como es uso y costumbre de los buenos andantes caballeros" ("All I say is, that if my master would take my advice, we would be now afield, redressing outrages and righting wrongs, as is the use and custom of good knights-errant," 2.4).

The island to be governed represents the more limited staying power of Sancho's imagination when compared with the radiant presence of Dulcinea in Don Quixote's; but it also represents his faith in the restoration of knight-errantry, a faith which might seem that of Don Quixote alone but which is no less Sancho's (in however blundering and approximate a fashion). Is it gullibility or, as in Don Quixote's own case, a will to believe? It might be thought that Sancho had followed his master along this road too; the astronomical and literary observations of Don Quixote during his "flight" on Clavileño contrast with the liveliness of the observations that Sancho Panza, Menippus redivivus, pretends to have made: the earth reduced for the eye of the voyager to a grain of sand, the Pleiades like goats in a lunar landscape (2.41). Sancho is now the equal of Don Quixote himself, as the latter recognizes.

The main change in Sancho, however, is effected at the pole of common sense; for common sense is shown to be, especially in the second part, authentic wisdom, a wisdom with *auctoritates* of its own: proverbs, the folk equivalent of Don Quixote's literary quotations. From the motivation of single acts, these become a whole philosophy of life. In an original *contaminatio* of the wisdom of rural tradition and Don Quixote's teaching, Sancho sketches out for his own use a book of manners and a table of values.

It is in this concerted movement toward wisdom that the near assimilation of prot- and deuteragonist is delineated, with the difference that Sancho is given the opportunity of exercising his wisdom in sovereign fashion, during his governorship of the island of Barataria. Is this an undeserved privilege, with respect to Don Quixote? A careful reading excludes such a hypothesis. The connection between Don Quixote and Panza is never so close as during their separation. To Panza, the solidly realistic, is rightly entrusted the task of putting into practice a wisdom which Don Quixote forever places on the plane of universality and abstraction. But when Sancho is about to take possession of his post, it is Don Quixote who provides him with his *Mirror of Princes* (2.42–43) with the addition, after his departure, of an epistolary codicil (2.51).

What characterizes the episode of Barataria is that in this government, born of a joke, Sancho reveals himself as a ridiculous and unregal Solomon, but nonetheless Solomon. Cervantes has put together and attributed to Sancho a whole anecdotage of ingenious solutions and far-sighted decisions, and he has Sancho soon win for himself as governor a dignity that places him far above the pompous duke who has contrived, within a series of adventures of the two heroes, Sancho's fictitious promotion as well. Thus as Sancho's steward observes (expressing in all likelihood Cervantes's own point of view), "las burlas se vuelven veras y los burladores se hallan burlados" (jokes become realities, and the jokers find the tables turned upon them," 2.49).

Sancho boasts of his nature as an "Old Christian," and his genealogical tree is more ramified than that of his master (which underlines, *e negativo*, the originality of the Quixote character). His immediate ancestor might well be the squire Ribaldo of the *Historia del caballero Cifar*: a sort of proverb-spouting *pícaro*, who flanks, in contrast, the more heroic Cifar (just as Sancho flanks Don Quixote). But the complexity of his humanity leads one rather to compare Sancho with the *bobo*, later the *gracioso*, of sixteenth- and seventeenth-century theater, whose forerunners are the slaves and servants of classical and Renaissance comedy, while his most brilliant representative is the Elizabethan fool.

The *gracioso*, cunningly accentuating an original dull-wittedness, is able to give expression to profound truths, not infrequently unwelcome ones. (Don Quixote too observes this: "Decir gracias y escribir donaires es de grandes ingenios: la más discreta figura de la comedia es la del bobo, porque no lo ha de ser el que quiere dar a entender que es simple": "To give expression to humor, and write in a strain of graceful pleasantry, is the gift of great geniuses. The cleverest character in comedy is the clown, for he who would make people take him for a fool, must not be one," 2.3). He enjoys an immunity justified by the fact that he lives on the fringes of society and social conventions. He exactly represents natural reality, which is repressed and ignored in the ceremoniousness of aristocratic society, or even the wisdom of ordinary people as contrasted with culture and its pretences.

It was the theater—from the time of the pastoral scenes in religious drama—which showed the way for appreciation and linguistic characterization of the wise rustic, the clown who, while he laughs, reveals profundity or passes judgment on the world. But the theater has its connections with a whole medieval literature dedicated to the peasant, the repository of beliefs elaborated over centuries of hard experience (from Marcolfus to Bertoldo). These beliefs find their quintessence in the proverb. It is no accident that paroemiology enjoyed such an upsurge of vitality at the close of the sixteenth century, with whole collections of *proverbios, refranes,* and the like.

Don Quixote, however, is in a class by itself. Sancho does not move on the fringes of or even within an event involving only the upper classes of literary characters; he accompanies, on a level of narrative equality, another *eslege,* Don Quixote himself. In other words, we have to do with two characters who break away from society (in opposite directions), while society in the book is represented only by secondary characters, or by the characters of the insertions. Instead of a norm and its infractions, we have two infractions against a norm, at opposite and substantially complementary poles. The kind of judgment on society implied thereby should by now begin to be clear.

6. *Don Quixote* is an expanding nebula. It moves out through writing time and through narrated time. Caught again in the sights of the telescope after a ten-year interval, it shows a much more advanced stage of an expansion which in the second part resumes its earlier rate. There are therefore linear movements forward (the horizontal succession of the episodes is broken up but also thrown into relief by insertions and occasional dovetailing) and movements into circular conformations which fill the space of ideas, relationships, and suggestions surrounding the nucleus of the plot.

These circular conformations have already suggested the image of the spiral several times. Cervantes in effect never takes up a preestablished point of view; he so orders things that persons and their attitudes, even the very means of expression, reflect backward and forward, rotating mirrors which fling whirling around us reality and imagination, truth and falsehood, tragedy and comedy, irony and poetry.

Of these spiral movements there is one which yet remains to be investigated, and it is perhaps the most important of all. Don Quixote, as we have seen, oscillates between madness and wisdom; he sees a barber's bowl and decides that it is a helmet; why not Mambrino's? For the others, of course, the bowl remains a bowl; finally Sancho, in brilliant linguistic mediation, christens it "baciyelmo" ("bowl-helmet," 1.44). In this instance the writer has quite clearly indicated the three points of view.

But the examples offered are often more complicated than this. The original surname of Don Quixote, given in the variants "Quijada," "Quesada," "Quejana" in 1.1 (so that we are led to postulate rich and conflicting oral traditions) is then repeated as "Quijano" at 2.74. Transformed by the aspiring knight himself to "Quijote" (1.1), probably under the influence of "Lanzarote" (Lancelot), it runs the risk of turning into "Quijotiz" in a project, immediately abandoned, of pastoral life (2.67). Furthermore, names are deformed through ignorance or in contempt and finally unfold their further possibilities in the etymological play to which they are subjected kaleidoscopically.

On the basis of this polyonomasiology, Spitzer proposed a global interpretation of *Don Quixote* based on the conception of "perspectivism." Things are represented in the book not as they are but as they are spoken of by the characters who come into contact with them; with this technique Cervantes has represented for us the variegated phantasmagoria of human contacts with reality. Behind it all stands the narrator-director, who holds all characters in the palm of his hand, controls their every mood, each thought, thereby celebrating his own omnipotence as creator.

The correspondence between narrative and linguistic perspectives has been definitively demonstrated. As for the conclusions we are to draw, I think there is still room for useful discussion. I would point out, meanwhile, that some of the onomastic oscillations, some of the contradictions of content, are the result of haste or carelessness. Now Cervantes, instead of correcting himself or relying on the absentmindedness of his readers, gives his contradictions official status, motivating them a posteriori and interjecting them into the narrative continuum. The consequence is that he himself becomes part of the shifting play of perspectives, encouraging their infinite multiplication.

Let us go beyond mere minor discrepancies. We have observed that the characters of Don Quixote and Sancho, together with the whole environment in which they act, have been transformed in the very act of drafting the book, most markedly so in the passage from the first to the second part. Of this too the author is well aware. He might have found biographical justifications, adapting to his own purposes the interpretative scheme of the *Bildungsroman*. Instead, he appeals to intentions of coherence, which he at once denies. I am thinking of the play he makes with the trustworthiness/untrustworthiness of his alleged source, of the chapters which Cervantes or perhaps Cide Hamete declares are in contrast with the rest of the book and which he thus defines as apocryphal (2.5, 24, etc.).

Perspectivism therefore exists not only at the level of the characters and their existential expression; it is found also at the level of the writer, who doubles with his pretended source and transfers the dilemma (trustworthiness/untrustworthiness) to still another level, the reader. He also complicates the dilemma with additional doubt rather than resolving it. By virtue of this fact, the madness/wisdom polarity is transferred from the protagonist to the writer and even to the reader. Don Quixote is a metaphor for our contacts with the world.

But is not this relativism in contrast with what has been observed up to now concerning Cervantes's poetics and his disciplined conception of relations between literature and reality? And is it not in contrast with the fact that the writer fairly clearly subscribes to the concepts of the Counter-Reformation?

In appearance, yes. Sufficient confirmation might be found in the hagiographic tone used to recount the knight's final return to right reason; for not content with renouncing his imaginings, his vainglory, the very name of warfare, he prepares for us a most exemplary death: with conscience at rest, the sacraments and comforts of the faith received with true unction and surrounded by the sincere sorrow of the onlookers—*retour à l'ordre* in the fullest sense of the word.

In truth, *Don Quixote* is balanced in an equilibrium of its own between programmatic affirmations and their negation, for they are hinted at, even put into effect, but never motivated. To speak of a double truth or of astute and prudent dissemination of doubt would be a somewhat heavy-handed solution. It is less imprecise, though still inadequate, to note the facilitation and freedom of expression afforded by a protagonist whose madness renders him irresponsible.

The fact remains, however, that there is no separation between author and character; but the character is nonetheless not the author's spokesman. Don Quixote is more exactly an extension of Cervantes's own intellectual experience: "Para mí sola nació don Quijote, y yo para él: él supo obrar, y yo escribir; solos los dos somos para en uno" ("For me alone [Cide Hamete's pen] was Don Quixote born, and I for him: it was his to act, mine to write; we two together make one," 2.74). By making use of Quixote the writer can make perilous assays in inaccessible or dubious spheres. The area frequented lies between two limits, poetic codification and explicit Tridentine dispositions, ethical and religious. The history of *Don Quixote*'s composition is a history of journeyings ever more wide-ranging and intense—wide-ranging, indeed, *because* intense—discovered and followed through within this area.

At the beginning, Renaissance poetics are at the front of the stage, and the madness of Don Quixote seems innocent enough when it confuses the relations of literature and life, the likely and the absurd, fantasy and reality. Poetics serve the author as a measuring instrument for Don Quixote's deviations, a "measuring stick" indeed against which to check things in the turmoil of values Don Quixote produces and disseminates abroad.

But already in this first phase the explosive force of Quixote's invention (and his inventiveness) brings to light unexpected elements, unsuspected viewpoints. Let us take landscape. Cervantes gives the impression of being still tied to the canons of Renaissance description, for which the *locus amoenus* of the classical tradition looms large. But when Don Quixote arrives on the scene, the brightness of the air is obscured by fog patches filled with dust; nocturnal landscapes abound, full of will-o'-the-wisp torches, glimmering with the whiteness of cowled ghosts. Often nature, no longer in concord, no longer well regulated, makes herself known by sounds alone, with fearful noises in the dark, or with breathless silence.

The contrast between a Renaissance and a baroque outlook is immediately recognizable, and we may well deduce that Don Quixote represents a tentacle reaching beyond the aesthetic barriers represented by Renaissance canons of taste, canons which in his initial declarations are shared by the knight, whose perorations develop themes that fit them perfectly: the Golden Age; good government; harmony of physical, moral, and intellectual qualities. Except, however, that madness divides what these canons had aimed to unite, breaking apart above all the instiutional premises they appealed to. The baroque character of the book is the product of Don Quixote's madness.

This holds still more for the weight to be given to the more corporeal, less pleasing aspects of reality. Cervantes still seems attracted by a stylization, or homogeneization, which will avoid excessive deviations toward tones that are too high or low; the constituent traits of Don Quixote, in particular his idealizing obstinacy, will by reaction call up the objects, gestures, attitudes, and environments that Renaissance literature so disdained (and had fenced off in an "apartheid" of satire, in the rustic "reserves" of the theater).

In the night of lust and illusion (1.16), the equivocations and bed swappings of Maritornes with the tussles that ensue follow a pattern fully worked out in popular narrative; they find their demiurge, however, in Don Quixote, who violently recruits the deformed and slatternly servant girl to play the role of "the chatelaine's daughter paying an amorous visit to the wounded knight"; he holds her in his arms, only to declare that his chastity is dedicated to Dulcinea. The servant girl's appointment with the mule driver, intruding on the horizon of the quixotic sublime, vomits forth all its potential vulgarity.

From the realistic to the bizarre, from the bizarre to the grotesque, the passage is immediate. The figure of the ancient country gentleman becomes more and more drawn, wooden, scruffy, even dirty, along the path of his imaginary *cursus honorum*; while patient nags are promoted to the status of steeds or adopt, on other occasions, the appearance of camels. Everything is deformed, as if in the power of some defamiliarization which at first cannot and then will not come to terms with the banality of the real.

The discoveries made by Cervantes, with the help of Don Quixote, are in the first instance artistic, another way of looking at things. But with the development and increasing complexity of the figure of the protagonist, this new way of looking at things faces problems of a moral and ideological order. A conspicuous part of the society of the time, with its customs and its conceptions, finds itself on Don Quixote's itinerary.

In particular, in the second part of the book the range of adventures broadens; once the almost domestic bounds of the first excursions have been crossed, the knight advances, self-assured, into the various regions of Spain, hurling himself (at least in imagination) headlong into chasms beyond human time (2.22–23), undertaking navigations beyond the equinox (2.29), riding through the stars (2.40–41). Earth, heaven, sea, the other world—nothing seems beyond the reach of this down-at-the-heels Odysseus, who moreover thinks himself entitled to orate from the height of an academic chair.

Don Quixote's judgment is now much more careful. But what is it he judges? The wider the reality to be faced, the more haphazard and elusive it reveals itself to be. Earlier there had been a within and a without: within madness, a relativism, an overturning of values, dissociation; without such madness there existed quite clearly criteria for evaluation, explicit paradigms. Now it is the whole world which multiplies, blurs, overlaps its shifting appearances.

The metaphor of the theater dominates the entire second part of the book. To begin with, there is the meeting with the car of "the Cortes of Death" (2.11). The passage from disguise (figures that seem to be a devil, Death, Cupid, etc.) to the real nature of the characters (actors in a company of strolling players) is embroidered upon in repeated linguistic changes on what they seem and what they are; changes that are played upon even after the discovery has been made, when the clown tumbles Rocinante and Don Quixote (Sancho describes him as a "devil," and Don Quixote is ready to search him out "en los más hondos y escuros calabozos del infierno": "in the deepest and darkest dungeons of hell"), while Sancho dissuades his enraged master from an encounter both because one cannot "acometer . . . a un ejército donde está la Muerte, y pelean en persona emperadores, y a quien ayudan los buenos y los malos ángeles" ("attack an army that has Death in it, and where emperors fight in person, with angels, good and bad, to help them") and because none of the players is a knight.

Then there is Maese Pedro with his puppets (2.25–26). These seem to be a folk-level materialization of the heroes of chivalry. Don Quixote intervenes quite competently in the production, until he is so carried away by the plot that he appears in it in person. But after the slaughter of the marionettes it is Maese Pedro who says, "No ha media hora . . . que me vi señor de reyes y de emperadores, llenas mis caballerizas" ("Not half an hour [ago] . . . I saw myself lord of kings and emperors, with my stables filled with countless horses"). In other words, it is he who identifies the symbol with the referent, while Don Quixote oscillates between a detached consideration of the "puppets," for whom he compensates the puppetmaster, and the certainty that Gaifero and Melisendra are in the process of making good their escape.

Finally, symbols rigidly fixed in their signification are the images carved in relief that peasants carry to their *retablo* (2.58). For each of them Don Quixote has some comment to make, and it invariably goes behind appearances and contingencies; the procession of saints closes with a splendid peroration on the part of the knight, who points out affinities between the soldiering of Christ and that of this world. And Sancho, reflecting not without insight, remarks on the character of this "adventure," totally contained within the bounds of reflection.

The three theatrical adventures unfold within the experience of Don Quixote and the others. Actors and puppets represent those same actions, whether human or supernatural, of which each is daily witness. The theatrical ritualization underlines the symbolic aspect of the contents represented, subjected to catharsis. If there is still anyone—especially Don Quixote—who confuses reality and representation, mere happening and explicit rite, the short-circuit does not overstep the bounds of the subjective.

We are confronted, however, with a different space, external to protagonist and deuteragonist, in all the adventures at the duke's and in Barcelona. It is Don Quixote and Sancho who this time find themselves on the stage, in the midst of actors whose only aim is to involve them in the play. The pranks contrived are in the most literal sense staged by the duke and duchess; the extemporaneous actors improvise and adapt their lines to the reactions of Don Quixote and Sancho, who have become unaware actors in a representation.

At this stage, few initiatives are left to Don Quixote's unaided imagination (and these are nearly all locutory); the imagination of the ducal pair is active, though as authors of a script much less genial and varied than the inventions of Don Quixote's first period. These scripts come closer to a taste for courtly ceremony than chivalry and are more inclined to search out visual and phonic effects and *coups de théâtre* than psychological and conceptual refinements.

Let us recall the three episodes of the car of Merlin (2.35), of Trifaldi (2.36–41), and Altisidora (2.69): ambitious episodes—in the intentions of those who have contrived them—with their magicians, enchantments, transformations, and, in the case of Altisidora, near resurrection. But they bear all the marks of courtly entertainment (the tradition of the *entremés*), with their disproportion between the pomp of disguise and stage machinery, the choreographic ambition of triumphal chariots, processions, and catafalques on one hand and the ridiculous nature of the contents on the other (the enchantment of Dulcinea broken by lashing Sancho's behind, the charm which puts long, manly beards on Trifaldi and her women, the slapping and pinching of Sancho which is to reawaken Altisidora). The taste which goes into making such scripts is sufficiently defined by the fact that they are conceived with Sancho in view even more than Don Quixote. In fact they foresee and encourage, as an extemporaneous element of the spectacle, the protests of the squire, the victim of side-splitting magic. If, however, we widen the horizon, we cannot but observe the substantially static nature of the execution: the choreography is the merest preliminary to high-flown and approximate harangue, which sufficiently serves to define the cultural level of these prankster courtiers.

At first, Don Quixote was victim of his own fantasies; to the choices that any stimulus naturally opens up were added, in his case, those suggested by the multiplicity of the simulacra. The world was doubled in the illusion. Now, however, Don Quixote is both manipulated and repressed by the imagination of others, and very narrow limits are set for his behavior. The world is elusive because illusionary.

That such a conclusion is not to be referred to the main character alone is made clear by his progressive return to sanity. From the moment at which the equivocations and illusions are no longer imputed to Don Quixote himself, he ceases to be an atypical (and comic) case and turns into a vexed and tormented Everyman (whence the reiterated disconsolate tone). The idea thus emerges that this conception of life as theater is being proposed by Cervantes in universal terms: a theater no longer under control, like that organized by men, it has now become a conditioning factor. Who is to assure us that the duke and duchess are not (unbeknownst to themselves) actors in a play organized around them, similar to the one they have contrived for our heroes? Does not the fact that the mockers end up morally the losers mean to suggest that he who mocks is in turn mocked, and perhaps that even the hands of the puppetmaster are themselves moved by invisible strings?

Once again a spiral pattern is presented, one which will link the greatest number of points within a given space. We find here its most complete and all-embracing actuation: we are dealing with the world itself. When he begins the book, Cervantes seems to recognize the existence of points of reference, of touchstones which lie outside a direct experience of life: there is madness and wisdom, falsehood and truth. In the descending parabola of the book, it is precisely when (and because) Don Quixote is found to be more wise than his hosts, who are childishly involved in enjoying his madness, that the opposing concepts become interchanged in continuation, in gnoseological phantasmagoria.

Cervantes has been caught out as well by his own acuteness. His aim was to expose to ridicule romances of chivalry with all their fantasies, and he has ended with a conception which rejects the concept of reality itself, recognizing instead the domination of an *ars combinatoria* of appearances within a relativism determined by point of view which infinitely transmutes potentials and relationships. He strove for a classical sense of proportion and ended by venturing into the realm of the grotesque and the asymmetrical; and in remaining there he found norms, however transient, and decorum, however precarious.

This itinerary subsumes and exhausts all possible judgments on the times and society. Certainly it is no accident that the exploration of the early seventeenth-century world is carried out by a near penniless hidalgo, knighted by an innkeeper, as makeshift seigneur, in a ceremony of blasphemous mummery. The author in this way strikes twice. He strikes first of all at the craze of aristocratic ambition (like the purity of the blood that Sancho boasts of so ingenuously). But indirectly and covertly, he also attacks all the characters in the book who are to any degree noble, for they are too idealistically inferior to the false knight who debases them by his very existence.

Sancho is the mouthpiece for critics of his master's doubtful blue blood: "Los hidalgos dicen que no conteniéndose vuesa merced en los límites de la hidalguía, se ha puesto *don* y se ha arremetido a caballero, con cuatro cepas y dos yugadas de tierra y con un trapo atrás y otro adelante. Dicen los caballeros que no querrían que los hidalgos se opusiesen a ellos, especialmente aquellos hidalgos escuderiles que dan humo a los zapatos y toman los puntos de las medias negras con seda verde" ("The hidalgos say that, not keeping within the bounds of your quality of gentleman, you have assumed the 'Don,' and made a knight of yourself at a jump, with four vine-stocks and a couple of acres of land, and never a shirt to your back. The caballeros say they do not want to have hidalgos setting up in opposition to them, particularly squire hidalgos who polish their own shoes and darn their black stockings with green silk," 2.2). But it is of course Don Quixote who proudly contrasts the "caballeros andantes verdaderos" ("true knights-errant") with the courtiers who, "sin salir de sus aposentos ni de los umbrales de la Corte, se pasean por todo el mundo, mirando un mapa,[3] sin costarles blanca, ni padecer calor ni frío, hambre ni sed" ("without quitting their chambers, or the threshold of the court, range the world over by looking at a map, without its costing them a farthing, and without suffering heat or cold, hunger or thirst") and who drag their merits in the dust, spending their time in "niñerías" and "las leyes de los desafíos" ("childish points or rules of single combat," 2.6; the whole chapter is fundamental as a treatise on the nobility).

The true nobility of Don Quixote, nobility of feeling and thought, finds itself surrounded by elements of very assorted social rank as he moves through the regions and environments of seventeenth-century Spain. The result is a faithful panorama of the Spain of Philip III, with its demographic crisis arising out of its wars and the expulsion of the *moriscos,* economic stagnation following the interruption of trade with Flanders, and the stifling climate of political absolutism allied to the religious. Above all the moral climate is in decline: instead of the productive activity earlier displayed by the *moriscos,* empty pomp and the *pundonore* are preferred; caviling verbosity marks the absence of speculative enterprise.

In inventing the figure of Don Quixote, Cervantes has shown his ability to grasp the crisis into which Spain was falling (and whose consequences he had himself experienced) but also his awareness that he as a writer had no alternative propositions to offer, no stimulating utopias. Don Quixote's utopia is one that turns back toward the past, and the absolute values it gives are tied to situations that cannot be repeated. Cervantes rejects a chivalric utopia but accepts, at least as a touchstone, the absolute values it implies. When he speaks rationally, Don Quixote is in some measure Cervantes's mouthpiece; but his sermon (as it is often called in jest) has the sound of a *vox clamantis in deserto*. For this reason Don Quixote must be defeated.

But his defeat is the victory of art. The mutability of Don Quixote's approaches to reality allow Cervantes to observe and judge the world of his time with all the lenses available (not the least of them madness), and with a liberty allowed by the absence of any official point of view. It is as if he were bringing into line with acceptable criteria of judgment those unbiased, nonconformist opinions which Cervantes would have been wary of formulating in his own voice.

Neither reformer nor revolutionary, Cervantes makes use of this delicate strategy for purely heuristic ends: he has found a key to penetrating the recesses of human life—in the historical situations known to him —and he joyfully puts it to use.

His conclusions, however, transcend time and space, to the point of constituting discoveries which belong in the number of human universals. And it would be interesting to compare Cervantes's techniques and solutions with those of the young Shakespeare, from the use of the madman as investigator of the more obscure corners of consciousness to the universalization of the metaphor of the theater. But more productive, perhaps, would be a comparison with the other arts.

We have seen that the drafting of *Don Quixote* corresponds to a path from Renaissance to baroque. This can easily be shown by a host of purely formal elements: an abundance of observations of effects of light and shade, a predilection for chiaroscuro, for nocturnal landscape; a full appreciation of phonic effects; attention to drapery (solemn and often heavy) and scenery; a taste for disguises, including transsexual, and a striving after surprise effects.

The world as it appears in the book can indeed be represented in terms of baroque architecture: there are the same infractions of a classicizing poetic, accepted, however, as a starting point (compare the breaking up of the classical "orders," which are still conserved in their morphology); "perspectivist" narrative techniques (analogous to the substitution of elliptical patterns, with an infinite variability of viewpoints, for the circular or quadrangular forms which entailed a preferred fixed standpoint); insistence on *trompe l'oeil* (the visual correlative to confusion between truth and dream).

Even the elimination of the antinomy of internal and external space effected by baroque architects corresponds strikingly to an inversion of perspective from within the contained viewpoint of personal perception to a system of those forces surrounding and determining the individual. It is an extension of effects and illusionisms from the subjective to the world itself, from psychology to ontology. People move among backdrops and colonnades, climb spiral staircases, move through the dark drawn by the glory of light; they descend amidst shrubs and fountains toward bridges and artificial grottos, moss-covered tree trunks—only to realize that it is all a pointless merry-go-round, that their wandering is aimless and meaningless. Madness then becomes a consoling illusion: Don Quixote's greatest defeat comes when he is brought to his senses.

Eight

The *Canção do exílio* of Gonçalves Dias, or Structure in Time

Analysis of the structures of a poetic text involves organizing its parts in terms of one or more expository models. Necessarily, this breaks up the succession of these parts within the text, even though case by case the description will take into account their respective ordering (but each time on the basis of an arrangement into categories). The way the parts of a text function is determined primarily by their position (which the author has established in view of the reactions he wishes to arouse in the reader); in other words, by the relations set up between each of them and those that precede and follow them. This succession of parts is institutionally temporal, since it coincides with the time the recipient takes to read the text as well as (and primarily) the author's own reading time from the moment he had the completed text before him.

Thus we are not dealing with a corollary of Saussure's theorem of synchrony and diachrony. Saussure opposed diachrony, which follows the development of a single element of language through time, to synchrony, which enables us to consider in their reciprocal relations all the elements of a language at a given moment. The work of art constitutes a "synchrony" in the sense that it fixes a complex act of *parole*, rendering it absolute; but it is a synchrony which can be perceived only in the temporal dimension of the act of reading.

To remain in the field of linguistic definition, the antimony between an extratemporal and a temporal vision of the text is implicit in the opposition between syntagm and paradigm; paradigmatic investigation necessarily takes us beyond the text we are examining, while a syntagmatic approach remains tied to the actual progression of the text, which is in the first instance syntactic and temporal.

But perhaps even closer to the problem I wish to emphasize here is Dilthey's insistence on the *Zirkel im Verstehen* so dear to Spitzer (from the whole to the parts, from the parts to the whole), except that for a fixed ontological whole we should substitute a whole perceived in the temporality of the eye that deciphers the text letter by letter (or the ear that listens to successive groups of sounds), thought that deduces meaning from an ordered connection of words into sentences, rhythmic sense that observes the persistence of or variations on a given prosodic pattern or the dovetailing of rhymes. These preliminaries are tied to a priori categories of space and time which are not susceptible of elimination (though it is not my intention to base my study of the text upon them *tout court*); they do nonetheless constitute a situation of fact which looms large in the experience of every writer or reader, to such an extent that not even the critic should feel authorized to violate it.

The importance of interpreting the text from within the time category has of course not escaped critics. Among the more recent we might quote Pagnini: "Another level of the literary work . . . is its *temporal dimension,* though this is presently seldom mentioned in various structuralist definitions, which have a Bergsonian, simultaneous conception of the work. Obviously enough, a poetic object is integrated into a paradigmatic structure, but it is through a syntagmatic experience that it is recognized and built up. Time spent reading is an adventure of meaning, its unfolding as something lived through: the participation of the reader in its constitution by means of various rhythmical phases: rite against revelation."[1] And Riffaterre says, "It is impossible to exaggerate the importance of a reading which moves in the same direction as the text itself, i.e., from the beginning to the end. Unless this 'one-way' movement is respected, an essential aspect of the literary phenomenon will be misunderstood—for a book unfolds (as in antiquity a *volumen* was literally unrolled), and the text is subjected to progressive discovery, a dynamic perception which is constantly changing, where the reader not only moves from surprise to surprise but also sees, as he moves progressively forward, a change in his understanding of what he is reading as each new element confers a new dimension on earlier elements, which it repeats or contradicts or develops. Awareness of one of these echoes involves a double reading of that part of the text, the second reading being retroactive. A third, all-embracing perception at the level of memory takes place when the reading is ended."[2]

The problem has thus been exactly defined. However, there does persist in these statements the axiom that a passage exists from a (perhaps repeated) reading, which constitutes an initial contact with the text, and a gradual uncovering of its message, to the final adding up of a total awareness, which is, it would seem, beyond time. I confess I am perplexed when faced with knowledge of this sort; either we are dealing with the quintessence of poetry—something rather like the *innere Sprach-form* of the idealists—which is finally able to leave aside the articulations of poetic discourse and all the "values" (lexical, syntactic, phonic, rhythmic, etc.) which constitute it, or else we are dealing with a "model" or pattern into which the elements of the text have been arranged: a model which allows, indeed obliges us to work our way again in temporal terms through all the parts of the text, along the lines laid down when these are determined by grouping the elements into classes. Such lines continue to intersect vertically the horizontal line which coincides with the linearity of the discourse constituting the text. One of the most valid gains of the structuralist approach is the axiom that the text itself must predominate. I maintain that there is an inescapable consequence: the corollary that the text is to be respected in all aspects, including the order of succession of its parts. A (temporal) reading is the first and most straightforward way of making contact with the text; after even the most refined analyses, we should still be left with a (temporal) reading, capable of highlighting what such analyses have gained.

In a final reading there is no longer an element of "discovery": it is like reading a novel whose plot is already known. But this comparison shows just how little is lost. Freed from the impatience of suspense, the reader is in a position to appreciate each subtle inflection of the narrative discourse in the light of the successive developments (not merely those that have to do with the plot) by which the author has prepared these inflections. In a simple first reading such inflections may well be misinterpreted or escape notice. On the other hand, in a final reading of a poetic text the critic is already well aware of the various phonic, rhythmic, and semantic strands of which each textual element forms a part. He is thus able to weigh each "function" with extreme[3] precision as he meets with it. But a total awareness of such series of strands should not result in a juxtaposition or an overlapping of them; rather, it should allow precise orientation of the elements within the context (i.e., with respect to the elements that precede and follow them). The temporal aspect alone allows—and makes sense of—this selection of functions with the maximum potentialization of each within its own particular sector of the context. This consequently achieves the fullest possible play for its power of suggestion.

Several recent attempts at analyzing the poetic text in its "narrative" aspect could perhaps already serve to confirm what I have just touched on. For my part, I shall undertake an examination of a composition of parallelistic structure, of the kind dealt with by the Russian Formalists and Jakobson and later by Americans like Samuel Levin. In my opinion, study of a parallelistic text can be conducted in many cases along the lines of set theory. If a series of recurrent phrases has a common element A, plus variables 1, 2, 3, n, it is probable that within the semiotic universe of the text to which 1, 2, 3, n belong A will constitute a class, so that the recurrent phrases can be reduced to a single phrase; for example, [A + 1, 2, 3, n], or else [A + 1] . . . [A + 2, 3, n], and so forth.

This preliminary conclusion leads to a series of deductions of a phonic, syntactic, and semantic order; it is nonetheless clear, indeed obvious, that the poetic effect of the text derives from the fact of its having divided (where the first formula obtains) the classeme [A + 1, 2, 3, n] into various classemes, (A + 2), (A + 3), (A + n), distributed harmoniously throughout the text to obtain both fragmented progressive information, with iteration of the common element A, and a rhythmic effect.

The *Canção do exílio* of Gonçalves Dias lends itself to such a project, despite the fact that it is a text in which, with exceptions to which due weight will be accorded, a repetition of identical phrases prevails. In any case, the rhythmical effect remains intact and is even reinforced, not to mention the semantic effect, which I shall also take into account. We are dealing with the fact that the semantic content of every phrase in a text is influenced and in a certain sense oriented by the surrounding phrases. It may thus undergo quite considerable transformations, despite the fact that the phrase itself remains unaltered. This kind of influence involves not only connotations but the denotative content itself. If it is then permissible in a preliminary listing to place side by side all like elements selected from the text, with the aim of describing the poem's structure from without, it will be no less essential as a second stage to reestablish these elements in their own place in the text and evaluate them within the discourse whose articulations they are. Such an analysis moves, despite the inevitable coming and going imposed by the nature of the signs, from the signifiers to what is signified and then to the sense.

The text of the poem follows, with the lines continuously numbered on the right. In the analysis, however, reference will be made to the separate stanzas by capital letters (on the left). Account will also be taken of the two groups of stanzas marked by Greek letters.

Kennst du das Land, wo die Zitronen blühen,
Im dunkeln Laub die Gold-Orangen glühen,
Kennst du es wohl?—dahin, dahin!
Möcht ich . . . ziehn.

GOETHE

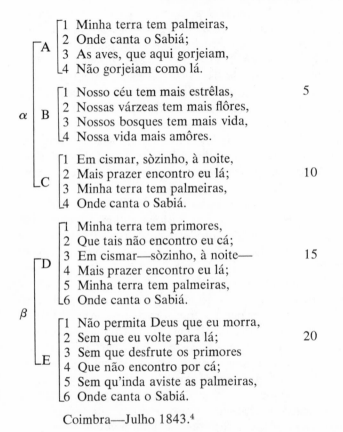

α A
1 Minha terra tem palmeiras,
2 Onde canta o Sabiá;
3 As aves, que aqui gorjeiam,
4 Não gorjeiam como lá.

B
1 Nosso céu tem mais estrêlas,   5
2 Nossas várzeas tem mais flôres,
3 Nossos bosques tem mais vida,
4 Nossa vida mais amôres.

C
1 Em cismar, sòzinho, à noite,
2 Mais prazer encontro eu lá;   10
3 Minha terra tem palmeiras,
4 Onde canta o Sabiá.

β D
1 Minha terra tem primores,
2 Que tais não encontro eu cá;
3 Em cismar—sòzinho, à noite—   15
4 Mais prazer encontro eu lá;
5 Minha terra tem palmeiras,
6 Onde canta o Sabiá.

E
1 Não permita Deus que eu morra,
2 Sem que eu volte para lá;   20
3 Sem que desfrute os primores
4 Que não encontro por cá;
5 Sem qu'inda aviste as palmeiras,
6 Onde canta o Sabiá.

Coimbra—Julho 1843.[4]

1.1. The poem is presented, with its epigraph from Goethe, as a contrasting reply. To the person who asks, "Kennst du das Land . . . ?" the poet speaks of his own land ("minha terra"). That is, to longing for a land of dreams he opposes homesickness for his own country, whose loss he mourns. This is confirmed by comparing the potential "dahin, dahin! / Möcht' ich . . . ziehn!" and the deprecative but essentially desiderative "Não permita Deus que eu morra, / Sem que eu volte para lá" and in particular by the substitution of "voltar" for "ziehen," for it implies an earlier presence.

The difference between longing and homesickness is shown too by the fact that the adverb of locale in the rhyme, though it is common to both poets, is always the same in Goethe ("dahin"), indeed it is reiterated as if the speaker were under the compulsion of a very strong feeling: this "there," in other words, is not explicitly confronted with any other.[5] In Gonçalves Dias, however, we find after two appearances of "lá" ("there," A4, C2), the first of which is in contrast with *aqui* (A3), a final contrast with the "cá" ("here") in chiastic form, as if to draw out all its latent potential ("cá," D2 ∼ "lá," D4; "lá," E2 ∼ "cá," E4); and the whole poem turns on a contrast between an idealized "lá" and a more modest "cá," the exile from which the poem is written.

These differences can be explained well enough if from the epigraph, which Gonçalves Dias has arranged to suit his own purposes, we pass to Goethe's own text. In Mignon's song two people are involved, although only one speaks: Mignon herself and the person who receives the invitation to the "Land wo die Zitronen blühn." We thus have Mignon : "dahin" = receiver : "here." This "dahin" is indicated in terms most likely to attract the other, precisely so he will decide to abandon his present "here." In contrast, in Gonçalves Dias it is the poetic "I" (in this case identical with the author) who finds himself in a dynamic position between two poles: he originated "lá," finds himself against his will "cá," and ardently desires to return "lá." Goethe's second person ("du"), as opposed to Gonçalves Dias's first person ("eu") shows well how this "dahin" is something alien to the receiver of the message, attractive though it be, and quite different from the "lá" which is, for Gonçalves Dias's homesick memory, more present in his emotion than the "cá" itself. This appears equally clearly in the contrast between "ziehen," which implies a relationship between two actors, and "voltar," which implies a single actor.

Again, from the epigraph we might take the syntactic scheme "das Land, wo," which is picked up but transformed by Gonçalves Dias, who links the relative of place not to the "terra" but to its content: "Minha *terra* tem *palmeiras, / Onde.*" It is also quite clear that the exotic "palmeiras" stand for the "Zitronen" or the "Goldorangen," southern fruit and hence exotic to a northerner like Goethe.

However, it should be observed that even though the palm is in a certain sense the heraldic tree of Brazil,[6] in the *Canção do exílio* its symbolic value is subordinated to that of the "Sabiá" which it bears; it is the "Sabiá" which becomes a symbol of his country, even though it sings from its special tree.[7] Thus "wo" leads into the list of trees in Mignon's song, and "onde" gives us the "Sabiá."

But the first stanza of Mignon's song is especially echoed in the *Canção* if we integrate it with lines not in the epigraph. Compare the following:

Das Land, wo die Zitronen blühn,	Minha terra tem palmeiras
In dunkeln Laub die Goldorangen glühn	. . . .
Ein sanfter Wind vom blauen Himmel weht	Nosso céu tem mais estrêlas
Die Myrte still und hoch der Lorbeer steht.	Nossas várzeas tem mais flôres
	Nossos bosques tem mais vida.

In both cases there is thus a synthesis of landscape which, starting out from a characteristic tree, moves from the sky to the vegetation, established by a few elements—except that in Mignon's song the trees are on the same visual level and the sky is indicated primarily as the source of the wind, even though the attribute "blauen" actualizes it in its chromatic aspect; whereas in the *Canção* we have an alignment of "céu," "várzeas," and "bosques," which (despite the insistent syntactic parallelism) isolates its elements as impossible to situate within a single, unified vision[8] (so true is this that the continuation, maintaining the scheme, is "Nossa vida mais amôres"). These last observations will be examined in more detail below (sec. 4.3).

1.2. The poem is made up of five stanzas, the first three of four lines (*quadras*), the last two of six (*sextetos*). The two blocks, α and β, are indicated as such by their identical beginnings ("Minha terra tem . . . ," A1, D1, a recurrent phrase, but only here at the beginning of the stanza) and endings ("Onde canta o Sabiá," C4, E6; and this also appears at the end of stanza D).

Block α is also characterized by the fact that its first and last two lines are identical and the scheme of the first member of the two couples, A1 and C3 (first-person possessive adjective + subject + "tem" + object), is taken up again with *variatio* in the central line B1–4, where the adjective is first-person plural and the objects are preceded by "mais."

Within the block, stanza B is characterized in three ways. There is a first-person possessive pronoun in the plural instead of the singular and in anaphora (always at the beginning of the line), with a kind of chiasmus, so that we have masc. sing. 1; fem. pl. 2; masc. pl. 3; fem. sing. 4, i.e., two cases with a final *s* in an internal position, and two externally; and an alternation of *z* and *ž* at the end of "mais," depending on whether what follows is a vowel (1, 4) or a consonant (2, 3).[9] Second, "mais" occurs in all the lines just before the final word, in the syntagm "tem mais" explicit in the first three lines and implicit in the last (where by zeugma "tem" is understood). Third, only nouns are in rhyme.

The stanzas of block β are characterized by their identical final lines and the same rhyme word at the end of the fifth line ("palmeiras"); by the mirror image of rhyme words at the end of the second and fourth lines ("cá"-"lá," "lá"-"cá"); and by the alternation of rhyme words to the point of building up a pattern which recalls the sestina:

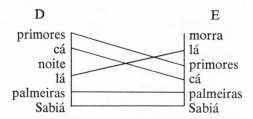

D   E
primores   morra
cá   lá
noite   primores
lá   cá
palmeiras   palmeiras
Sabiá   Sabiá

Here only the end words "noite" in D and "morra" in E remain without correspondences, although "noite" echoes C1, while "morra" is in partial alliteration and also assonance with "primores."

Within α, A and B are assimilated by the representation as an internal rhyme word of line 4 the (word-)rhyme which ends line 3 (respectively, "gorjeiam" and "vida")[10] and by similarly patterned first lines (with the exception of first-person singular and plural possessives and the presence of "mais"), with objects located on the same semantic axis: "terra"-"céu." This, however, is more a polarization of the signifiers than of the signified, given that "terra" stands metonymically for "country" and "céu" retains its proper sense, indeed so closely defined— it is the sky of Brazil—as to stand in paradigmatic relation to "várzeas" and "bosques" (and "vida") and in syntagmatic relation with "estrêlas," like "várzeas" with "flôres," etc. (see sec. 3.1).

Stanzas B and C are linked by the reappearance of "mais" from B1–4 in C2, by the alliteration "amôres":"cismar," and by the correspondence between "céu" (B1), which is clearly a night sky, since it has "estrêlas," and the "noite" of C1.

What links D and E to constitute block β is the reappearance of two pairs of lines with virtually identical second lines and different first lines, except for the final word:

(Minha terra tem) primores
Que tais não encontro eu cá [D1–2]

(Sem que desfrute os) primores
que não encontro por cá [E3–4]

(Minha terra tem) palmeiras,
Onde canta o Sabiá [D5–6]

(Sem qu'inda aviste as) palmeiras
Onde canta o Sabiá [E5–6].

Here it should be noted that in both cases we find elimination of the same segment of the phrase and its substitution with segments which are syntactically analogous.

There are also further relations of similarity and difference. For example, stanza D takes up "minha," from the beginning of line 1, at the beginning of line 5, while E anaphorically repeats "sem que" at the beginning of lines 2, 3, and 5 in a series that by implication embraces the whole complex 2–6, in which 4 and 6 are made up of secondary relations. The triple initial "sem" of E takes up as if in echo (vowel identity) the double "tem" of D within the lines (1, 5) in a distributive relationship which is certainly not accidental when the "palmeiras" line, which invariably contains "tem" in the other stanzas (A1, C3, D5), lacks it only in E5. It should be noted that whereas D's "minha" lines are almost identical ("Minha terra tem" segment), those with "sem" in E are alike in syntactic structure ("Sem" + "que" + verb in the first-person present subjunctive; 3 and 5 follow this with an object in the plural) and differentiated by the presence of "eu" (2) and "inda" (5).

Block β, then, naturally enough has connections with block α. The two last lines of D are identical with the initial lines of A and the last lines of C; rhyme words are repeated not only in these lines but also in A4, C2, D4, and E2 ("lá") and in C1 and D3 ("noite"); there is rhyme at a distance of "primores" (D1, E3), "flôres" (B2), and "amôres" (B4); and finally, line D3 ("Em cismar—sòzinho, à noite") repeats line C1 ("Em cismar, sòzinho, à noite").

1.3. However, the lyric contains elements which allow a different segmentation. In particular, it should be noted that stanzas A and B are differentiated from the stanzas which follow, C included, by the absence of first-person singular verbs; their verbs are exclusively third-person singular ("tem," A1; "canta," A2; "tem," B1) and plural ("gorjeiam," A3, A4; "tem," B2, B3); compare, by way of contrast, the other stanzas: "encontro," C2, D2, D4; "morra," E1; "volte," E2; "desfrute," E3; "encontro," E4; and "aviste," E5. This difference is accentuated in stanzas C–E by an expressed first-person pronoun (C2, D2, D4, E1,

E2). The first person is present in A and B only in the possessives "minha" (A1) and forms of "nosso" (B1–4). Furthermore, there is a particular link between D and C: all C lines have been repeated verbatim in D: C1–2 = D3–4; C3–4 = D5–6; and we should add that of D's other two lines one (D1) is a *variatio* of C3 ("Minha terra tem palmeiras/primores"), while the other (D2) takes on a contrasted similarity to C2 = D4 ("Mais prazer encontro eu lá/Que tais não encontro eu cá").

These links between C and D are rendered even more clear by the fact that E is from many points of view in opposition to all the other stanzas. In them the finite verbs are always in the present indicative ("tem," A1; "canta," A2; "gorjeiam," A3–4; "tem," B1–3; "encontro," C2; "tem," C3; "canta," C4; "tem," D1; "encontro," D2, D4; "tem," D5; "canta," D6); furthermore, every stanza contains "tem." In E, however, the present subjunctive predominates ("permita," E1; "morra," E1; "volte," E2; "desfrute," E3; "aviste," E5), and the verbs which appear in the subjunctive are all different from those of the other stanzas; from the others only the present forms "encontro" and "canta" come down into E.

As for the absence of the verb "ter," it permits us to seize on a further element which characterizes E. In stanzas C and D, "ter" and "encontrar" indicate, in the first case, the possession of certain attributes by the distant country; in the second, the poet's movement of search: a "discovery" of disappointing attributes in the country in which he finds himself and a mental "discovery," which is indeed close to a "seeking out with the imagination" the attributes of his own country ("não encontro eu cá," D2 ~ "encontro eu lá," C2, D4). Now in E we have "encontrar" and not "ter," always in a negative context (E4). It would seem that we are to deduce that this negativity depends upon the absence of "ter" and its subject (the distant land); it is, however, correlated with the exclusive "sem," followed by an adverbial mention ("lá") of the distant country, in a fabric of negations of the negations:

Não permita Deus que eu morra,
Sem que eu volte para lá;
Sem que . . .
Sem qu'inda aviste as palmeiras
Onde canta o Sabiá.

If now we set out from line 6, which equals A2, C4, and D6 (and note that here alone it is not preceded by "Minha terra tem palmeiras"), we deduce that "aviste" is here the substitute for "tem"; in other words, that the correlation "tem-encontro" is replaced by "encontro-aviste": "seeking out with the imagination" comes to its climax here at last with a visual discovery ("aviste").

In short, we have found a double articulation of the poem. On one hand—and this aspect is the most stylistically marked—ABC versus DE; on the other—and this corresponds more closely to the semantic shifts—AB versus CD versus E. This second articulation will be reexamined below in sections 4.2–5, while in 1.4 we shall find an analogous phenomenon.

1.4. The number of lines constituting the two blocks α and β is the same: twelve. But a change in the length of the stanzas, though the same rhyme scheme is maintained, is effected in such a way as to allude to the possibility, rejected by the poet, of continuing with quatrains. Behind the 6 + 6 grouping of DE one glimpses a possible 4 + 4 + 4 arrangement, which would have rendered β equal to α in terms of stanzas. Let us make an attempt at distributing the lines of stanzas DE as quatrains D*, E*, and F*:

D*
1 Minha terra tem primores,
2 Que tais não encontro eu cá;
3 Em cismar—sòzinho, à noite—
4 Mais prazer encontro eu lá;

E*
1 Minha terra tem palmeiras,
2 Onde canta o Sabiá.
3 Não permita Deus que eu morra,
4 Sem que eu volte para lá;

F*
1 Sem que desfrute os primores
2 Que não encontro por cá;
3 Sem qu'inda aviste as palmeiras,
4 Onde canta o Sabiá.

We shall observe that (*a*) D5, now it has become E*1, has a beginning identical with D1: two successive stanzas with a similar beginning (further, E*1–2 would have the same beginning as A1–2); (*b*) E3, which has now become F*1, picks up E*4 as if establishing a refrain ("Sem que" . . . "Sem que") and repeats the final word of D1 (D*1): the first line of the first and third stanzas would have the same final word, with rhyme over a distance; (*c*) E4, now F*2, is almost identical with D2 (D*2), so that we shall have between the first and last stanzas of the group near identity of the second line; (*d*) E2, now E*4, has the same rhyme as D4 (D*4): two successive stanzas will end with the same rhyme word; and (*e*) F* is composed (except for the final recurrent and invariable line) entirely of octosyllables *a maiori*.

2.1. There is an element common to all the stanzas: the even lines are all rhymed on an accented "a" (with the exception of stanza B, where the rhyme is in "-ôres"), on the basis of a reiteration of the "Sabiá," A2, C4, D6, E6; "lá," A4, C2, D4, E2; and "cá," D2, E4.

In the odd lines there are at times imperfect assonances within the same stanza: "palmeiras":"gorjeiam," A1, 3; "primores":"noite," D1 (3 even less clear-cut is the relation of similarity, though it is compensated for by alliteration, between "morra" and "primores," E1, E3). At other times, however, there exists a relationship from one stanza to another ("palmeiras":"gorjeiam," A1, A3: "estrêlas," B1), and then not only the rhyme is involved but entire words as well: "palmeiras," A1, C3, D5, E5; "noite," C1, D3; "primores," D1, E3. It should be noted, as Aurélio Buarque de Hollanda has pointed out,[11] that "palmeiras" and "primores" have the same consonant at the beginning of each of their three syllables.

The fact that we find in final position in the line not just rhymes but whole words should lead us to dwell particularly on the recurrence of the words themselves in this position. Nor is this all: as we move back into the line, it becomes clear that the repetition is not of words alone but of whole lines. The situation is the following: "Minha terra tem palmeiras," A1, C3, D5 (and further, with "primores" as object, D1); "Onde canta o Sabiá," A2, C4, D6, E6; "Em cismar, sòzinho, à noite," C1, D3; "Mais prazer encontro eu lá," C2, D4. Nearly identical are "Que tais não encontro eu cá" (D2) and "Que não encontro por cá" (E4).

This obsessive but well controlled repetition of words and lines can be schematized as follows (solid rules indicate the repetition of entire lines; broken rules, repetition of final words alone):

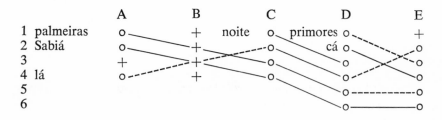

Only six lines out of twenty-four contain end words which are not re-peated somewhere in the poem (A3, B1–4, E1). The repeated words usually appear in a repeated line, while we have repetition of the final word alone at A4, C2 = D4, E2; D1, E3; and D5, E5. One notices at once a tendency of the final words and the lines in which they belong to "descend." When whole lines are in question, we find no exceptions: the pair A1–2 moves down to C3–4 (quatrain) and to D5–6 (sestet), and C1–2 moves down to D3–4. As for C1–2, only the final word of its first line comes down to E3, whereas the second line comes down almost un-changed to E4. On the other hand, the behavior of the final "lá" is symptomatic: it moves from A4 up to C2 and from D4 to E2, while when it goes down from C2 to D4, it does so in the repetition of the whole line. Such behavior will be studied in relation to the "cá-lá" inter-change in the second and fourth collocation of D and E (see sec. 4.3).

2.2. The deliberate restriction of the poem's lexical horizon can be seen not only in the recurrence of whole sentences but also in the fre-quency with which single words are repeated. It may be synthesized in the following diagram, in which the solid rule corresponds to the per-centage of new words used in each stanza, while the broken rule corre-sponds to the percentage of words in a single stanza which are found again in the stanza or stanzas which follow.[12]

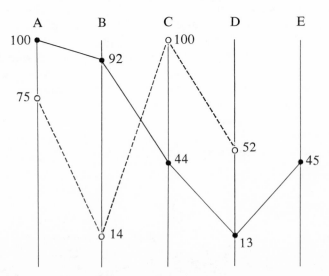

The first line measures innovation; the second, irradiation (always within the confines of the composition).

Following out the innovation line, along which the first stanza naturally enough has a percentage of 100, we notice that the value remains quite high (92 percent) in B, a stanza absorbing very little from A (i.e., "tem"), while, as might be expected, it descends in the stanzas that follow and make progressive use of materials from preceding stanzas. The sudden upward leap of E is characteristic; it passes from 13 to 45 percent, with innovation in nearly one-half of its words.

With regard to the irradiation line, we see that it is high in A and very high indeed in C (which is all the more characteristic in that there are four stanzas after A and only two after C). Further, if it is natural that the line should descend in D, which is followed by a single stanza, that it should be so low in B (14 percent) is less obvious, when there are three stanzas still to come. A comparative examination reveals that relative to their position, stanzas B and E are the most innovative, while stanzas A and C are the most irradiating and stanza B the least. We are left with the impression that B and E are the stanzas least subject to the repetition technique of composition, an impression which analyses at a syntactic and semantic level will confirm (see secs. 3.1, 4.3, and 4.5).

3.1. The first four stanzas of the lyric (A–D) constitute, by repetition or variation of elements or concepts already expressed, a wide-ranging comparison between the lamented native land and the land in which the poet finds himself as in exile. Means of effecting this comparison are the quantitatives "mais" and "não . . . como" and the adverbs of place "lá," "cá," and "aqui." For the moment, I am not taking into consideration first-person possessives because—and the reasons for this will be seen—they never stand in opposition to any "they"; in only a single case (D1–2) is "minha" correlated with "cá"; but the rhyme position and the complementarity of lines D2 and D4 polarize the "cá," opposing it instead to the "lá" of D4.

Even within so narrow a range, Gonçalves Dias effects a certain *variatio*:

	mais	não . . . como	cá, aqui	lá
A		+	+	+
B	+			
C	+			+
D	+	+	+	+

In other words, while A and D present not only quantitatives but also the opposing pair of adverbs of place (with the difference that D uses both the quantitatives "mais" and "não . . . como," and A uses only the second), B uses "mais" without adverbs of place, and C uses the quantitative and only one adverb, "lá."

Naturally the compartments of B and C remain empty only because of the extension over the two stanzas of full-scale explication of the comparison which had been effected in A: explications which are such as to predispose, by indicating its terms, the variety of ways in which the following stanzas will be realized.

In fact A is made up of two periods, the first purely asseverative, the second comparative. The connection between the two periods, which retrosemanticizes the first in comparative terms, is made by two techniques: (a) a passage from individual to class ("Sabiá" → "aves"), where "aqui" the "aves" trill less movingly than those "lá" (in "minha terra"), because the "Sabiá" is not among them; and (b) a parallelism, *"o Sabiá canta": *"as aves gorjeiam."

Throughout the poem we find different degrees of comparative actualization involving parallel periods linked vertically by the existence of classes which contain the respective subjects and objects of the periods.[13] In fact as many as eight of the poem's twenty-four lines fall within a single broad comparison:[14]

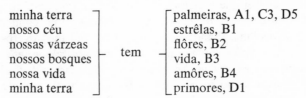

minha terra ⎤
nosso céu ⎥
nossas várzeas ⎥ tem
nossos bosques ⎥
nossa vida ⎥
minha terra ⎦

⎡ palmeiras, A1, C3, D5
⎢ estrêlas, B1
⎢ flôres, B2
⎢ vida, B3
⎢ amôres, B4
⎣ primores, D1

Indeed the last of these recurrences[15] encloses in a unifying whole all those preceding it:

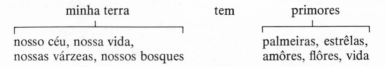

| minha terra | tem | primores |

nosso céu, nossa vida,
nossas várzeas, nossos bosques

palmeiras, estrêlas,
amôres, flôres, vida

The pacemaker function of line D1 is emphasized by structural devices. While "Minha terra tem palmeiras" assumes a rhythmical-obsessive dominance (it is repeated three times without variation), "Minha terra tem primores," in symmetry with "Minha terra tem palmeiras," opens the second part of the poem. Furthermore, the two lines appear together in a complementary relationship in stanza D (lines 5 and 1). "Palmeiras" and "primores," by means of the very similarity of their consonants, come to represent two extremes, the specific and concrete and the generic and abstract.

The development of the poem is facilitated by the different positions of generic or abstract, specific or concrete nouns along the chain of subjects and objects. In A we have a generic and abstract subject ("terra," "country") placed alongside an object that is defined and concrete ("palmeiras"), by antonomasia, Brazilian flora; in B, a series of concrete subjects ("céu," "várzeas") with concrete objects ("estrêlas," "flôres"), then a concrete subject ("bosques") with a generic object ("vida"), and last, a generic subject ("vida") with a generic object ("amôres"). In stanzas D and E there is a calculated alternation of the generic "primores" (D1, E3) and the concrete "palmeiras" (D5, E5); in D the formula "minha terra tem" always precedes, while the formulae are changed in E (see sec. 4.5).

But whereas "Minha terra tem palmeiras" is purely assertive, all the propositions which make up B contain "tem," expressed or understood, followed by a "mais" with no second term of comparison: it may be taken as implicit only by virtue of the explicitation of comparison of "aqui" with "lá" in A3–4. In other words, the assertive moment and comparative moments, separate in A, are fused in B to such a degree that it even allows of partial ellipsis.

In D, in a different form, "mais" without a term of comparison is used again; only the adverb "lá" appears, and it is explained by the "minha terra" of the following line. Comparison with "aqui" is always implied by the "aqui" of A3: "Mais prazer encontro eu lá," C2. But at this point another series of parallelisms is begun:

	Mais prazer encontro eu lá,	C2
(primores)	Que tais não encontro eu cá,	D2
	Mais prazer encontro eu lá,	D4
(primores)	Que não encontro por cá,	E4

As the verb "encontro" ("eu") remains unvaried, we find in two cases a principal proposition with "prazer" as its object and "lá" as its localization and in two cases a relative proposition in which "encontro" is preceded by "não." Since the relative is susceptible of transformation, in terms of generative grammar, into a nuclear sentence (*"não encontro [tais] primores [por] cá"), and since a secondary role, at least in this phase, is played by the presence or absence of "tais" and "por" before "cá," the parallel verses can be reduced to two nearly equipollent types:

1. Mais prazer encontro eu lá
2. não encontro (tais) primores eu (por) cá

Here the line joining "prazer" and "primores" has as its directions the subjective and the objective, whereas that which unites "mais" and "não" ("tais") has the relative and the absolute. Therefore

1. relative   →   subjective
2. absolute   →   objective

At this point it should be clear why stanza D contains the fullest repertory of techniques. It is a synthesis of all those used earlier: the opposition of "cá" and "lá," plus the possessive "minha," for the comparison effected in either a relative ("mais") or an absolute form ("tais não"), between the extremes of the specific and concrete "palmeiras" and the generic and abstract "primores." Let us bear in mind, however, the fact that D shares in this parallelism with one absolute and objective phrase ("Que não encontro por cá").

3.2. Stanza E makes a substantial contribution to the poem's series of parallelisms: half of its lines, in fact, are constructed in an identical manner:

Sem que eu volte para lá,   2
Sem que desfrute os primores,   3
Sem qu'inda aviste as palmeiras,   5

However, unlike other parallel lines, they cannot be arranged into a static whole, since they indicate actions that are of necessity successive: "volte" does not imply "desfrute" and "aviste" but constitutes their necessary premise on a referential plane.

The heterogeneity of "volte" on one hand and "desfrute" and "aviste" on the other is underlined by another syntactic fact: the second and third lines, unlike the first, are completed by relative propositions, and these too are heterogeneous, a fact which becomes clear particularly when they are transformed into nuclear sentences:

*não encontro por cá os primores
*o Sabiá canta nas (sobre as) palmeiras

4.1. And now the time has come to reintegrate our findings into a reading of the poem. But it is essential to insist at the outset on a fact to which sufficient weight is not always given: one must consider as an integral part of a composition its title and epigraph.

The poem's *ex abrupto* opening can be explained by the fact that it may be read as a sort of reply to Goethe's lines, "Kennst du das Land . . . ?" "Minha terra tem palmeiras. . . ." On the other hand, there is a difference in situations (see sec. 1.1)—in the first case, an invitation to Italy, a land of dreams which is neither the native country nor the home of the person addressed; in the second, the homesickness for his own far-off country, Brazil, of a poet who is living temporarily in Portugal (the *cançao* is dated "Coimbra—July 1843"). This difference is already announced in the title, which sums up Gonçalves Dias's expatriate situation (not without exaggeration: he was not in exile, having gone to Portugal in 1838 to complete his studies, though the death of his father and his stepmother's refusal of financial aid rendered his situation precarious; but the exaggeration lends justification to his desperate homesickness).

4.2. On the basis of the poet's standpoint with respect to his material, three principal moments can be recognized: an enunciative moment (stanzas A, B), where the verbs are all third-person singular or plural; a subjective moment (stanzas C, D) in which verbs of static content in the first-person singular appear, followed by the pronoun "eu" (always "encontro," C2, D2, D4), and one adjective stands out, the only one in the *canção*,[16] and qualifies a state of feeling ("sòzinho," C1, D3); and a desiderative moment (stanza E), in which a "helper" appears, "Deus" (E1), who is capable, through the jussive subjunctive "permita," of provoking the movements[17] and actions of the poet (i.e., of the first person "eu [E2], always in the subjunctive: "volte," 2; "desfrute," 3; "aviste," 5).

4.3. The opening of the poem is apodeictic. Its first two lines, precisely because of this apodeictic character, will become in the stanzas that follow a sort of almost obsessive refrain and at the same time a reference to the lost land through antonomastic citation of characteristic trees ("palmeiras"), a bird ("Sabiá"), and a slight vibration of joy ("canta"). I have already remarked (sec. 1.1) that these two lines reach their climax in the sabiá, for whom the "palmeira," characteristic though it is, is only the support. It should also be made clear that what distinguishes the sabiá is its song, not its appearance, for the latter is not striking. "Canta" stands here not as a generic indication of the bird's most readily perceived activity but as its most distinctive and ennobling trait.[18]

The two other lines of stanza A have two interconnected functions, highlighting the comparative value of the first two lines and actualizing, by reference to what is near at hand, what is affirmed of things far away.

The comparison is found in an autonomous form in lines 3–4. These reflect the preceding lines by recalling "canta" in "gorjeiam" and "Sabiá" in "aves." As a consequence of this, the opposition "aqui" ∼ "lá" is completed in "aqui ∼ lá (minha terra)." The line "Onde canta o Sabiá," which will become descriptive in subsequent stanzas, here takes on an evident resonance, reinforced by the repetition of "gorjeiam," so that "as aves" are, with the sabiá (leaving out of account, obviously, the poet himself and God) the only animate beings to appear in the poem.[19] Such resonance is, however, only mental: the present "gorjeiam" is quite as durative as (i.e., is no more momentary than) "canta"; the difference is that the first verb concerns the country "of exile" and is thus susceptible of direct experiment, while the second is relegated to an unattainable distance. The passage from mental to practicable definitions is marked metrically by the prosody of line 3, with its accents on the second and fifth.[20]

Stanza B is made up of four perfectly parallelistic lines which are parallel in turn to A1 (see sec. 3.1). In fact the four lines explicate A1's affirmation, adding no more than a comparative element, "mais," whose second term of comparison may be taken as given, since stanza A has already revealed it. It is for this reason, its integrative and explicative nature, that this stanza is the only one which does not contain the matrix line "Minha terra tem palmeiras" (for stanza E, see sec. 4.5).

This stanza is also enunciative in character and seems to be confirmed as such by the generic nature of the objects: the sky, naturally filled with stars,[21] the fields, naturally filled with flowers, the woods. Up to here the point of view seems to coincide with that of Goethe, its model. However, a sudden rhythmical acceleration follows, marked by the stylistic repetition of "vida" and the ellipsis of "tem"; and such acceleration is to be found in the conceptual associations as well. The "vida" is that of those who frequent "bosques" and whose hedonistic aims in so doing are well defined: Gonçalves Dias imagines young Brazilians who go to the woods to make love: in the line which follows the object of "vida" will be in fact the "amôres" which bring the stanza to a close full of rich allusion.[22]

This same asymmetrical extension is represented in the stanza by a failure to complete "mais"; while the anaphora on the possessive "nosso" and the iteration of "mais" are, more than the nouns themselves, the fulcrum of the statement. This explains the contrast between the strongly innovative character of the stanza (sec. 2.2) and its nature as explanatory appendix: we find an unusual display, for this poem, of isolated rhymes (sec. 2.1) and nouns used only here, but these nouns are generic and in part heterogeneous. In effect, we are dealing here with a long parenthesis, whose cohesion and effectiveness of allusion are to be found in an idea which lies beneath the surface: a handful of symbol-objects are enough to show that everything to be found in Brazil is better than what is found in Portugal. It was essential to repeat this single, dominant idea with the insistence of anaphora[23] and parallelism.

4.4. The initial line of the third stanza concentrates within itself all the psychological notions which form the nucleus of stanzas A–D. We are told that the poem is being written—or that we are to think of it as being written—at night ("à noite"), i.e., at a time which tends to allow introspection and melancholy ("em cismar") free rein,[24] and in absolute solitude ("sòzinho"). The vector of comparison ("mais") with the poet's own country ("lá") is now more direct and personalized ("eu") than earlier, where there was recourse only to the first-person pronouns "minha" and "nosso"—moving from a verb of relation ("encontro") between subject and object, which is an abstract of considerable capacity ("prazer"), so much so, indeed, that it constitutes a first synthesis of all the objects earlier indicated ("palmeiras," "estrêlas," "flôres," "vida," "amôres"). With an effective *hysteron proteron* we have first the poet's considerations (A–B) and then the situation in which they were formulated: *these considerations take on a posteriori the value of exclamations.* Once again "mais" is without a term of comparison; in B1–4 it had at least been objectified by the opposition of "aqui" and "lá"; now this "lá," prepared for by the series "Nosso," "-a," "-os," "-as" and reactivated by the refrain "Minha terra . . . ," finds itself in contrast with a "here" inclusively represented by the nocturnal and solitary anguish of the poet in exile. This more personal register (for expression of a totally private torment) is well indicated by the lexical choice as well: "cismar" and "sòzinho" belong to a more familiar (more modest) level than the other words used in the poem.

Stanza C comes to a close with the same two lines which open A— the mirror image is perfect. They no longer have the informative value inherent in their nature as initial affirmation. But there is a corresponding increase at the level of feeling: the "palmeiras" and the song of the sabiá are a symbolic synthesis of the "prazer" found by the poet in his lonely "cismar": the continuity between "lá" and "minha terra" represents the tension of desire exactly. But even more important is a clue at the level of musicality: repeated at the end of the stanza, the two lines, already familiar to the reader (or hearer), take on the function of refrain and appear as a thematic, rhythmical, and sentimental contrast, preparing the way for further repetitions, which occur regularly: in short, a leitmotiv. At this point we should remark that the sabiá is the only element which in absolute characterizes Brazil; in the other cases ("céu," "várzeas," "bosques," "vida," "prazer," "primores") Brazil is characterized only in comparative terms ("mais," "tais não"). It is thus not only by number but by virtue of their marked symbolic force that the sabiá lines dominate the whole *canção.*

In repeating the same first three words of the "refrain" ("minha terra tem") while replacing "palmeiras" with "primores," the initial line of D makes a break with what has gone before: i.e., on one hand it marks a turning point in its parallelistic course (no sooner has the phrase "minha terra tem" established itself as a refrain than it serves to start a new stanza from a different standpoint); on the other hand it provides new information. In the first place "primores" includes within a yet wider whole a class already defined by "prazer," "palmeiras," "estrêlas," "flôres,'" "vida," and "amôres." Further, if the "prazer" in C was characterized as being present ("lá") in "minha terra," so that "encontrar" was the result of an act of memory, now the "primores" are characterized in terms of their absence ("cá"): "encontrar" preceded by a negation indicates a frustrated action, with an iconic correlation of the accents on the second and fifth found only in line A3, whose iconic function is nearly identical (see sec. 4.2).

The rest of the stanza is made up of an integral repetition of stanza C, constituting almost a more lengthy four-line refrain. However, lines 3–4 here come to integrate lines 1–2, providing "cá" with its correspective "lá" and following up the enunciation of absence in the "cá" lines ("não encontro") with enunciation of presence in the "lá" lines ("encontro"), and finally developing the whole range of means of comparison employed in stanzas A–C (see sec. 3.1). In other words, stanza D provides the most complete working out of ideas previously only partly expressed: the presence in Brazil of perfections lacking in Portugal, the meditation of the poet, and his striving toward the "prazer" which in memory his own country offers: antonomastic image of the "palmeiras" and the sabiá.

This development rests on an accentuation of elements of feeling, in terms of a climax anticipated in the preceding stanza. The first two lines of D are enunciative, and their localization is real ("cá"); lines 3–4 embrace the nocturnal "cismar" of the poet, and their localization is mental, memorial ("lá"); last, "lá" is rendered concrete in the image of the "palmeiras" and the lonely, intense song of the sabiá. Two observations should not be left out of account. First, "primores," abstractly positive, contrasts in "cá" lines with "prazer," subjectively positive in the "lá" lines; the words have an identical initial consonant cluster, "pr-."[25] Further, the adverbial attribute and its complement ("sòzinho," "à noite") which in C1 were separated from their immediate context by commas only, are now isolated and emphasized by dashes, doubtless to suggest a longer pause and a greater resonance, in the reading.[26]

4.5. As was the case with other elements (see secs. 1.3, 2.2), the orientation of stanza E is quite different. From the outset it assumes a deprecating tone rendered by "não permita" followed immediately by the helper "Deus." The whole stanza depends syntactically on this "não permita" as well; it is made up of a single complex period—a principal clause, "Não permita Deus . . . "; a first-rank dependent clause, "que eu morra"; second-rank dependent clauses, "Sem que eu volte . . . ," "Sem que desfrute . . . ," and "Sem qu'inda aviste . . . "; and relative third-rank dependent clauses, "Que não encontro . . . " and "Onde canta. . . ." The deprecating form is the effective transformation of a desiderative subject matter expressed through the negations of negations (see sec. 1.3), where "morra" introduces a further element of pathos, with the same exaggeration which presents a period of study as a form of exile (see sec. 4.1).[27] This manner of expressing an affirmative content negatively repeats the definition of Brazil *e negativo* in terms of the "primores" that are *not* found in Portugal.

It is symptomatic that the *cá* ∼ *lá* contrast is now turned upside down. The poet already seems to lean toward "lá," thanks to the meaning and the subjunctive tense of "volte"; "cá" serves to verify for the last time the absence of the Brazilian "primores," toward which Gonçalves Dias also tends through a further subjunctive, "desfrute." This inversion is thus related to an insistence on verbs of marked personal participation ("volte," "desfrute," "aviste") which surface at the moment in which distance and separation begin to be surmounted, at least in desire. Intensity of longing is represented iconically by parallelism with anaphora ("Sem que . . . ," "Sem que . . . ," "Sem que . . . "). Nor should the "realistic" precision of the verb "avistar" be lost sight of: Gonçalves Dias sees himself already on board the ship from which he will catch sight of his palm-covered country.

The stanza thus takes up again, in its presentation and orientation, elements expressed in preceding stanzas: it is characteristic that five rhyme words out of the six in D and E are maintained, but with their position altered (see secs. 1.2, 2.1). The points at which this technique is most effective are lines 3–4 and 5–6. In the latter, the identical repetition three times of the refrain phrase "Minha terra tem palmeiras / Onde canta o Sabiá" is interrupted, and the more dense segment ("palmeiras . . . Sabiá") is inserted into the single period of which the stanza consists. Further, a comparison of the two competing segments

Minha terra tem
Sem qu'inda aviste

underlines the shift from a description which has turned into a recurring
musical motif to an experience calling for realization and already anticipated in desire.

Lines 3–4 present a noticeably similar phenomenon: here too the
object ("primores") and the secondary relative, only slightly varied
("tais não . . . eu" $\sim$ "não . . . por"), are retained from D1–2, while
the beginning of the first line is replaced, with identical results:

Minha terra tem
Sem que desfrute

Nonetheless, the surprise is less marked on the verbal plane, because
the D1–2 pair do not recur (in this sense, there is thus a reinforcement
of the use of the same technique in 3–4 and 5–6); but the surprise is
considerable on a semantic plane, since E3–4 insert into the desiderative
syntax and lexis the affirmation of D1–2.

Lines 3–6 thus constitute an innovation in the lyric's tissue of verbal
iteration, an innovation which is also rhythmical. Lines 3–5 stand alone
in having accents on the fourth and seventh syllables; furthermore, lines
3 and 5, with paroxytone endings, embrace 4 with its oxytone ending.
Such shifting and retardation of the rhythm coincides with those lines
in which, by means of carefully selected images, one enjoys in anticipation the experiences of the exile come home. The wheel has come full
circle. The heraldic "Sabiá" of the first descriptive-exclamatory lines is
now, in the last two, the living sabiá itself, whose singing will reach the
poet at the very moment he will see again the "palmeiras" of his own
country.

5. The limited confines of my approach in this chapter hardly permit
even a rapid survey of the success of the *canção*, for it was immense.
Imitated and echoed countless times,[28] parodied particularly by the
Modernists (though this too is evidence of success, of a vitality which
can be irritating), memorized in Brazilian schools, it has even become
part of the Brazilian national anthem.[29]

Investigation of this success and the outline of a value judgment are
undertakings to which my critical discussion may contribute at least in
part. Success here will depend primarily upon the simplicity and musicality of this small hymn to Brazil, rendered intense by the viewpoint of
"the exile." The simplicity is that of the linguistic means adopted: a
spare lexis with almost no adjectives, in which every word is capable

of becoming an emblem or symbol, and an elementary syntax, with periods which do not exceed two octosyllables, except in the last stanza. Its musical character is that of the octosyllables themselves, with accents only rarely varied; of the repetition of the same words in rhymes; of the motif refrains, frequently repeated and perhaps integrated with further hints of refrain—a perfect text to be learned by heart.

A further fact, historical and cultural in character, must be added. This lyric is the quintessence of the *ufanismo* which is such a constant in Brazilian literature: not generic nationalism but a comparison with Portugal, the linguistic homeland, in an attempt to counterpose its glories, its traditions with the natural beauty, lush fertility, and vast spaces of Brazil. With a few well-judged touches, Gonçalves Dias has found expression for this feeling, displaying it in a light which makes it inevitable and alive, apart from any discussion or uncertainty: homesickness, *Heimweh, mal du pays, saudade.* We might think that he has perhaps deliberately filled a need (as Salles suggests)[30] felt often by others before him, from the Portuguese Almeida Garrett, who accuses the Brazilians of not yet having sung what was most characteristic of their own land:

> For my part, if I were to have any complaint to make against him [Tomás Antonio Gonzaga], I should complain not of what he has done but of what he has failed to do. Let me explain: I wish that, instead of painting Arcadian scenes in Brazil for us, pictures entirely European, he had painted pictures with the colors of the country in which they were situated. Oh! how much his poetry lost by this fatal error! If only this ingenuous Marilia had come, like Saint-Pierre's Virginie, to sit in the shade of the palm trees [*á sombra das palmeiras*] while around her there flew the *cardeal soberbo* in its royal purple, the sabiá tender and melodious [*o Sabiá terno e melodioso*] . . .[31]

down to the Brazilian Gonçalves de Magalhães: "The poetry of Brazil is not a civilized native; it is a Greek attired as a Frenchwoman and a Portuguese, and acclimatized to Brazil; it is a virgin from Helicon who, sitting in the shade of the American palm trees [*sentada à sombra das palmeiras*], takes for a nightingale the sabiá which trills [*o sabiá que gorjeia*] among the orange boughs."[32] Thus the success of the *Canção do exílo* had commenced even before the text had been written, though this of course does not in any way underrate personal influences or the subjective value of the poem. It is a single expression, not an abstract celebration, of homesickness.[33]

Critics have remarked how this composition, in its simplicity, has skillfully touched emotional chords. Buarque de Hollanda points out that the nouns employed are "beings and things of nature, for the most part, or abstractions: elements which, unadorned as they are, gain depth in intensity and impose themselves all the more effectively on their own terms."[34] And Merquior confirms that the nouns are arranged in an "unadorned and abstract" fashion activated expressively by a feeling of *saudade*.[35] An absence of qualifiers[36] corresponds to this use of nouns, and this "evidences strikingly the substantives of the poem, throwing them into relief, opening out their emotional resonance."[37] Naturally the importance of the repetition of verses has been underlined as well. They seem almost obsessive in relation to the poem's subject matter, a "memory transformed into an obsession."[38]

However, not enough weight has been given to the mechanism which picks up single words and whole lines. This is what I have tried to do here. If in a first approximation they can be termed "refrains," it should be clear that in the strictest sense, we are not really dealing with refrains. The repeated verses are always inserted into the stanzas and semantically tied to them. Despite the limitations involved in placing heteronomous (though cognate) arts side by side, I would suggest that the recurring verses in the *canção* actuate a "fugal" structure. The two lines "Minha terra tem palmeiras, / Onde canta o Sabiá" constitute the subject which is then developed through *divertimenti*, though these remain closely linked to the opening theme; in the last stanza, we return, varying rhythm and attack, to the subject, thereby constituting a *stretta*. It will be remembered that the fugue originated as a development of the *ricercare*, and this poem of Gonçalves Dias is indeed a searching out of all the evocative potential implicit in its two opening lines.

The dignity of the *canção* lies predominantly perhaps in this fugal character, especially as its musical values are so finely calculated in the shifting accentuation of the octosyllables themselves. However, such harmonization, which the linearity of verbal discourse cannot hope to attain, is present in some measure as a result of the overlapping of the different transstanzaic structures. This overlapping operates within the poem as a whole, where it is possible to arrange the stanzas into groupings ABC, DE, but also into groupings AB, CD, E; and it operates no less in the second grouping where, behind the sestets D and E, possible quatrains D*, E*, and F* can be divined. Structures superimposed in this manner are obviously the result of a dense reiteration of lines, which permits a variety of sections, depending on which similarities are held to be the most significant. For the reader, however, the "possible" groupings which show through the geometry of the stanza divisions set in motion a play of persistences and interruptions, breaking and flowing in the fabric of memory which skillfully imitates the initiation and the immediate exhaustion of discourse developments, as these grow from the obsessive and exclusive unity of a single feeling, *saudade*, and the image in which it initially and definitively assumed concrete form.

Nine

The Function of Language in Samuel Beckett's *Acte sans paroles*

Beckett's *Acte sans paroles* seems by its very title to proclaim the degradation of language to a secondary function. If "paroles" is read as "discourse" (or more specifically "monologue," since there is only one character), then the play has no words at all. Furthermore, *Acte* is intended for theatrical representation, so that the linguistic expression of the printed text serves merely to describe movements which will realize on the stage a text finally liberated from all linguistic support.

On the other hand, Beckett has published *Acte* several times and by so doing has endowed his text with independent existence as literature: the words which compose it make it in every sense one of Beckett's works. And so we find ourselves straight away with two contrapositions: abstention from language (on the stage)/use of language (on the printed page) and subordinate function of the text (instructions)/autonomy of the text (message).

Even if the text of *Acte* is approached in its subordinate function, it betrays its lack of univocal status. The sentences of which it is composed, primarily instructions for staging, occupy a position of dependence with respect to the sum of the gestures, movements, and sounds which constitute the play. But the same sentences might also be viewed as a description—or, rather, a statement—of these same gestures, movements, and sounds. In other words,

(linguistic) text → gestures, movements, sounds
(theatrical text) → (linguistic) text

These oppositions and bivalencies cannot be made to cancel each other out on the empirical plane simply by discovering, for example, whether Beckett's written text preceded its first staging or not, or by leaving it to the reader to choose his own standpoint for a reading: a producer whose aim is to stage the work would regard the text as a "palimpsest" of instructions; the owner of the book which contains it would view it as autonomous; a spectator of the play might use the text as a reminder or as a means for evaluating the success of its realization.

The oppositions are constituent and can be clarified by defining relationships of meaning among the conceptual, verbal, and gestural planes, for it is on these planes that the text is actually or potentially developed.

Having recourse to a commonly accepted terminology, I shall use "Sense" to stand for the overall meaning produced by the series of literal linguistic signifiers; in so doing I include those signifiers which are implicit in the movements and sounds which make up our play. I suggest the following diagram:

$$\frac{\text{series of visual signifiers vs. written text} \left\{ \dfrac{\text{verbal signifiers}}{\text{verbal signified}} \right.}{\dfrac{\text{series of dramatic signified}}{\text{Sense}}}$$

The problem is thus not whether the words come before or after the theatrical action but, rather, the part they play in establishing the Sense. It is in fact clear that if the series of visual meanings (signified) can be regarded as the equivalent of the written text in its meaningful dramatic content, a further bifurcation of the text into signifiers and signified (by subdivision, into discrete meaningful units, more minute and precise than would be possible with a posteriori divisions of stage action) might well lead to an increase in Sense or to its closer definition.

This semiotic framework is valid only if it takes us beyond a possible comparison (not readily viable as a practical project) of a performance and a reading of *Acte*. The written text imposes strict limits on the actor's freedom of interpretation: every unforeseen move or gesture can distort the intentions (and thus the message) of the author. As I shall show, the written text in its turn contains indications which are not easily translatable into gestural terms.

Whether the text is ideally located before or after its performance, what still needs clarification is whether, by its very constitution, it can contain a stock of meanings and sense which, on the first hypothesis, will be of assistance in producing the work on the stage and, on the second, will reveal or define semiotic values. It is the aim of the present chapter to investigate this stock of meanings.

1.1. First the content of the play must be described in terms of its invariable elements, whether the mode of their realization is verbal or scenic.[1] There is a single male character (I shall call him C) on a bare, brightly lit stage (apparently a desert). He responds to the stimulus of whistle blasts. In the first four sequences and in two of the last, whistle blasts from the wings represent a recall order. In all other sequences, whistle blasts from above draw C's attention to objects which descend from the flies and which he would not have noticed if the sound had not drawn his attention to them.

The difference in function of the whistle blasts corresponds to a difference of situation. Whistle blasts from the wings involve C in a consideration of space: each time he moves right or left toward the wings, and each time he is repelled. The aim is thus to indicate to him the limits of the area accorded him: the stage. Whistle blasts from above, on the other hand, draw C's attention to objects he might make use of within the area assigned.

When he receives a whistle blast stimulus from the wings, C's reaction is constant at first: he runs toward it; but he meets a counterforce which brings him unceremoniously back onstage. On the fourth occasion, he stops short of the wings and returns at once, stumbling as he had on previous occasions. The reaction, we may say, has been interiorized.

The whistle blasts from above segment a more complex series of situations and decisions. A tree comes down from the ceiling; C sees that it will serve to shade him and approaches it, but soon its branch bends and the shade disappears; scissors descend, and C uses them to cut his nails; a carafe of water descends, and he tries in vain to seize it; a cube comes down, and C tries to climb on to it in order to reach the carafe— once more in vain; a second cube comes down; after several attempts C understands that the small cube must be placed on the large one; and by climbing on it he should be able to reach the carafe, except that this ascends a little and so remains out of reach. A third cube descends, but now, as in the case of the whistle blasts from the wings, C has learned his lesson and no longer tries; the cube ascends once more.

The descent of a rope dangling from above suggests to C a whole series of movements. First he tries to climb up it to reach the carafe, but the rope grows slack. Then he cuts off a piece with the scissors and uses it as a lasso to get hold of the carafe; the carafe, however, rises yet higher and disappears from sight. Now quite without hope, C decides to hang himself, but he is stopped by the branch of the tree, which bends again.

Two whistle blasts from the wings stimulate C's initial reactions once; the second time, he does not move. There is a final series of actions with the scissors: C cuts his nails and then decides to cut his throat, but the

small cube ascends, removing the scissors and lasso as well as the handkerchief C has been continually folding and unfolding; the large cube
also goes away, knocking over C, who was sitting on it. Only the tree
remains on the stage, which the carafe, now back again, rejoins. The
carafe now comes closer and closer to C, tempting him, and though he
has it within easy reach, he refrains from seizing it; it disappears. The
tree once again offers its shade (the branch has righted itself); but C
stays where he is, quite alone; the tree disappears. C looks at his hands
as he did when the tree first descended to the stage.

	Orders		Objects Desired		Instruments							Possession
	Ws	Wa	Ca	B	T	S	Cu^1	Cu^2	Cu^3	R	L	H
1												+
2	+											+
3	+											+
4	+											+
5		+		+	+							+
6a		+		+	+	+						+
6b					+	+						+
7			+	+	+	+						+
8a		+	+		+	+	+					+
8b			+		+	+	+					+
9a		+	+		+	+	+	+				+
9b			+		+	+	+	+				+
9c			+		+	+	+	+				+
9d			+		+	+	+	+				+
10		+	+		+	+	+	+	+			+
11a		+	+		+	+	+	+		+		+
11b			+		+	+	+	+		+	+	+
11c			+		+	+	+	+			+	+
11d				+	+	+	+	+			+	+
11e					+	+	+	+			+	+
12	+				+	+	+	+			+	+
13a	+				+	+	+	+			+	+
13b					+	+	+	+			+	+
13c					+	+	+	+			+	+
13d					+	+						
14		+	+		+							
15a		+		+	+							
15b												

1.2. What has been summarized here can be more clearly represented
in a table, which lists the orders C receives (Ws = whistle blast from
the side; Wa = whistle blast from above), objects desired (Ca = carafe; B = branch, as shade producer or support for hanging), instruments at C's disposal (S = scissors; Cu^1 = large cube; Cu^2 = medium
cube; Cu^3 = small cube; R = rope, which when cut provides L =
lasso; and T = tree, as support of B, even though T itself has no function), and C's only possession (H = handkerchief). Also listed are C's
actions and their results (Recoil = C is brought back onstage; Fail =

Actions	Results		
	Recoil	Fail	Removal
(Movement right)	+		
Movement right	+		
Movement left	+		
Incomplete movement left	+		
Seeks shade; looks at hands			
Takes S and cuts nails			B
Drops S			
Tries to get Ca		+	
Climbs on Cu^1; tries to get Ca		+	
Replaces Cu^1			
Climbs on Cu^2; tries to get Ca		+	
Puts Cu^1 on Cu^2; climbs up; falls		+	
Puts Cu^2 on Cu^1; climbs up; tries to get Ca			Ca*
Puts cubes away			
Thinks without moving			Cu^3
Climbs up rope			R
With S cuts L from R			R
Tries to get Ca with L			Ca
Putting Cu^2 on Cu^1, tries to hang self from B with L			B
Puts back cubes and L			
Movement right	+		
No movement			
Looks at hands; begins cutting nails			
Puts S and H on Cu^2; prepares to cut throat			Cu^2, S, L, H
Sits on Cu^1			Cu^1
Does not try to get Ca			Ca
Does not seek shade of B			T, B
Looks at hands			

failure; Removal = of objects or instruments). In the columns which precede the list of actions a plus sign indicates the kind of command which provoked the action and the objects, instruments, and possession present onstage. The same sign indicates results, whether Recoil or Fail; while for Removal the object or instrument is listed, an asterisk indicating that the removal is not total disappearance. Actions have been numbered to correspond to orders; thus if C performs more than one action after a single whistle blast, these are marked by the same number, followed by *a, b, c,* etc.

2.1.   Beckett's characters often move toward silence, restricting themselves to movements and gestures (or even to grunting and monosyllables or short sentences). On other occasions too we find a single character on the scene. Here, however, solitude and silence are complete (*sans paroles*). The result is a distinct dehumanization of C, and this seems to follow a regression on the evolutionary scale of *homo sapiens* (I remark above all the absence—or at least the nonexpression—of memories, which are a sort of retrospective hope for so many Beckett characters). We might even doubt whether C really is a man and not, let us say, an anthropomorphic ape, were it not for his familiar gesture of folding and unfolding his handkerchief, his careful nail cutting, and the pathetic sense of order which leads him to rearrange the cubes or roll up the lasso after his unsuccessful attempts.

Indeed it should be noted that the only freedom of movement allowed the actor, with respect to precise instructions, concerns this handkerchief. Beckett describes the character as follows: "Un homme. Geste familier: il plie et déplie son mouchoir." Then the handkerchief is not mentioned again except for C's using it to clean the scissors he intends to cut his throat with (action 13), when it is immediately taken away from him.

Of course, even C's movements are not necessarily human: his reaction to the stimulus of whistle blasts from the wings are those of an animal whose reflexes are being conditioned; his use of instruments is that of a chimpanzee whose intelligence is being measured (especially regarding the cubes: that it is useful to pile them up he understands by trial and error, as also the need to arrange them in descending order of size).

In short, it looks as if Beckett has here replaced the physical decadence to which his characters are usually subject with a lowly position on the evolutionary scale. On the other hand, it should be noted that physical decadence in Beckett is regularly accompanied by a new awareness (of tragedy or ineluctability); here awareness, inexpressible given C's mutism, has been made to coincide with a development of intelligence which can be ascertained from behavior.

I would stress the function of the whistle because it can be evaluated comparatively. In *Happy Days*, Winnie too lives to the rhythm of the ringing of a bell, but in the kind of limbo in which she lives it symbolizes the beginning of day and night (not otherwise distinguished); it thus takes on the value of an intellectual metaphor.

We should not, however, investigate too closely who blows the whistle. We are dealing with an entity (which I shall call G) whose consistency is relational. He can play with a man (with Man) as with a puppet; he decides not only the man's destiny but also the punishments which are to occupy his life, rendering them as varied as they are numerous. In other plays of Beckett a certain religious preoccupation together with biblical references allow us to call this entity God; here this would be too narrow a definition. . . .

2.2. It is now legitimate to conclude that despite appearances the play has two characters, C and G, a fact which in no way modifies C's state of solitude. For C, G is a force (or sum of forces) in whose power he finds himself. Between C and the force(s) there is no communication except that which is identified with behavior. G's language consists of whistle blasts and those of his actions which involve C: the attribution of this language to a single source is for C identical with the discovery of his own lack of liberty. This deciphering and attribution of language to a single source interrupt and block C's actions.

The connection between C and G is much more evident to that spectator/reader whom the (likely) premise that the play will not lack some sense predisposes to a search for causal connections, and who is inclined to search for narrative logic since the very nature of the play is narrative (narration of thoughts, if not of events). An intersecting relationship is thus established: in the fiction, between C and G; in the action onstage, between a sender (the author) and a receiver (the spectator/reader). The sender expresses himself by means of the relations between C (fictitious receiver) and G (fictitious sender); decoding his message means, first, deciphering G's language by placing oneself in C's position; second, deciphering from a detached standpoint the type of communication to which G and C's behavior belongs; and third, defining the laws of such communication.

As for the existence of G and his position with respect to C, the spectator/reader (like C himself) may advance the following arguments:

2.3. If the actions of *Acte* are divided into two large groups, according to whether the whistle blasts come from the side (Ws) or above (Wa), there are two types of process:

Ws: invitation – acceptance – rejection
Wa: offering of objects – acceptance – withdrawal of objects

Invitation and offer alike imply both a Giver (G) and a Receiver (C). Rejection and withdrawal, for their part, imply an Opponent: indeed the play tells of C's discovery of this Opponent and his norms for C's behavior. The immediacy of the stimulus-reaction-consequence relationship makes it likely, and increasingly evident, that the Opponent is G himself.

Obviously, the terms "invitation" and "offering of objects" are exact only from C's point of view. In reality, the whistle blasts are mere *signals* by whose means G draws C's attention to the norms he is about to enunciate: i.e., prohibitions against approaching the wings, and making use of desirable objects. But the signal constitutes the first element of a prohibition formula only if C interprets it as an invitation or an offer. It is in fact well known that in analogical language it is difficult to communicate the sign *not*.[2] G expresses it by having a rejection follow an apparent invitation, a withdrawal succeed an apparent offer.

The three stages represented earlier thus coincide with the three phases of C's understanding of the norm: first he hears a signal; then he interprets it as a command; last, he discovers that it is a negative command (a prohibition). Thus:

	Signal	*Command*	*Prohibition*
Ws	invitation	acceptance	rejection
Wa	offering of objects	acceptance	withdrawal of objects

Thus the pedagogic fashion in which he proclaims his rules is basic to G's way of proceeding. While for the invitation-rejection series he considers it sufficient to confirm the indissolubility of the reaction-consequence connection, for the case of offer-withdrawal, he has retained a more cruel, more detailed didactic technique. He offers not only the objects of desire (Ca, B) but also the instruments that would seem to enable their enjoyment (Cu^1, Cu^2, Cu^3, S, R). Thus C is able to verify the inflexibility of the norm after he has exerted himself as much as he could to obtain what seemed to be offered.

3.1. The pedagogic treatment C is made to undergo can be read from our earlier table. Up to action 7, C does nothing more than obey stimuli or indulge in noninventive actions. probably habitual (nail cutting). The failure of the shade at the end of 6a is already a warning sign, but it is not such that he sees it as connected with his actions. It is between 8 and 13 that C develops to the full his talent and activities (quantitatively, we have seventeen actions to six commands: thus C's autonomous actions are more numerous than those directly stimulated by the whistle blasts).

The progress of C's inventiveness is proportionally related to the seriousness of his failures of achievement: there is indeed a crescendo from actions 7–9b, where C may well attribute his failure to the objective difficulties of the situation, to actions 9c–11b, where it becomes clear that an Opponent is at work increasing the difficulties each time by shifting the limits of the possible further and further away. When despite his increasingly cunning use of cubes, rope, and lasso he has obtained from the rope by using the scissors, C must recognize the fact that the carafe first moves off and then is taken entirely away from him, he makes up his mind to commit suicide. It must be remarked, too, that in his attempt to do so C is no less inventive than when he tried to seize the carafe; the end result, however, is even more cruel, taking the form of a punishment which deprives C not only of the instruments earlier given him but even of his talisman-consolation, his handkerchief.

The results column is symptomatic: the best result, zero, follows sterile actions, for the most part actions of rearrangement (6b, 8b, 9d, 11e) or of attention to or reflection on the body (5, contemplating hands; 13b, cutting nails; at 6a the branch bends naturally because shade is looked for, 5, but not because nails are pared); constructive or self-destructive actions are the ones which invariably result in rejection or the withdrawal of objects.

But most remarkable of all for the play's sense is the withdrawal of objects and instruments to which C is condemned even when he decides not to act at all: a preliminary warning is that of action 10, when following C's puzzled perplexity the smallest cube, which has just appeared onstage, disappears again behind the flies; the greatest extension of the norm is found at the end when C seems finally to have decided not to react to any kind of stimulus at all, and the carafe disappears, after offering itself within easy reach (14), and then even the tree vanishes (15).

Acte is clearly a brief apologue; its atemporal value is signified by the incomplete nature of actions 1 (C is repelled from the wings right; there is no representation of the preceding moment, that of the whistle blast) and 15*b* (C contemplates his hands as in action 5, when the objects began to descend to the stage). The connection between progress in intelligence and progress in awareness is indicated by the different outcome of the lateral whistle blasts of actions 2–4 (in addition obviously to 1, where the preceding sound is understood) and 12–13*a*: in the first series C obeys three consecutive identical stimuli and only on the fourth occasion does he give signs of being more on guard, though he is still docile; in the second series, he gives up unhesitatingly after the second stimulus.

In C's consciousness two kinds of experience alternate in the form 1-2-1-2: the first kind concerns the stimulus-reaction-consequence connection and serves to inculcate the unfathomability of G's will; the second kind concerns the connection of offering-acceptance-withdrawal and serves to show him the law according to which acceptance excludes attainment. Thus all industry is vain, including attempts to withdraw from the game itself by suicide. It is after his attempt at hanging himself that the first type of experience reappears (actions 12, 13*a*); and it is after this, when he has recognized the impossibility of seeking out a different space and has established the tantalizing function of the objects of desire and the instruments which would seem apt for their attainment, that C concludes that the only possible reaction is to remain inactive.

The condemnation is a double one: condemned to a nonsatisfaction of appositely stimulated desires and to nonwithdrawal from the punishment, though C twice attempts it through suicide. The attempt indeed provokes an extra punishment: withdrawal of the handkerchief, one of those objects to which so many Beckett characters remain attached as if they were the archaeological evidence of their civilization, aids to self-possession, ways of passing the time and keeping up a pretense of a nonexistent activity. The loss of his handkerchief has only one possible meaning for C: despair.

3.2. It is important to distinguish the different functions of removing the objects from C's reach and taking them away altogether. Mere withdrawal seems to maintain the offer-withdrawal scheme; in other words it seems to reaffirm a negative norm (actions 9*c*, 11*a*): with the object offstage the norm would no longer be applicable. Complete disappearance punishes C for his obstinate persistence in seeking possession of the object (considered as an infraction of the norm: actions 11*b*–*c*) or, more severely (since it goes together with withdrawal of the handkerchief), for his attempts at suicide, another way of refusing obedience (11*d*, 13*c*–*d*). Last, there is withdrawal par excellence, which crown's G's didactic work: the object is taken away because C has learned not to react to the stimuli (10, 14, 15a).

In substance, C is made to undergo what in communication pragmatics is called "paradoxical injunction." He is placed within a framework of reference where he must choose between "wanting the object" and "not wanting it." The contradiction is twofold: (1) the objects presented to C (a branch, thus shade; a carafe and instruments for seizing it) are *desirable* by definition (it should be remembered that the scene is a blazing desert), so C is unable "not to want" them: (2) it is precisely the paradoxical alternative which C must choose: that of "not wanting." In other words, the norm imposed by G is "Thou shalt not want that which thou desirest."

When C has understood the norm beyond any possibility of doubt, he decides to escape from the scheme of reference established by G by committing suicide. In impeding this suicide and punishing C for the attempt, G teaches him the second norm: "Thou shalt not seek to escape from the scheme of reference I impose upon thee." This is exactly the situation psychiatrists call "the double bind."[3] It implies the existence of two or more persons involved in an intense relationship which in turn implies the psychological or even physical survival of one of them; the sending of a contradictory message or injunction; and a refusal to allow the receiver of the message to escape from the given scheme of reference.

If we refer to a hierarchy of modal values (want to, know how to, be able to, do), we find that G, in his initial role of seeming Giver, provokes C to "want"; thus he "makes C want." But in his role of Legislator (for C, of Opponent), he makes C "not able." Between the two extremes of "want to do" and "not be able to do," the training of C involves an ever increasing development of "know how to" (appropriate use of instruments: blocks, rope, etc.). We have, in short,

want to do ($\rightarrow$ know how to do) $\rightarrow$ not be able to do

In the first series of attempts, C connects his own "not doing" with a "not being able to do" attributed to objective elements. Only when a change in his disfavor of the objective elements shows him that his "not being able to do" is "being stopped from doing" does he go back to the first element in the chain, replacing an induced "want to" ("make to want to") with a "not want to." But does this "not want to" represent the only possible affirmation of freedom, or is it a conditioned consequence of G's didactic procedure and thus the result of a paradoxical "not make to want" (make not to want what one has been made to want)? I shall attempt a reply to this question further on; if definition of the laws of behavior of C and G is to seize the sense of the play, then the moment for this reply has not yet come.

4. Considered in its written form, *Acte* has an exactly corresponding precedent: the stage direction. Instead of directions set amidst dialogue in a relationship which serves to integrate words and movements or gestures, what is relevant here are those directions, often quite lengthy, which precede the opening of the dialogue in such plays as *Fin de partie*, *Krapp's Last Tape*, and *Happy Days* (note that *Acte* and *Fin de partie* are contemporary, having had their first performances together on 1 April 1957). *Acte* might be viewed as the development of initial stage directions of this kind for two reasons. One is specifically theatrical: in the plays just cited the stage directions give rise to a dumb show of some length. The other reason is stylistic: the language, the syntax in particular, is clearly similar.

The mechanical nature of the characters' movements (they are robot- or puppet-like) has as its correspective in these texts the brevity of sentences in the present tense juxtaposed and linked with an invariable subject, "il." Repetition of identical movements is indicated by the successive employment of the same sentence. Sentences are often made up of nouns, as if to avoid the responsibility of predicating them to a subject. Short, recurrent sentences are frequent: they allude to tics, almost gestural refrains, or to the fatal convergence of the characters' agitation in situations which will remain unchanging.

5.1. Even more than in his stage directions in *Acte*, Beckett aims at a language without resonance or color. Adjectives are extremely rare, mainly serving to define: "droite," "gauche," "petit," "grand," "seule," "maigre," "légère," "rigide," "fixe," "second." Only in the preliminary notes on character and scenery, i.e., prior to the text properly so called, do we find that the "éclairage" is "éblouissant," a fact which serves to confirm the importance of lighting in Beckett's plays.

The author has thus in general remained faithful to his intention of offering enunciations uncontaminated by subjective traits: instructions, in fact. But his participation, despite everything and counter to all his proposals, is noticeable. The message bears the (mental) fingerprints of its sender; the writing is autograph, despite the block capitals which aim at anonymity. And so the sense of the play can be helped to emerge further by the words that are *not* pronounced in it.

I will indicate the most significant of these epiphanies of Sense.

5.2. The Exclusive Role of C

Onstage appears the man (C) with his handkerchief; then progressively objects of desire and instruments come down from the flies and are used or transformed by the man (the lasso from the rope) in order to reach the objects. The objects are withdrawn or brought closer by an external entity, G, who ends by removing them as well as the instruments altogether from C.

But attention must be focused on C; each event is presented from his point of view. G himself emerges from deductions for which no explicit support is offered. Beckett shows the central position of C in the diegetic perspective with a perfectly simple grammatical procedure: after having designated him "l'homme" in the second line of the text, he then refers to C invariably by the pronoun "il"; in those cases where a masculine noun just used ("sifflet," "arbre," "sol," "tronc," etc.) might claim the attribution of the pronoun, the unequivocalness of of the function "il" = "the man" is effected by virtue of the fact that C is the only animate being present on stage.

5.3. Rhythmic Mimesis

In *Acte* the technique of repetition of identical sentences or phrases is predominant. From a functional point of view it might be said that Beckett has laid down for himself the following norm: for identical movements, identical words. Thus of the first four actions, 2 and 3 are described by the same sentence ("Rejeté aussitôt en scène, il trébuche, tombe, se relève aussitôt, s'époussette, réfléchit") and 1 and 4 by sentences initially different—since the beginning of the action is different—and then identical with the sentence quoted for 2 and 3 from "trébuche" on.

These directions are redundant only in appearance, since two precise motivations can be found for them. Iconic: the constancy of the gesture-word, action-sentence connections sets out to establish an exact equivalence between the text of the play and its performance. Stylistic: repetition of words and sentences in direct relation to the gestures the actor must make creates an obsession with recurrence which becomes tragicomedy (C is a sort of puppet forced to repeat the inevitable awkwardness of his movements).

This recurrence is undoubtedly more marked in the written text than it would be in performance. The written text brings recurrence to bear not only on more clearly segmented elements (words as compared with gestures) but also on a more minute segmentation (sounds and letters), and this has no correspondence in performance. Moreover, recurrence involves a sum of discrete, measurable elements which is much greater and more readily perceived than anything possible in stage presentation.

5.4. Dramatic Values

A point is reached where the very segmentation goes beyond any correspondence to live performance and assumes a dramatic function which a seeming impassibility of description does nothing to disguise. Let us take action 14, whose sentences can be listed as follows:

i.   La carafe descend, s'immobilise à un demi-mètre de son corps.
ii.   Il ne bouge pas.
iii.   Coup de sifflet en haut.
iv.   Il ne bouge pas.
v.   La carafe descend encore, se balance autour de son visage.
vi.   Il ne bouge pas.
vii.   La carafe remonte et disparaît dans les cintres.

It is normal that at i C should not react; he notices the objects only when the whistle calls his attention to them. This however, does nothing to diminish the greater resonance given to C's resignation and immobility by the reiterated "Il ne bouge pas" (ii, iv), even if strictly speaking only in case 4 is it legitimate to speak of resignation. Even more effective is the distinction made between the slight movements of the carafe, although they belong to the same action: first "à un demi-mètre de son corps," then "autour de son visage"; the distinction and relative separation allow a further repetition (vi) of "Il ne bouge pas." C's education is complete: an insignificant gesture is, or seems to be, all that is required to take hold of the carafe. And yet he does not make it.

5.5. Mental Action

Given the narrative-descriptive character of this text, references to mental action might seem out of place. And so they are, but in terms of a precisely calculated effect, in phrases in which reflection is placed on the same level as the gestures, there being no hierarchy of duration or importance: "Il *réfléchit*, va vers la coulisse gauche, s'arrête avant de l'atteindre, se jette en arrière, trébuche, tombe, se relève aussitôt, s'époussette, *réfléchit*" (4). It is "reflection" by fits and starts, mechanical and subhuman.

But even the use of "réfléchir" has been carefully calculated by Beckett. The function of the verb is demarcation: it initiates and concludes actions 2–7; Then, while other formulae take the first position, it serves as a conclusion up to 13a (it had also concluded action 1). Nor is this all. Since the objects that descend from the flies are perceived by C only after the whistle blast, the repetition of "réfléchit" before and after the descent of the objects indicates the continuity of the reflection (the second "réfléchit" is always followed by "toujours"). The formula is thus

Il [series of verbs], réfléchit.
[Descent of object or instrument.]
Il réfléchit toujours.

It is used in actions 5, 6b, 7, 8a, 10, and 11a. Its interruption coincides with an end to the descent of objects and instruments.

Let us go back for a moment to the "réfléchit" which inaugurates action. After the whistle blasts from the wings (2–4), the absolute beginning has the form "Il réfléchit." After the descent of the objects and the whistle blasts from above, formulae of the following kind are met with:

Il se retourne, voit . . . , réfléchit. [5, 7, 9a, 10, 11a]
Il lève la tête, voit . . . , réfléchit. [6a]
Il lève les yeux, voit . . . , réfléchit. [6b]

In actions 7, 9a, and 11d a simple "réfléchir" is replaced by a gesturalization of reflection. These are the moments of maximum combinatory effort. What is to be envisaged in the cubes and their piling up is the possibility of climbing on them to shorten C's distance from the carafe or to reach the branch. This effort at rational connection is represented by bringing the verb "regarder" progressively to bear on the instruments and objects to be connected: "Il se retourne, voit le cube, le *regarde*, *regarde* la carafe, prend le cube . . . " (7); "Lasso en main il va vers l'arbre, *regarde* la branche, se retourne, *regarde* les cubes, *regarde* de nouveau la branche . . . " (13). In the successive phases, the effort is represented by a connection between initial mistaken movements, governed by "vouloir," and a "se raviser," two entirely mental verbs: "Il se retourne, voit le second cube . . . *veut* rapporter le cube à sa place, *se ravise*, le dépose, va chercher le grand cube . . . " (8a); "il . . . va vers les cubes, prend le petit et le porte sous la branche, retourne prende le grand et le porte sous la branche, *veut* placer le grand sur le petit, *se ravise*, place le petit sur le grand . . . " (13). In short, mental processes have been subjected to careful distinction. This is obtained either by juxtaposition with descriptive verbs or by means of alternation with verbs which represent reflection in material terms ("regarder") or with verbs clearly not representational ("vouloir," "se raviser").

These distinctions follow exactly C's position within the action of the play. We have just seen that their range is widest at those moments in which C's inventiveness is most fully employed. Between 9*b* and 11*d*, C finds that he is called upon to resolve other problems, and we have a new use of "réfléchir" which we might describe as transitional.

From 9*c* on, C's failures no longer present a neutral appearance (objective difficulties) but show themselves as the work of an Opponent. The first episode is that of the carafe: it moves away from C at the very moment at which, having climbed on to the two cubes, he is about to seize it. He climbs down from the cubes, reflects, puts them back where they were, and then "[il] se détourne, réfléchit." This formula indicates, then, a moment of reflection between insight gained and further possible initiatives. We find it again, in fact, at 11*b* (between the rope's slackening and the search for the scissors to cut it), at 11*c* (after the carafe has ascended into the flies), twice at 11*d–e* (after the branch in bending has prevented C's hanging himself and after he has most neatly rearranged cubes and rope); and the series reaches its end with actions 12 and 13*a*, provoked by whistle blasts from the side.

There is thus nothing that needs pointing out at the beginning of action 12, for the following succession:

Il se détourne, réfléchit.
Coup de sifflet coulisse droite.
Il réfléchit, sort à droite.

In this case, a transition is effected between two phases of a succession changed from outside: the "réfléchir" that precedes the whistle blast carries over into that which precedes the movement of reaction. Much more interesting is the succession relative to the descent of the third cube:

Il réfléchit toujours.
Coup de sifflet en haut.
Il *se retourne*, voit le troisième cube, le regarde, *réfléchit*, se *détourne*, *réfléchit*.
Le troisième cube remonte et disparaît dans les cintres.

Here between "retourner" and "détourner," between "regarder," "réfléchir," and once again "réfléchir," what is being described is an internal resistence; the formula "il se détourne, réfléchit" acts as a transition to zero movement: C moves his head, but his body stays rigid. The formula is contenutistically (but not psychologically) the equivalent of that which will be adopted at 13*a*, 14, and 15*a*: "il ne bouge pas."

In actions 11*d* and 13*c* a new verb appears, "constater." We are dealing with the two attempts at suicide. The Opponent withdraws from C not only the objects of desire but also the instruments which would free him from his torment: the branch on which to hang the lasso, the scissors to cut his throat. On both occasions C turns toward the place chosen for his execution and then stops when he realizes that the suicide has become impossible to effect because the instruments have been removed: "Il se redresse, le lasso à la main, *se retourne, constate*" (11*d*); "Il *se retourne* pour reprendre les ciseaux, *constate*, s'assied sur le grand cube" (13*d*).

These two uses of "constate" spark a final insight. In fact they bring to an end the more complex intellectual actions, those in which all modes of reflection, enunciative and gestural, are present: ". . . Il va vers l'arbre, *regarde* la branche . . . *regarde* les cubes, *regarde* de nouveau la branche . . . *veut* placer le grand sur le petit, *se ravise* . . . *regarde* la branche . . ." (11*d*); "Il *regarde* ses mains, *cherche des yeux* les ciseaux . . . *réfléchit* . . ." (13*c*). In the second action, indeed, the detailed description of movements renders iconic all the paths, all the interlinkings of the thought. Let us reread it: "Il regarde ses mains, cherche des yeux les ciseaux, les voit, va les ramasser, commence à se tailler les ongles, s'arrête, réfléchit, passe le doigt sur la lame des ciseaux, l'essuie avec son mouchoir, va poser ciseaux et mouchoir sur le petit cube, se détourne, ouvre son col, dégage son cou et le palpe . . . " (13*b–c*).

The final insight is the renunciation not only of action but of thought as well. The sentences in which C is the subject are now no more than three:

Il reste allongé sur le flanc, face à la salle, le regard fixe.
Il ne bouge pas. [Repeated four times.]
Il regarde ses mains.

It is easy enough to show by commutation the sense of "Il ne bouge pas." We need only compare the following succession:

Coup de sifflet en haut.
Il se retourne, voit l'arbre, réfléchit. . . . [5]

Coup de sifflet en haut.
Il lève les yeux, voit la carafe, réfléchit. . . . [6*b*]

Coup de sifflet en haut.
Il ne bouge pas. [14]

"Il ne bouge pas" renounces the reflection which had preceded every initiative and the initiative itself. C knows that should he move, the object of desire would once more escape from him. The only act left him, discouraging because sterile, is that of looking at his hands. It was the first instinctive act, after the discovery of the shade, in action 5; an act not prohibited, like cutting his nails (6*a*). So true is this that the scissors remain onstage and are used again for the same purpose (13*b*); they are only taken away from him when, in a burst of initiative, he decides to use them to take his life (13*c*). It is a punishment, as is the contemporaneous confiscation of his handkerchief: C can only look at his hands, look within himself, feel. Nothing else.

6. *Acte* has thus been the theater of a strange struggle between referential function and poetic function. Beckett has striven to make his text conform exclusively to the former; but it is the latter which has gained the upper hand, despite him and fortunately for us. The verbs denoting mental actions are in themselves enough to show that Beckett has not managed to keep to his project of a tightly knit word-gesture equivalence: the straightforward instruction manual character which he appears to be offering in the play.

Among clues to this poetic function I have been content to note those which seemed to bear the heaviest burden of Sense. A stylistic analysis would provide a fuller documentation; but for our purposes it is enough to be able to affirm that the text does indeed fall under the jurisdiction of style, which implies that the Sense breaks bounds above and beyond literal meanings.

Against the widely accepted thesis poetic function → stylistic deviation, we have found that in *Acte* Beckett creates his effects by means of techniques which are almost all achieved along the linearity (syntagmatic and trans-sentential) of the discourse and not by *in absentia* relations with the paradigm: in substance, the effects are obtained by juxtapositions of verbs within the sentence or by the total or partial repetition of sentences or phrases or, finally, by the substitution (with progression) of parts within sentences otherwise equal or of different sentences with partly similar functions. There is still more; these effects are activated by the neutral tone of the discourse itself, by the choice of a middle style, an impersonal vocabulary (observations which might be extended to other works of Beckett as well, to their cold-blooded desperation and impassive humor).

But rather than a demonstration based on elements of style, I prefer (because it is more succinct and conclusive) one that can be given at the level of Sense. In paragraph 3.2 several problems were left unresolved: Does C's final inactivity lead him to an area of freedom, or does it condemn him to an area of conditioning? Is his "not wanting" a "not wanting to want" or a "being made not to want" by G?

An outline solution (still not very clear) is suggested by the structure of the play. Given that the whistle blasts from the side allude more clearly than the others to the technique of conditioned reflexes, their repetition toward the end of the action (12, 13a) would seem to show on G's part a menacing reaffirmation of his power and on C's part a greater readiness to allow himself to be negatively conditioned. While in 4 he responded only partially to the command, in 13a he does not respond at all.

But the indications in the text are much more clear. C's reaction to the final whistle blast from the side ("Il ne bouge pas") is exactly the same as that evoked by the whistle blast from above when it drew his attention to the final offer of the carafe and the shade (14, 15a). It is the first time that his reaction to both types of command is the same: a clear sign that C has been conditioned in both cases not to want. His mental itinerary, however, still awaits explanation. Here too data of a verbal order throw light on the Sense: on one hand there is the delayed appearance of "constater" after a series of instances of "réfléchir"; on the other, the expression "le regard fixe" (13d) after several instances of "voir" and "regarder." These are signs of a slowing down, then of a block, in exploratory, inventive activity, which does not mean a block in intelligence. "Il constate" is the last mental action attributed to C (13d) prior to his renunciation of any kind of physical action whatsoever.

Now we know that C finds himself in a "double bind" (sec. 3.2), which usually brings about schizophrenia. Further, the state itself is induced by means of conditioned-reflex procedures. We are thus dealing with Pavlov's "experimental schizophrenia." C's final behavior corresponds exactly to what psychiatrists call a catatonic state, one of the commonest effects of schizophrenia. I am not claiming that Beckett modeled C's behavior on that of schizophrenics (even if his work as a whole does rather remind one of a procession of schizophrenics); I am claiming, and this is more far reaching, that Beckett has seen in the "double bind" a characteristic element of the human condition.

The cruelty of the treatment meted out to C lies in having stimulated his intelligence (a human trait) in order to repress his will; and not this alone: in having brought conditioning to bear on the will (a human trait) instead of on instinct, thereby depriving C of hope (a human trait) but not of suffering. It is made clear, once again by stylistic means (we have noted in sec. 5.4 the desolate tone of the renunciations described in the actions or, rather, nonactions from 14 on), that C remains subject to desire: to quench his thirst, to withdraw from light and heat. The "not wanting" to which he has been conditioned is terrible because it in no sense coincides with a "not desiring." We might, in short, most aptly fill out the scheme of values of section 3.2 with the insertion of "desiring," but with this contradictory pattern, which is the result of conditioning:

$$\left.\begin{array}{c} \text{desiring} \\ \downarrow \\ \text{knowing how to} \end{array}\right\} \rightarrow \text{not wanting ("being made not to want")}$$

Such is the circumstantial message, the negative gospel, the bad news that Beckett has managed to hide between the lines of his instructions for the gestures, puppet-like and ridiculous, of a silent actor.

Notes

Chapter One

1. T. Todorov, "Le categorie del racconto letterario," in *L'analisi del racconto* (Milan, 1969; the essay was first published in French in 1966), p. 231.
2. G. Genette, *Figures III* (Paris, 1972), p. 72.
3. C. Bremond, *Logique du récit* (Paris 1973), p. 321, n. 1.
4. The description proposed by Yu. M. Lotman (*La struttura del testo poetico* [Milan, 1972; first published in Russian in 1970], p. 98) is excellent: "A structure of relations is not a sum of material particulars but a stock of relationships which is of primary importance in the work of art and constitutes its basis, its reality. But this stock is structured not as a many-tiered hierarchy with no internal intersections; it is, rather, a complex structure of reciprocally intersecting substructures, with reiterated interventions now of one element, now of another, in various constructive contexts. It is these intersections which constitute the 'reality' of the artistic text, its material polymorphism, which repels the bizarre, asystematic character of the surrounding world with such verisimilitude that there is created in the inattentive reader an illusion, a belief in the identity of this causality, this final individuality of the artistic text, and the properties of the reality that is represented." For successive references to transformational grammar, see N. Ruwet, *Langage, musique, poésie* (Paris, 1972), p. 199.
5. We shall see that matters are made even more complicated by the fact that, though reading time is undoubtedly progressive, it is not uniform (sec. 2.1).
6. The bibliography here is virtually limitless; I mention only S. R. Levin, *Linguistic Structures in Poetry* (The Hague, 1962); W. A. Koch, *Recurrence and a Three-modal Approach to Poetry* (The Hague, 1966); R. Jakobson, *Essais de linguistique générale* (Paris, 1963); and Lotman.
7. V. Erlich, *Il formalismo russo* (Milan, 1966; first published in English in 1964), p. 259.
8. V. B. Shklovsky, *Una teoria della prosa* (Bari, 1966; first published in Russian in 1925), p. 34.
9. Ibid.
10. Cited in Erlich, p. 260.
11. Shklovsky, p. 178 (the chapter is dated 1921).
12. B. V. Tomashevsky, "La costruzione dell'intreccio," in *I formalisti russi: teoria della letteratura e metodo critico*, ed. T. Todorov (Turin, 1968; the essay was first published in Russian in 1925), pp. 311, 314.
13. Ibid., pp. 314–15.

14. Ibid., pp. 316–18.
15. V. Ya. Propp, *Morfologia della fiaba* (Turin, 1966; first published in Russian in 1928), p. 27.
16. V. Ya. Propp, "Struttura e storia nello studio della favola," ibid., p. 219. (This essay was not included in the original 1928 edition.)
17. Ibid., p. 27.
18. Ibid., pp. 27, 72.
19. "Struttura e storia," p. 217.
20. Ibid., pp. 208–9.
21. Ibid., p. 227.
22. *Morfologia della fiaba*, pp. 80–81, 93; my italics.
23. Ibid., p. 96; italics in original.
24. L. Dolezhel ("From Motifemes to Motifs," *Poetics* 4 [1972]: 55–90) proposes a threefold division in place of my fourfold one: *motif texture* (= discourse), *motif structure* (= plot), and *fabula* (= narrative model), made up of *motifemes*. I should add that for Dolezhel "motif" corresponds more or less to "unity of content," and "motifeme" to "function" (the term is taken from A. Dundes, *The Morphology of North American Indian Folktales*, Folklore Fellows Communications, vol. 81, no. 195 [Helsinki, 1964]; see my sec. 6.1 below). In identifying III and IV, Dolezhel does not record the phase of logical and chronological reorganization of the actions in their etic aspect, though this must precede the passage from the specific to the generic, from the etic to the emic (see my sec. 3.1). Thus in the figure on p. 61 Dolezhel gives only the specification relationship between fabula and motif structure and the verbalization relationship between motif and motif texture. The schema of G. Genot ("Della scomposizione letteraria," *Sigma* 25 [1970]: 3–38) is also threefold, although differently conceived: *plot, fabula,* and *argument.* The omission of discourse (Dolezhel's motif texture) is merely terminological and has little weight; what is missing, however, as it is missing from Dolezhel and almost all other researchers, is a distinction between fabula and narrative model. The new element in Genot's list is the argument, or pseudo referent. "The argument," he writes, "is the 'second' figurative guise which gives the illusion of being concrete and which, in its reference to a cultural, psychological, ethical, etc. system, enables the narrative to conform to the institutionalized modes of an extraliterary code that is already in some measure discursive" (p. 20). It is not my impression that the argument can be situated at the same level as the other two terms, along a line of increasing abstraction; I suspect that its nonhomogeneous nature destines it, rather, for the sphere of the plot, part of whose material it would furnish.
25. P. N. Johnson-Laird, "The Perception and Memory of Sentences," in *New Horizons in Linguistics*, ed. J. Lyons, 3d ed. (Baltimore, 1972), pp. 269–70.
26. For the concept of memorial synthesis, see C. Segre, *Semiotics and Literary Criticism* (The Hague, 1973), p. 65. See also T. A. Van Dijk, *Some Aspects of Text Grammars: A Study in Theoretical Linguistics and Poetics* (The Hague, 1972), pp. 133, 140 ("Texts have to be conceived of as having a surface structure of sentences and a global deep structure which can be considered to be a semantic abstract underlying the text").

27. "Although on its reception the message appears as an articulated succession of significations, i.e., in its diachronic state, reception can be achieved only when the succession is transformed into simultaneity, from pseudo diachrony to synchrony. Brøndal has it that synchronic perception can only grasp at most six terms at a time. If one thus establishes as a primary condition the principle of simultaneous grasping of meaning, applicable to all levels of the manifestation, not only does the message appear as an achronic unit of manifestation, but every organization of the manifestation, i.e., in a broad sense the whole immanent syntax, must be conceived of as articulation of content in view of its reception" (A.-J. Greimas, *Semantica strutturale* [Milan, 1969; first published in French in 1966], p. 152). For deductions in the field of analysis of tales, see S. Jansen, "Esquisse d'une théorie de la forme dramatique," *Langages* 12 (1968): 71–93; and G. Genot, *Analyse structurelle de "Pinocchio"* (Florence, 1970), pp. 22–25.

28. See chaps. 7 and 8, which give example of prose and poetry, respectively.

29. For this new branch of linguistics, whose founder is Z. S. Harris but which has developed most especially in Germany and Holland, see W. Dressler, *Introduzione alla linguistica del testo* (Rome, 1974; first published in German in 1972), from whom I derive, with some retouching, a list of the problems it deals with. Its most advanced representative is perhaps J. S. Petöfi (*Transformationsgrammatiken und eine ko-textuelle Texttheorie* [Frankfurt, 1971] and "Grammatische Beschreibung, Interpretation, Intersubjektivität" [unpublished manuscript, 1973]).

30. A pair of terms introduced by V. Mathesius: see J. Vachek, *The Linguistic School of Prague* (London, 1966), pp. 18, 77, 89.

31. Dressler, p. 63.

32. Van Dijk, p. 4.

33. Shklovsky, p. 43. It should be noted that here, paradoxically, Shklovsky takes the real text as a decomposition of the fabula which is a pure invention of the critic, however fundamental it may be.

34. Ibid., pp. 72, 158.

35. The novella, for example, is in general "a combination of circular composition and step construction, further complicated by the development of various motifs" (ibid., p. 78).

36. Ibid., pp. 184–85.

37. Tomashevsky, pp. 314–15.

38. Ibid., p. 316.

39. Ibid., p. 314.

40. Ibid.

41. See Segre, pp. 65–66.

42. There has been some talk of "deferred" or "suspended" meaning: see J.-Y. Tadié, *Proust et le roman* (Paris, 1971), p. 124; and Genette, p. 97.

43. See Ch. Todorov, "Le hiérarchie des liens dans le récit," *Semiotica* 3 (1971): 127; but Todorov leaves out of account another, more readily utilizable function of the fabula, that of a theoretical hypothesis formulated by the critic for descriptive purposes.

44. For narrative point of view, see the summing up by F. Van Rossum-Guyon in "Point de vue en perspective narrative," *Poétique* 1 (1970): 476–97; the whole of *Poétique*, vol. 1, no. 4 (1970); the Russian texts presented by Todorov in *Poétique*, vol. 3, no. 9 (1972); Genette, pp. 206 ff; and B. A. Uspensky, *Study of Point of View: Spatial and Temporal Form* (Urbino, 1973).

45. There is an elementary but well-articulated synthesis in R. Bourneuf and R. Ouellet, *L'univers du roman* (Paris, 1972).

46. Genette, *Figures III*.

47. Here Genette (p. 187) proposes a formula (*information* + *informateur* = *C*, where *C* stands for *Constante*) and at once declares it inapplicable to Proust, whom he thereby considers an exception or paradox. I believe that such a formula is hardly ever valid. We might just say (although it would be obvious) that *information* + *sélection* = *C*.

48. The bibliography is immense. I mention only K. Hamburger, *Die Logik der Dichtung*, 2d ed. (Stuttgart, 1968); F. Stanzel, "Epischer Praeteritum: Erlebte Rede, Historisches Praesens," reprinted in *Zur Poetik des Romans*, ed. V. Klotz (Darmstadt, 1965; the essay was first published in 1959); W. J. M. Bronzwaer, *Tense in the Novel* (Groningen, 1970); and H. Weinrich, *Tempus: Besprochene und erzählte Welt* (Stuttgart, 1971). There are additional references in Van Dijk, p. 290, n. 2.

49. On phase differences between meanings on setting out and meanings on arrival, see Segre, pp. 74–77.

50. Ibid., p. 90. A similar observation by O. Burgelin is cited by Genot, *Analyse structurelle de "Pinocchio,"* p. 32.

51. See Genot, *Analyse structurelle de "Pinocchio,"* p. 22.

52. We might recall that Aristotle had already distinguished within tragedy not only spectacle and song but also plot, character, diction, and thought, dealing with them in a most illuminating manner (*Poetics*, 1450a).

53. Erlich, pp. 78–79.

54. V. B. Shklovsky, "Pil'njak," *Rassegna sovietica* 16 (1965): 75, 78.

55. As I have observed (Segre, p. 234) in the case of Shklovsky's *Sentimental Journey*.

56. P. Zumthor, *Lingua e tecniche poetiche nell'età romanica (secoli XI-XIII)* (Bologna, 1973; first published in French in 1963), p. 155.

57. P. Zumthor, *Semiologia e poetica medievale* (Milan, 1973; first published in French in 1972), p. 239.

58. T. Todorov, "Poétique," in *Qu'est-ce que le structuralisme?* (Paris, 1968), pp. 108–16.

59. See chap. 3, sec. 10 below.

60. See E. M. Meletinsky, S. Yu. Neklyudov, E. S. Novik, and D. M. Segal, "La folclorica russa e i problemi del metodo strutturale," in *Ricerche semiotiche: nuove tendenze delle scienze umane nell'URSS*, ed. Yu. M. Lotman and B. A. Uspensky (Turin, 1973).

61. Bremond, *Logique du récit*, p. 12.

62. Ibid., p. 25.

63. Ibid., p. 35; also p. 30.

64. Ibid., p. 47. The definition proposed by Lotman is similar but neater: "How does an event present itself when it is a unit of plot composition? *In*

the text the event is the transference of the character beyond the confines of the semantic field" (italics in original). From this comes a whole symptomatic series of affirmations regarding the plot: "Displacement of the hero within the space assigned him does not constitute an event. It thus becomes clear that the concept of event depends on the spatial structure of the text, on its classificatory component. Hence the plot can concentrate on the main episode, which is the intersection of the main topological limit and the spatial structure" (p. 281). "Inevitable elements in every plot are (1) a semantic field divided into two reciprocally complementary subsystems; (2) a boundary between the two subsystems which under ordinary conditions cannot be crossed but in the given case (a plot text always hinges on a given case) can be crossed by the hero-agent (the protagonist); and (3) the hero-agent" (p 283).

65. Bremond, *Logique du récit*, p. 46.
66. C. Bremond, "La logica dei possibili narrativi," in *L'analisi del racconto*, p. 99. (The essay was first published in French in 1966.)
67. Ibid., p. 102.
68. Propp, *Morfologia della fiaba*, p. 98. Tomashevsky spoke instead (but with respect to literary texts) of passages from states of contradiction to final reconciliation, or from loss of equilibrium to its reestablishment (or some part thereof; p. 313).
69. Bremond, "La logica," pp. 120–21.
70. Excluding the opening part of the essay, where there is an increase in specificity between *virtuality* and *improvement to be obtained* or *deterioration foreseeable*.
71. V. Ya. Propp, "La trasformazione delle fiabe di magia," in *I formalisti russi*, ed. Todorov, p. 278. (The essay was first published in Russian in 1928.)
72. This, it appears, is Lotman's opinion; see n. 64 above.
73. *Poetics* 1450b (*Aristotle's Theory of Poetry and Fine Art*, trans. S. H. Butcher, 4th ed. [London, 1951]).
74. Propp, *Morfologia della fiaba*, chap. 6.
75. Ibid., p. 121.
76. T. Todorov, *Grammaire du "Décaméron"* (The Hague and Paris, 1969), p. 28. The problem is examined more broadly and less unilaterally in the appendix on "Les hommes-récits," pp. 85–97.
77. See P. W. M. De Meijer in *Het Franse Boek* 41, no. 1 (1971): 5–11; and Bremond, *Logique du récit*, pp. 103–28.
78. Todorov, *Grammaire du "Décaméron,"* pp. 34–41. Earlier Todorov (*Littérature et signification* [Paris, 1967]) had synthesized the verbal world of *Les liaisons dangereuses* in the triad *désir, participation*, and *communication*, to which rules of derivation were applicable: opposition and passive (pp. 58–61); hence a whole case classification, with the aim of defining the behavioral code of the *Liaisons* (p. 66).
79. Bremond, *Logique du récit*, pp. 129–333.
80. Ibid., pp. 132–33.
81. Ibid., pp. 309 ff.
82. Ibid., pp. 137–38.
83. Tomashevsky, p. 337.

84. The experiment of A. Rossi ("La combinatoria decameroniana: Andreuccio," *Strumenti critici* 7 [1973]: 1–51) is most illuminating.
85. Homer *Iliad* 1.17–42; English translation by A. T. Murray (Cambridge, Mass., 1924); Plato *Republic* 3.393–94; Jowett translation.
86. Genette, pp. 190–91. He gives only the second sentence, as he does not quote the whole passage.
87. W. O. Hendricks, "On the Notion 'Beyond the Sentence,'" *Linguistics* 37 (1967): 12–51.
88. W. O. Hendricks, "Methodology of Narrative Structural Analysis," *Semiotica* 7 (1973): 163–84.
89. Ibid., p. 175.
90. Ibid., p. 178.
91. Mentioned in Todorov, *Littérature et signification*, p. 57.
92. Propp, *Morfologia della fiaba*, p. 121.
93. E. M. Meletinsky, "L'étude structurale et typologique du conte," in appendix to V. Propp, *Morphologie du conte* (Paris, 1970; first published in Russian in 1969), p. 207.
94. Todorov, *Grammaire du "Décaméron,"* p. 19.
95. Ibid., p. 16.
96. See De Meijer (n. 77 above).
97. Bremond, *Logique du récit*, pp. 196–97.
98. Propp, *Morfologia della fiaba*, pp. 102–5.
99. Bremond, *Logique du récit*, pp. 22–25.
100. Hendricks, "'Beyond the Sentence.'"
101. Propp, *Morfologia della fiaba*, pp. 36, 41, 42.
102. See E. Dorfman, *The Narreme in the Medieval Romance Epic: An Introduction to Narrative Structures* (Manchester, 1969). Dorfman uses the term "narreme" for large textual sections which can be unified under a heading.
103. C. Lévi-Strauss, "La struttura e la forma," in Propp, *Morfologia della fiaba* (the essay was first published in French in 1960).
104. C. Lévi-Strauss, *Antropologia strutturale* (Milan, 1966; first published in French in 1958), pp. 227–55.
105. Lévi-Strauss, "La struttura e la forma," pp. 166–67.
106. Lévi-Strauss, *Antropologia strutturale*, p. 233. *Parole* and *langue* are used in Saussure's sense.
107. Which I think can be defined as "content units" at the level of the fabula.
108. Lévi-Strauss, "La struttura e la forma," p. 192.
109. Ibid., p. 181.
110. Ibid., p. 191.
111. Lévi-Strauss, *Antropologia strutturale*, pp. 240–42.
112. Propp, "Struttura e storia," in *Morfologia della fiaba*, p. 218.
113. Ibid., p. 219.
114. As excellently expounded by Meletinsky.
115. For more detailed information, see ibid.; Meletinsky et al.; S. Miceli, *Struttura e senso del mito* (Palermo, 1973); and M. Pop, "Neue Methoden zur Erforschung der Struktur der Märchen," in *Wege der Märchenforschung* (Darmstadt, 1973).

116. Propp, *Morfologia della fiaba*, p. 116.
117. Bremond, *Logique du récit*, p. 122.
118. With an interesting forerunner in R. P. Armstrong, "Content Analysis in Folkloristics," in *Trends in Content Analysis* (Urbana, Ill., 1959).
119. M. Pop, "Aspects actuels des recherches sur la structure des contes," *Fabula* 9 (1967): 1–3; and "Neue Methoden zur Erforschung," p. 434.
120. Bremond, *Logique du récit*, pp. 59–80.
121. Meletinsky, p. 243.
122. Ibid., p. 244.
123. Meletinsky et al., p. 422.
124. W. Labov and J. Waletzky, "Narrative Analysis: Oral Versions of Personal Experience," in *Essays on the Verbal and Visual Arts*, ed. J. Helm (Seattle, 1967).
125. See Van Dijk, pp. 136–37, 293–94, with logical retranscription to involve the protagonist.
126. D. M. Segal, "Il nesso tra la semantica e la struttura formale del testo," in *I sistemi di segni e lo strutturalismo sovietico*, ed. R. Faccani and U. Eco (Milan, 1969; the essay was first published in Russian in 1966). The quotation is on p. 335.
127. Greimas, pp. 192–203.
128. A.-J. Greimas, *Del senso* (Milan, 1974; first published in French in 1970), p. 191.
129. Ibid., p. 182.
130. Ibid., p. 176.
131. Ibid., pp. 185–230, 157–83.
132. Ibid., p. 187.
133. Ibid., p. 196.
134. Ibid., p. 197.
135. Ibid., pp. 158–59; italics in original.
136. Ibid., p. 161.
137. Ibid., p. 164.
138. Ibid., p. 173.
139. Ibid., p. 174.
140. Ibid., p. 166.
141. L. Hjelmslev, *I fondamenti della teoria del linguaggio* (Turin, 1968; first published in Danish in 1943), p. 58.
142. Ibid., pp. 76–77.
143. See, e.g., chap. 6 below.
144. Greimas, *Del senso*, p. 167.
145. Bremond, *Logique du récit*, p. 93, has many important observations.
146. R. Barthes, "Introduzione all'analisi strutturale dei racconti," in *L'analisi del racconto*, p. 25.
147. Ibid., p. 18.
148. Ibid., p. 21.
149. Ibid., p. 19. The distinctions made by Tomashevsky (pp. 316–17) between *free*, *bound*, *dynamic*, and *static motives* are similar. See sec. 1.1 above.
150. See chap. 2.
151. See chap. 3. An excellent attempt along the same lines is made by S.

Alexandrescu in "A Project in the Semantic Analysis of the Characters in William Faulkner's Work," *Semiotica* 6 (1971): 37–51.

152. See chap. 3, sec. 6. Relation between the polygon of the characters and the fabula had already been glimpsed by Tomashevsky (p. 312): "Mutual relationships between the characters at each determined moment constitute a *situation*: e.g., the hero loves the heroine, but she loves his rival. Here we have three characters, the hero, the rival, and the heroine, while the relationships are the love of the hero for the heroine and hers for the rival. A typical situation is one which contains contrasting relationships: the different characters, in this case, wish to transform it in different ways. . . . We may therefore define the unfolding of the fabula as the passage from one situation to another, where each situation is characterized by a clash of interests, by collision and struggle between characters."

153. S. D. Avalle, "L'ultimo viaggio di Ulisse," *Studi danteschi* 43 (1966): 35–68. See also the highly elaborate analyses of G. Genot, "Teoria del testo e prassi descrittiva," *Strumenti critici* 5 (1971): 152–77; and "Le récit (du) déclassé," *Revue romane* 7 (1972): 204–32. The second of Genot's essays brilliantly confirms the possible utilizations of analyses of the tale in the comparative field (see chap. 4, nn. 3, 6, 8, 9, 17, 19, and p. 119 below).

154. See V. V. Ivanov, V. N. Toporov, and A. A. Zaliznyak, "Possibilità di uno studio tipologico-strutturale di alcuni sistemi semiotici modellizzanti," in *I sistemi di segni*, ed. Faccani and Eco (Milan, 1969; the essay was first published in Russian in 1962). Further information regarding these researches is found in D. M. Segal, "Le ricerche sovietiche nel campo della semiotica negli ultimi anni," in *Ricerche semiotiche*, ed. Lotman and Uspensky.

Chapter Two

1. J. Frappier, *Le mort le roi Artu: roman du XIIIe siècle*, 3d ed., Textes littéraires français (Geneva and Paris, 1964).

2. "A poi que ge ne di que les aventures recommencent" ("I would almost say that adventures are beginning again"), Gawain exclaims upon seeing the ship.

3. In *La prosa del duecento*, ed. C. Segre and M. Marti (Milan and Naples, 1959), pp. 868–69.

4. See R. Besthorn, *Ursprung und Eigenart der älteren italienischen Novelle* (Halle, 1935), pp. 111–12.

5. I refer to letters such as those contained in *Sommetta ad ammaestramento di comporre volgarmente lettere (1284–1287)*, ed. H. Wieruszowski, in *Archivio italiano per la storia della Pietà*, 2:193–98; or the two love letters published by J. Ruggieri in *Archivum romanicum* 24 (1940): 92–94.

Chapter Three

1. The best edition is that of Franca Ageno: G. Boccaccio, *L'elegia di Madonna Fiammetta*, with an afterword by A. Schiaffini, "Autobiografia e stile

del Boccaccio dal *Filocolo* alla *Fiammetta*" (Paris, 1954). The text (divided into paragraphs) is reproduced in Boccaccio, *Opere*, ed. Cesare Segre, commentary by Maria Segre Consigli and Antonia Benvenuti (Milan, 1966), pp. 943–1080. I have used the latter edition because Ageno's is not readily available. For the classical sources, the commentary of Maria Segre Consigli is still the most complete.
2. Developments in critical work are helpfully described by D. Rastelli in "La modernità della *Fiammetta*," *Convivium*, r.n. 1 (1947), pp. 703–15; and "Le 'fonti' autobiografiche nell'*Elegia di Madonna Fiammetta*," *Humanitas* 3 (1948): 790–802. See also, by the same author, "Boccaccio rétore nel 'Prologo' della *Fiammetta*," *Saggi di umanesimo cristiano* 2 (1947): 10–18; "*L'elegia di Fiammetta*: il mito mondano e la caratterizzazione psicologica della protagonista," *Studia ghisleriana*, ser. 2, 1 (1950): 151–73; and "Spunti lirici e narrativi, motivi stilistici nella *Fiammetta* di G. Boccaccio," *Lettere italiane* 3 (1951): 83–98.
3. The theoretical problem sketched out here is dealt with appositely in chap. 8.
4. See V. Crescini, *Contributo agli studi sul Boccaccio con documenti inediti* (Turin 1887), pp. 149–64, and the articles cited in n. 21 below. The many French and Italian vernacular versions of the *Heroides* should be recalled; one of them, attributed to Filippo Ceffi, is perhaps earlier than the *Fiammetta*; see E. Bellorini, *Note sulle traduzioni italiane delle "Eroidi" d'Ovidio anteriori al Rinascimento* (Turin, 1900).
5. For this reason, the other models followed by Fiammetta should remain in the background; the same is true for those traits of Dido whose presence in Fiammetta is emphasized by W. Pabst, *Venus als Heilige und Furie in Boccaccios "Fiammetta"-Dichtung* (Krefeld, 1958), and B. König, *Die Begegnung im Tempel* (Hamburg, 1960).
6. See P. Rajna, in *Studi danteschi* 4 (1921): 33. Dante, however, is not without forerunners, as P. V. Mengaldo points out in "L'elegia 'umile,'" *Giornale storico della letteratura italiana* 143 (1966): 177–98; this adds considerably to our list of medieval definitions of elegy. For a convincing explanation of the Dante passage, Mengaldo should be compared and integrated with the suggestions of F. Quadlbauer, *Die antike Theorie der "Genera dicendi" im lateinischen Mittelalter* (Vienna, 1962), pp. 150–57.
7. See, however, the way in which this sentence is qualified by M. Marti (it is of "preeminently psychological value") in the introduction to G. Boccaccio, *Opere minori in volgare* (Milan, 1969), 1:41, where one finds other observations worthy of note.
8. But the whole sentence—"A' casi infelici, onde io con ragione piango, con lagrimevole stilo seguirò come io posso" ("The unhappy events over which I justifiably weep I shall follow as I may, with sorrowful pen and style")— seems to allude also to *Heroides* 15.7: "Flendus amor meus est; elegia flebile carmen."
9. See V. Branca, *Boccaccio medievale*, 3d ed. (Florence, 1970), p. 88.
10. See C. Dionisotti, "Appunti su antichi testi," *Italia medioevale e umanistica* 7 (1964): 77–131. With regard to French models for the ottava, see A. Roncaglia, "Per la storia dell'ottava rima," *Cultura neolatina* 25 (1965): 5–14.

11. "The *Fiammetta* falls generally within the *Heroides genre*" (Crescini, p. 156).

12. See N. Sapegno, *Storia letteraria del Trecento*, La letteratura italiana: storia e testi (Milan and Naples, 1963), p. 306; Sapegno further notes references to Tristan and Yseut and the reading of "franceschi romanzi" by Fiammetta (8.7).

13. See S. Battaglia, "Il significato della Fiammetta" (1944), in *La coscienza letteraria del Medioevo* (Naples, 1965): "The *Elegia* of Boccaccio is not merely a song of love and separation but a precise investigation of a moment of passion, carried out with breathless patience, indeed with exasperated and painful exactitude. He conceived it with all the rigor of a treatise, with that exhaustive curiosity of an encyclopedic and classificatory cast which recalls the methods of the medieval scholastic mind: but it is alive and moves free as a result of its contemporary urgency, and this assures its value for us today" (p. 661).

14. For numerical values in the *Decameron*, see G. Billanovich, *Restauri boccacceschi* (Rome, 1945), pp. 156–57.

15. In the *Filocolo*, however, the *commiato* is inserted into book 5, and in the *Teseida* into book 10.

16. As well as in the classics: there is one in the *Aeneid* (twelve books) at the beginning of book 8 (lines 37–45).

17. G. De Robertis, *Studi* (Florence, 1944), p. 52.

18. Billanovich puts it excellently: "The energic attraction of the *Elegia di Madonna Fiammetta*, particularly in the first part, where the diary treats of a passion which is repressed, though intense, derives first of all from the isolation of the protagonist: ill and prey to her own fears, with the unhappiness of recognizing the disease and calculating its inexorable advance. In a state of hallucination, Fiammetta feeds on solitude" (p. 11). See Battaglia: "The *Elegia di Madonna Fiammetta* is a book of heartsick meditation: the effects of love and meditation on them are alike immersed in this climate of evocative isolation. The lyric tone of the elegy is to be found here: love relived, in estrangement and at a distance, as a feeling that is traced back to its source through its reflected images" (p. 664).

19. The opposition of Venus and Tisiphone can turn into an identity if we follow up the clue of a suspicion Fiammetta herself—with the wisdom of hindsight—expresses concerning the apparition of Venus: "Ohimè misera! che io non dubito che, le cose seguite mirando, non Venere costei che m'apparve, ma Tesifone fosse piuttosto" ("Alas, unhappy creature that I am! For I have no doubt, when I see what followed, that it was not Venus who appeared to me but, rather, Tisiphone," 1.21). The suspicion is taken up and elaborated upon by Pabst and König. To my mind, Fiammetta's exclamation falls in line with a whole series of recriminations against everything which has aided the development of her love: "O *infernal furia* o inimica fortuna" ("Either *hellish fury* or hostile Fortune," 1.8); "[Amore] da *infernale furia* sospinto" ("[Love] by *hellish fury* driven," 1.15). (It is the Nurse, Fiammetta's conscience, who is speaking here; hence one is not authorized to formalize a discourse on the identification of Venus and Tisiphone.)

20. On borrowings from Seneca's tragedies, see Crescini, pp. 160–62; A. S. Cook, "Boccaccio: *Fiammetta*, Chapter 1, and Seneca: *Hippolytus*, Act 1,"

American Journal of Philology 28 (1907): 200–204; V. Crescini, "Il primo atto della *Phaedra* di Seneca nel primo capitolo della *Fiammetta* del Boccaccio," *Atti del R. Ist. Ven. di Scienze, Lettere ed Arti* 70 (1920–21): 455–66; and M. Serafini, "Le tragedie di Seneca nella *Fiammetta* di Giovanni Boccaccio," *Giornale storico della letteratura italiana* 126 (1948): 95–105.

21. See A. Seroni, "In margine a un commento: sulle fonti del sonetto 'Al sonno' di G. della Casa," *Studi di filologia italiana* 7 (1944): 173–81; A. Roncaglia, "Sulle fonti del sonetto 'Al sonno' di Giovanni della Casa," *Giornale storico della letteratura italiana* 125 (1947): 42–54. See also C. C. Coulter, "Statius, *Silvae*, 5.4, and Fiammetta's Prayer to Sleep," *American Journal of Philology* 80 (1959): 390–95.

22. In confirmation, it might be noted how in the *Filocolo*, despite its extremely classicizing cast, the falling in love in church, described in a way that is very similar to *Fiammetta*, ennobles with periphrases but does not hide the Christian allusions: "Io, della presente opera componitore, mi ritrovai in un grazioso e bel tempio in Partenope, nominato da colui che per deificare sostenne che fosse fatto di lui sacrificio sopra la grata; e quivi con canto pieno di dolce melodia ascoltava l'uficio che in tale giorno si canta, celebrato da' sacerdoti successori di colui che prima la corda cinse umilemente essaltando la povertade e quella seguendo" ("I, the compiler of the present work, found myself in a gracious and beautiful temple in Parthenope, named for one [Saint Lawrence] who, for his deification, allowed himself to be sacrificed on a gridiron; here was singing full of sweet melody, and I listened to the office sung on that day, celebrated by priests who were successors of him [Saint Francis] who first humbly girded himself with the cord exalting poverty and followed it," 1.1).

23. Good observations on this aspect can be found in F. Flora, *Storia della letteratura italiana*, 11th ed. (Milan, 1959), 1:308.

24. See in confirmation this declaration of Fiammetta: "In libri diversi ricercando l'altrui miserie e quelle alle mie conformando, quasi accompagnata sentendomi, con meno noia il tempo passava" ("Seeking out in various books the sufferings of others and comparing them with my own, I felt myself in company, as it were, and so time passed less heavily," 3.2).

25. With touches which go beyond the fragile walls within which courtly love retires, in Boccaccio's version mercantile and naturalistic to boot. Twice the Nurse expresses the opinion that amorous coquetry is part and parcel of the vices of the rich (1.15), of the leisure only they can allow themselves (6.15)—a touch that will reappear in the *proemio* of the *Decameron*, X.12; it it echoed by Fiammetta herself, though she takes her cue from Lucan, at 5.30.

26. The first comparison is found in R. Renier, *"La vita nuova" e la "Fiammetta"* (Turin, 1879), p. 274 (points of contact with the *Vita nuova* are even more evident in the similar scene of falling in love in church in *Filocolo*, 1.1). There is a further comparison in the commentary of N. Zingarelli on a selection of Boccaccio's *Opere* (Naples, 1913).

27. On this stylistic formula in the *Vita nuova*, see A. Schiaffini, *Tradizione e poesia nella prosa d'arte italiana dalla latinità medievale al Boccaccio*, 2d ed. (Rome, 1969), pp. 101–4; and B. Terracini, *Pagine e appunti di linguistica storica* (Florence, 1957), p. 265 (who here judges it a biblically derived

trait), and *Analisi stilistica: teoria, storia, problemi* (Milan, 1966), p. 219.
28. These can be arrived at by setting out from the commentary on the *Rime* by V. Branca (Padua, 1958).
29. The dream in 1.1 has some of the characteristics of Dante's Matelda (*Purgatorio*, 28), as noted by H. Hauvette (*Boccace* [Paris, 1914], p. 145, n. 1). But words, images, and stylemes from Dante need to be pointed out systematically, as Zingarelli does for the chap. 3 he publishes.
30. The Petrarchan borrowings are striking; see C. Muscetta, *Giovanni Boccaccio e i novellieri*, in E. Cecchi and N. Sapegno, eds., *Storia della letteratura italiana* (Milan, 1965), 2:356–57. Among medieval Latin sources, G. Velli singles out the *De planctu naturae* of Alain de Lille (*Studi sul Boccaccio* 4 [1967]: 254, n. 2).
31. Apostrophe is one of the techniques of *amplificatio* which was most appreciated in the Middle Ages: see, e.g., the *Poetria nova* of Geoffrey de Vinsauf (264–460) in E. Faral, *Les arts poétiques du XIIᵉ et du XIIIᵉ siècle* (Paris, 1942).

Chapter Four

1. I quote from the fifth edition of V. Branca (Florence, 1965).
2. Following the terminology of Greimas, *Du sens*, p. 253, *actants* are the characters to the extent that they are semantic units of the tale's framework; *actors* are the characters to the extent that they are lexicalized units. My analysis is carried out at the level of *actors*, given that the respective roles of H, W, and L are identical with their legal (or illegal!) position, and this is necessarily lexicalized.
3. Motivations and vectors (or, if it is preferred, causes and means of the *beffa*) coincide in tale II. In this tale, clearly characterized sociologically, the poverty which drives the woman into the arms of a lover is also that which allows the betrayal: "Con ciò fosse cosa che il marito di lei si levasse ogni mattina per tempo per andare a lavorare o a trovar lavorio, che il giovane . . . uscito lui, egli in casa di lei se n'entrasse" ("Her husband being wont to rise betimes of a morning to go to work or seek for work, the gallant . . . was to come into the house as soon as her husband was well out of it," 9; all quotations from the *Decameron* are from the translation of J. M. Rigg, Everyman's Library edition). The same poverty induces the husband to sell the tun in which the lover, suddenly become a scrupulous buyer, is hiding (vectors: "andare a lavorare o a trovar lavorio": "to go to work or seek for work," 9; "tu non vuogli oggi far nulla": "thou hast a mind to make this a holiday," 14; "non fo il dì e la notte altro che filare": "day and night I do naught else but spin," 14; "To dovresti essere a lavorare": "Thou shouldest be at work," 15; "Tu dei essere a lavorare": "Thou oughtest to be at work," 18; "andai per lavorare": "I went out to work," 20; etc. It should be noted (in the play of sentiments too the cause of betrayal is by means of the *beffa*) that although the woman stresses (14–18) the miseries and hardships of her existence to cover her own fault with her husband's remorse, there is no doubt that the miseries and hardships are real enough. This is a procedure that differentiates the tale markedly from its source (Apuleius *Metamorphoses* 9.5),

where the woman is "postrema lascivia famigerabilis," and her recriminations concerning her domestic hardships are quite unfounded.

4. For the *beffa*, see A. Fontes-Baratto, "Le thème de la *beffa* dans le
Décaméron," in *Formes et significations de la "beffa" dans la littérature
italienne de la Renaissance*, ed. A. Rochon (Paris, 1972).

5. In this tale the contrast between the "courtly" tone of the opening and
the cruelty of the *beffa* creates a break that is also stylistic, well noted by
Branca in *Boccaccio medievale*, pp. 127–32.

6. This is Boccaccio's successful innovation with respect to his source, the
Comedia Lidiae of Matthew of Vendôme (in E. Du Méril, *Poésies inédites
du Moyen Age* [Paris 1854]), in an attempt to justify the wife's behavior at
least in part. Original too is the reference by the servant go-between Lusca
to class antagonism, in order to disarm Pirro's scruples: "Speri tu, se tu
avessi o bella moglie o madre o figliuola o sorella che a Nicostrato piacesse,
ch'egli andasse la lealtà ritrovando che tu serbar vuoi a lui della sua donna?
. . . Trattiamo adunque loro *e le lor cose come* essi noi e le nostre trattano"
("Thinkest thou, that, if thou hadst a fair wife or mother or daughter or sister
that found favour in Nicostratus' eyes, he would be so scrupulous on the
point of loyalty as thou art disposed to be in regard of his lady? . . . Observe
we, then, towards them and theirs the same rule which they observe towards
us and ours," 24–26).

7. A retaliation pointed up stylistically (see U. Bosco, *Il Decameron: saggio*
[Rieti, 1929], p. 183) is that of tale VIII, where the betrayed husband who
believes he has beaten his wife (in reality the servant girl), "dicendole la
maggior villania che mai a cattiva femina si dicesse" ("rating her the while
like the vilest woman that ever was," 19), will find her relations turning upon
him with "la maggior villania che mai a niun cattivo uomo si dicesse" ("the
soundest rating that ever was bestowed upon caitiff," 49).

8. Absent from Apuleius's *Metamorphoses*.

9. Only the first of these particulars is in Matthew of Vendôme: Boccaccio's
reiteration is significant.

10. *Poetics* 1450b.

11. C. Bremond, *La logica*, pp. 100, 104, 106.

12. I am borrowing here from linguistics the terms *etic* and *emic*, derived
from *(phon)etic* and *(phon)emic*, to represent any kind of opposition of this
type.

13. Indeed all the discourses of friar and godfather, as G. Petronio notes in
his commentary to the *Decameron* (Turin, 1950), 2:67, are full of religious
unction, "to exploit and sneer at the religiousness of this plaster saint."

14. G. Getto (*Vita di forme e forme di vita nel "Decameron*," 2d ed. [Turin,
1966], pp. 165 ff.) speaks of "exchange between illusion and reality." He
treats tales IV and VIII with considerable insight, sensing exactly that in
the day as a whole the exchange involves, according to the tale, only the
neighbors or the husband, in a variety of gradations (p. 175).

15. In tale IX, which (as has been noted) constitutes in practice a fusion of
two tales, the preliminary tale (the three proofs the wife provides for the
future lover to the husband's disadvantage) serves to predispose the husband
to this confusion of f and t. Note in particular the third proof, where the

signs that will convince the husband about his decayed tooth are carefully prepared. And note how, to avoid any possible suspicion, the wife demonstrates herself ill on the day when under the "enchanted" tree she gives herself up to the embraces of Pirro.

16. See Getto, p. 173.

17. It is worth noting that the immediate source for this tale, exemplum 14 of the *Disciplina clericalis*, ed. A. Hilka and W. Söderhjelm (Heidelberg, 1911), does not give this accusation but that of "frequenting prostitutes" ("meretrices adire"). It should be remembered that the wife, both in the tale and in the exemplum, is in the habit of neutralizing her husband by making him drunk: Boccaccio has thus perfected the technique of turning the tables by having the wife blame the husband for what had served her as an expedient when she wished to put into effect a blameworthy project of her own: adultery.

18. See Petronio's note to the *Decameron*, p. 70.

19. This too is one of Boccaccio's innovations. In the source the neighbors are not present, and it is the "parentes" who take the part of the wife.

20. We are, in short, in the semantic category of the "disguise": see Todorov, *Grammaire du "Décaméron,"* pp. 35–36.

21. Furthermore, in the logic of the characters (as in Matthew of Vendôme) the *beffa* is presented as the main demonstration of how easy betrayal is. Lidia, undertaking to provide Pirro with the three proofs he has asked for, "gli mandò dicendo che quello che egli aveva addimandato pienamente fornirebbe, e tosto; e oltre a ciò per ciò che egli così savio reputava Nicostrato, disse che in presenza di lui con Pirro si sollazzerebbe e a Nicostrato farebbe credere che ciò non fosse vero" ("and therewithal she told him, that, as he deemed Nicostratus so wise, she would contrive that they should enjoy one another in Nicostratus' presence, and that Nicostratus should believe that 'twas a mere show," 31).

22. See L. Di Francia, "Alcune novelle del *Decameron* illustrate nelle fonti," *Giornale storico della letteratura italiana* 44 (1904): 80–94.

Chapter Five

1. While not aiming at bibliographical completeness, I hope I have brought together a sufficiently wide range of interpretations and judgments on the tale of Alatiel: G. Almansi, "Lettura della novella di Alatiel," *Paragone* 22, no. 252 (1971): 26–40, reprinted in *L'estetica dell'osceno* (Turin, 1974]; M. Baratto, *Realtà e stile nel "Decameron"* (Vicenza, 1970), pp. 96–101; Bosco, pp. 95–97; Flora, p. 325; Getto, pp. 96, 259–60; C. Grabher, *Giovanni Boccaccio* (Turin, 1941), pp. 147–48; Hauvette, pp. 264–65; Muscetta, pp. 394–97; Petronio, 1:242; and N. Sapegno, *Il Trecento* 3d ed. (Milan, 1966), p. 341. For the text of the *Decameron* I use the Branca edition.

2. Here is how B. Lavagnini describes it in *Enciclopedia italiana*, 30:78–79: "the adventures of a pair of lovers who divided by an infinitude of trials and tribulations, occasioned now by the will of men, now by the caprice or persecution of fortune, manage to remain faithful, overcoming the most exacting

trials, and find themselves at last, beyond their wildest hopes, brought together again."

3. This is most effectively stressed by V. Shklovsky in *Lettura del "Decameron"* (Bologna, 1969; first published 1961), pp. 222–24. The parodic nature of our tale was earlier announced by Shklovsky in *Una teoria della prosa*, pp. 58–59, despite the fact that, ill supplied with information or perhaps in haste, he believes that Alatiel kept her chastity.

4. Shklovsky (*Una teoria della prosa*, p. 95) would call it brochette structure (but he does not refer to the tale).

5. Muscetta, p. 394.

6. The system enucleated, no less than the *Decameron*, excludes a *stil novo* interpretation of "cosa" ("e par che sia una *cosa* venuta / di cielo in terra a miracol mostrare"). A *stil novo* conception perhaps lies behind Riggs's "creature."

7. It is no accident, then, that Alatiel is named in only two sections, the opening and closing paragraphs (9, 95).

8. The expression is Todorov's (*Grammaire du "Décaméron,"* p. 36).

9. More detailed indications are noted in chap. 4 above.

10. See V. Russo, "Il senso del tragico nel *Decameron*," *Filologia e letteratura* 11 (1965): pp. 55–58.

11. One might indeed see in the shipwreck episode a fairly detailed kind of prefiguration: the men, active and ferocious ("quantunque quelli che prima nel paliscalmo eran discesi colle coltella in mano il contraddicessero": "though the first comers sought with knives in their hands to bar the passage of the rest"), all die in their desperate anxiety to save themselves ("credendosi la morte fuggire, in quella incapparono": "found the death which they hoped to escape"); but Alatiel is saved, though she remained helpless in the ship which ran "velocissimamente" ("with prodigious velocity") before the wind.

Chapter Six

1. Essential bibliography: A. A. Parker, "Themes and Imagery in Garcilaso's First Eclogue," *Bulletin of Spanish Studies* 25 (1948): 222–27; M. Arce, "La égloga primera de Garcilaso," *La torre* 1, no. 2 (1953): 31–68; E. L. Rivers, "Las églogas de Garcilaso: ensayo de una trayectoria espiritual," *Atena* 151 (1963): 54–64; and R. Lapesa, *La trayectoria poética de Garcilaso*, 2d ed. (Madrid, 1968), pp. 130–47. The Spanish text I have used is Garcilaso de la Vega, *Obras completas*, ed. E. L. Rivers (Madrid 1964); and the translation is that of J. M. Cohen in *The Penguin Book of Spanish Verse* (Harmondsworth, Middx., 1956). The *editio minor* of Garcilaso (*Poesías castellanas completas* [Madrid, 1969]) helpfully numbers the stanzas but modernizes the spelling. A contribution to the philological reconstruction of the text has been made by A. Blecua in *En el texto de Garcilaso* (Madrid, 1970), pp. 115–47.

2. The commentaries of Brocense, Fernando de Herrera, Tamayo de Vargas, and Azara have been collected by A. Gallego Morell in *Garcilaso de la Vega y sus comentaristas*, 2d ed. (Granada, 1972).

3. Only stanza 20, with its extra line, modifies this schema (A11 B11 C11 B11 A11 C11 c7 d7 d7 E11 E11 F11 G11 f7 G11). A further irregularity should perhaps be attributed to early editors. Line 263, a septenary in the 1549 edition and in Rivers, is the hendecasyllable the scheme requires in other texts ("más convenible fuera aquesta suerte"): see Blecua, pp. 120–21. Lapesa, n. 172, defends the infraction.

4. Similar to that of Vergil's eighth eclogue in Juan del Encina's translation, which I quote from *Cancionero de Juan del Encina* (1496; facsimile ed., Madrid, 1928). Garcilaso must have borne this translation in mind (see nn. 12, 13 below). The distribution is the following: argument, stanza 1; dedication, stanzas 2–4; narration, stanza 5; Damon's lament, stanzas 6–14; narration, stanza 15; Alphesiboeus's lament, stanzas 16–25. The stanzas, all octosyllabic, have the following schema: a b c a b c c d e c d e, with a refrain in in the laments (x y y).

5. See the schema of Arce, pp. 34–35. There are excellent pages in A. Prieto, *Ensayo semiológico de sistemas literarios* (Barcelona, 1972), pp. 171–75, where he works out a description of the two laments as *canzoni* "in vita" and "in morte": a reliving of the Petrarchan model.

6. This should be corrected to "orladas," according to Blecua, pp. 132–35.

7. See, e.g., Vergil's eclogues, with the sunset at the close of the first (82–83), the second (67–68) and the tenth (77); the eighth, which Garcilaso has particularly in mind, begins with a description of the dawn (14–16). The symmetrical description of dawn and sunset is Garcilaso's innovation.

8. The following graphic conventions are adopted in this chapter: two vertical rules indicate separation; an arrow indicates movement. The arrow is broken when the movement has yet to take place.

9. Note that the effect of "bolver" as it is referred to Galatea's eyes is quite opposite: "Tus claros ojos a quién los bolviste?" 128.

10. For this point see Arce, pp. 48, 54.

11. See Parker, who, however, does not distinguish clearly enough the different attitudes of Salicio and Nemoroso.

12. The idea probably came from Juan del Encina's translation of Vergil's eighth eclogue (which has no more than "Mopso Nysa datur: quid non speremus amantes? / Iungentur iam grypes equis," lines 26–27): "A Mosso Nisa fue dada / Que razon pudo *juntallos* / Amadores que esperamos / La *contrariedad juntada* / Los grifos con los cavallos" (stanza 8).

13. A phenomenon which is, however, related to the model. In Vergil's eighth eclogue there is a recurrent identical line (21, 25, 31, 36, etc.) which changes at the end of Damón's song (61). Juan del Encina too ends each stanza of Damón's lament except the last (14) with a refrain x y y.

Chapter Seven

1. I have used John Ormsby's translation of Cervantes (Chicago, 1951).
2. Note the descent from "se tiene por ciérto" to "dicen."
3. Is this a reference to Ariosto's *Satire* 3, lines 61–66?

Chapter Eight

1. M. Pagnini, "La critica letteraria come integrazione dei livelli dell'opera," in *Critica e storia letteraria: studi offerti a Mario Fubini* (Padua, 1970), 1:91.
2. M. Riffaterre, *Essai de stylistique structurale* (Paris, 1971), pp. 327–28; but cf. pp. 66–68. Lessing provides an interesting comparison (*Laokoon*, 17) between the figurative arts and poetry ("that which the eye takes in in a single moment [the poet] enumerates slowly and progressively"). Last, see J. Geninasca, who touches on this point in A.-J. Greimas, ed., *Essais de sémiotique poétique* (Paris, 1971), p. 48.
3. I do not say *absolute* because there does not exist, in my opinion, a *total*, definitive interpretation: the text lives parallel to us; it is an experience which grows richer with each new experience (see Segre, 1:4).
4. Here is a literal translation of the text: "In my country there are palm trees / where sings the sabiá [a kind of blackbird]; / the birds which here [in Portugal] trill / do not trill as they do there [in Brazil]. / In our sky there are more stars, / in our fields more flowers, / in our woods more life, / in our life more love. / In meditating, all alone at night, / more pleasure I find there; / in my country there are palm trees / where sings the sabiá. / In my country there are qualities / such as I do not find here; / in meditating, all alone at night, / I find more pleasure there. / In my country there are palm trees / where sings the sabiá. / God grant that I do not die / without returning there again, / without enjoying the qualities / that I do not find here, / without seeing again the palm trees / where sings the sabiá." For bibliography regarding Gonçalves Dias, see L. Stegagno Picchio, *La letteratura brasiliana* (Florence, 1972), pp. 228–29; pp. 175–82 give an accurate profile of the poet. The *canção* is quoted, as are his other poems, from Gonçalves Dias, *Poesia completa e prosa escolhida* (Rio de Janeiro, 1959); the lack of any distinction between "tem" and "têm" should be particularly noted; for this point, see the commentary of A. Houaiss, ibid., p. 81.
5. So far I have cited the Goethe epigraph as Gonçalves Dias gives it. A. Meyer ("Sobre uma epígrafe," in *A chave e a máscara* [Rio de Janeiro, 1964], pp. 95–99) points out that, consciously or unconsciously, Gonçalves Dias has retouched Goethe's verses, turning them into "uma espécie de 'canção do exílio' em alemão." Apart from "blühen" and "glühen" in place of "blühn" and "glühn," he unites with a comma and follows with an exclamation mark the two "dahin," whereas in Goethe the exclamation mark comes after the first "dahin," while the second begins the sentence "Dahin / Möcht'ich mit dir, o mein Geliebter, ziehn!" When one thinks of the significance these retouchings have for the poet, one can only be astonished at Meyer's proposal that the Goethe epigraph should be restored to its original form.
6. See Gonçalves Dias's own introduction to his *Timbiras*: "Não me assentei nos cimos do Parnaso, / Nem vi correr a linfa da Castália. / Cantor das selvas, entre bravas matas / Áspero tronco da palmeira escolho. / Unido a êle soltarei meu canto" (*Poesia completa*, p. 476). It is for this reason, indeed, and not merely to keep his distance from Goethe's text with its *Zitronen*, that Gonçalves Dias has his sabiá living in the *palmeiras*, despite the

fact that the sabiá that lives in the palm tree is, as it happens, the only kind which does *not* sing; while the kind that does, the "sabiá-piranga," lives in orange trees: see D. Salles, in *Suplemento literário Minas Gerais*, 11 October 1969. In more recent authors it is the *buriti*, i.e., a particular species of palm tree, which takes the place of the general term *palmeira*.

7. Palm trees also exist in Portugal, though if I am correct, not among the green willows of Coimbra, where Gonçalves Dias wrote the *canção*.

8. But here is a kind of key to this "chaotic enumeration": "Tudo me arrouba e enleva, / Mar e terra, nuvens, céus, / Estrêla, flor, planta e selva, / Tudo quanto vem de Deus, / Quanto nos olhos reluz, / Quanto o mundo exterior / Do belo em formas traduz," *Ciúmes*, in *Poesia completa*, p. 643.

9. This is true at least in terms of Portuguese pronunciation. It should be remembered that the poet was the son of a Portuguese immigrant and returned to Portugal in his fifteenth year, five years before he wrote the *canção*. In any event, since precise indications regarding Gonçalves Dias's pronunciation do not exist, I limit my phonetic observations accordingly.

10. Only the internal rhyming of "vida" with itself is noted by J. G. Merquior, "O poema do *lá*" (1964; reprinted in *Razão do poema: ensaios de crítica e de estética* [Rio de Janeiro, 1965], p. 43).

11. A. Buarque de Hollanda, "À margem da *Canção do exílio*" (1944; reprinted in *Território lírico: ensaios* [Rio de Janeiro, 1958], p. 30).

12. I take into account all words, articles included, and distinguish singular from plural, masculine from feminine: whatever kind of division is employed would in any case be open to criticism. Words used in A: "minha," "terra," "tem," "palmeiras," "onde," "canta," "o," "sabiá," "as," "aves," "que," "aqui," "gorjeiam," "não," "como," "lá" (16 = 100 percent, since this is the opening stanza). Words which recur in the other stanzas: "minha," "terra," "tem," "palmeiras," "onde," "canta," "o," "sabiá," "as," "que," "não," "lá" (12 = 75 percent). Words used in B: "nosso," "céu," "tem," "mais," "estrêlas," "nossas," "varzeas," "flôres," "nossos," "bosques," "vida," "nossa," "amôres" (total 13). New words: "nosso," "céu," "mais," "estrêlas," "nossas," "várzeas," "flôres," "nossos," "bosques," "vida," "nossa," "amôres" (12 = 92 percent). Words which recur in other stanzas: "tem," "mais" (2 = 15 percent). Words used in C: "em," "cismar," "sòzinho," "à," "noite," "mais," "prazer," "encontro," "eu," "lá," "minha," "terra," "tem," "palmeiras," "onde," "canta," "o," "sabiá" (18). New words: "em," "cismar," "sòzinho," "à," "noite," "prazer," "encontro," "eu" (8 = 44 percent). Words which recur in other stanzas: all 18 (100 percent). Words used in D: "minha," "terra," "tem," "primores," "que," "tais," "não," "encontro," "eu," "cá," "em," "cismar," "sòzinho," "à," "noite," "mais," "prazer," "lá," "palmeiras," "onde," "canta," "o," "sabiá" (23). New words: "primores," "tais," "cá" (3 = 13 percent). Words which recur in the following stanza: "primores," "que," "não," "encontro," "eu," "cá," "lá," "palmeiras," "onde," "canta," "o," "sabiá" (12 = 52 percent). Words used in E: "não," "permita," "Deus," "que," "eu," "morra," "sem," "volte," "para," "lá," "desfrute," "os," "primores," "encontro," "por," "cá," "inda," "aviste," "as," "palmeiras," "onde," "canta," "o," "sabiá" (24). New words: "permita," "Deus," "morra," "sem," "volte," "para," "desfrute," "os," "por," "inda," "aviste" (11 = 45 percent).

13. Buarque de Hollanda (p. 27) notes that similes in the *canção* are more often implicit than explicit.

14. As pointed out in n. 4 above, "tem" in Gonçalves Dias's spelling is either singular or plural; obviously the difference of pronunciation remains.

15. It might be recalled, though the fact is not relevant here, that in B4 "tem" is understood.

16. As remarked by Buarque de Hollanda (p. 26), who goes on to add that "sòzinho" is without "essência pictural" (p. 28). This almost total absence of adjectives is all the more significant if we take into account the fact that Gonçalves Dias habitually employs a singularly rich adjectivism: though his statistics are not definitive, O. Moacyr Garcia (*Luz e fogo no lirismo de Gonçalves Dias* [Rio de Janeiro, 1956], p. 23) credits him with an adjective percentage of 18 (greater than the 15 percent of contemporary lyric production).

17. Although the only verb of movement is "voltar": see Merquior, p. 49.

18. See R. C. B. Avé Lallemant, "O sabiá cantando," in *Reise durch Nord-Brasilien im Jahre 1859* (Leipzig, 1860), quoted in the Brazilian translation (Rio de Janeiro, 1961) by L. da Câmara Cascudo in *Antologia do folclore brasileiro*, 4th ed. (São Paolo, 1971), pp. 130–31, where it is stated that the sabiá "é uma espécie de melro" and there is a musical transcription of its melody. For the "prehistory" of the sabiá in Brazilian literature and in particular for the page dedicated to it by Antônio do Rosário (seventeenth century), see Hélio Lopes, in *Suplemento literário Minas Gerais*," 6 December 1969.

19. Buarque de Hollanda (p. 31), while stressing that "aves" in the plural is generic, reaches the point of saying that the sabiá is the only living creature represented in the *canção*. For line 3 (and for B2), see *Adeus* (*Poesia completa*, p. 206): "Onde não crescem perfumadas flôres, / Nem tenras aves seus gorjeios soltam."

20. For the scansion of line 3, see Merquior, p. 44; for D3 (see sec. 4.5), p. 47.

21. See *Tristeza* (*Poesia completa*, p. 134): "em céu diverso / Luzem com luz diversa estrêlas d'ambos."

22. For curiosity's sake I might draw attention to the fact that one of Gonçalves Dias's poems is entitled *Minha vida e meus amôres* (*Poesia completa*, p. 130).

23. On the use of anaphora in Gonçalves Dias's poetry, see F. Ackermann, *A obra poética de A. G. D*, trans. E. Schaden (São Paulo, 1964; original ed. 1938), pp. 159–61.

24. This is a constant in Gonçalves Dias's poetry: "A paisagem noturna e o entardecer lhe provocam sentimentos de tristeza compassiva mas não desesperada" (Moacyr Garcia, p. 48).

25. Observed by Buarque de Hollanda, p. 30.

26. For the strength of pathetic feeling attributed by the poet to the adjective "sòzinho," see his 1845 letter from Caxias (*Poesia completa*, p. 799): "Sòzinho em terra que, apesar de minha, eu posso chamar estranha," etc.; and Aires de Mata Machado, *Crítica de estilos* (Rio de Janeiro, 1956), p. 26.

27. There is a very similar structure at the beginning of *Desejo* (*Poesia completa*, p. 125): "Ah! *que eu não morra* sem provar, ao menos / Sequer

por um instante, nesta vida / Amor igual ao meu! / *Dá*, Senhor *Deus*, que eu sôbre a terra encontre / Um anjo, uma mulher."

28. One might recall at least Gonçalves Dias's imitation in the lyric which bears the symptomatic title *Minha terra* (*Poesia completa*, pp. 656–57), written in Paris in 1864, noting "Sob um céu menos querido," "em tristes serões d'inverno," "Meu êste sol que me aclara, / Minha esta brisa, êstes céus: / Estas praias, bosques, fontes," "Mais os amo quando volte," etc. Among the moderns we might list Manuel Bandeira, Juó Bananére, Oswald de Andrade, Guilherme de Almeida, Murilo Mendes, Carlos Drummond de Andrade, Ribeiro Couto, Cassiano Ricardo, Mario Quintana, Vinícius de Morais, A. C. Jobim, and Chico Buarque de Hollanda. See Aires de Mata Machado, passim.

29. The words, by the Parnassian J. Osório Duque Estrada (1870–1927), have been adapted to the music composed by Francisco Manuel da Silva for the proclamation (1831) of Dom Pedro II, which became the anthem of the republic in 1890. Duque Estrada's text, winner of a national contest, was made official in 1922. See in particular the stanza "Do que a terra mais garrida / Teus risonhos, lindos *campos têm mais flores*; / *Nossos bosques têm mais vida*," "*nossa vida* no teu seio *mais amôres*." There are echoes of the *canção* in the hymn of the Brazilian expeditionary forces in the Second World War, which is by Guilherme de Almeida.

30. N. 6 above.

31. *Obras completas* (Lisbon, 1904), 2:357.

32. D. Gonçalves de Magalhães, "Ensaio sôbre a literatura no Brasil," *Niteroi*, vol. 1.

33. A point expressed, in direct contrast to the articles of Salles in *Suplemento literário Minas Gerais* (11 October 1969, 6 June 1970), by J. G. Merquior, ibid. (4 April, 12 September 1970).

34. Buarque de Hollanda, p. 28.

35. Merquior, "O poema do *lá*," p. 43.

36. Except for "sòzinho," which qualifies objectively: see sec. 4.4 and Merquior, "O poema do *lá*."

37. Buarque de Hollanda, p. 26.

38. Merquior, "O poema do *lá*," pp. 46, 44.

Chapter Nine

1. *Acte sans paroles* was first performed in England, together with *Fin de partie* (in French): "créé . . . à Londres, et repris le même mois . . . à Paris." The present article is based on the French text (Paris, 1957) rather than the English (London, 1958), since the latter differs in some respects: e.g., in the absence of the handkerchief.

2. See P. Watzlawick, J. H. Beavin, and D. D. Jackson, *Pragmatic of Human Communication: A Study in Interactional Patterns, Pathologies, and Paradoxes* (New York, 1967).

3. G. Bateson, D. Jackson, J. Haley, and J. Weakland, "Toward a Theory of Schizophrenia," *Behavioral Science* (1956).

Index